LE
VOYAGEUR
FRANÇAIS.

THE FRENCH TRAVELER

ALSO BY WILLIAM D. GAIRDNER

The Critical Wager
ECW Press, 1982 — Toronto

The Trouble With Canada: A Citizen Speaks Out
Stoddart, 1990, and BPS Books, 2007 — Toronto

The War Against the Family:
A Citizen Speaks Out On the Political, Economic,
and Social Policies That Threaten Us All
Stoddart, 1992, and BPS Books, 2007 — Toronto

Constitutional Crack-Up:
Canada, And the Coming Showdown With Quebec
Stoddart, 1994 — Toronto

On Higher Ground: Reclaiming A Civil Society
Stoddart, 1996 — Toronto

After Liberalism
Stoddart, 1998 — Toronto

Canada's Founding Debates
Stoddart, 1999, and University of Toronto Press, 2003 — Toronto

The Trouble With Democracy: A Citizen Speaks Out
Stoddart, 2001, and BPS Books, 2007 — Toronto

The Book of Absolutes:
A Critique of Relativism, and a Defence of Universals
McGill-Queen's University Press, 2008 — Montreal/Kingston

OH, OH, Canada: A Voice From the Conservative Resistance
BPS Books, 2008 — Toronto

The Trouble With Canada ... Still!
Key Porter Books, 2010 — Toronto

The Great Divide:
Why Liberals and Conservatives Will Never, Ever Agree
Encounter Books, 2015 — New York

DISRUPTIVE ESSAYS:
There Are No Safe Spaces in This Book!
Kinetics Design, KDbooks.ca, 2018 — Toronto

THE FRENCH TRAVELER

Letters to "Chère Madame"

ADVENTURE
EXPLORATION & INDIAN LIFE
IN EIGHTEENTH-CENTURY CANADA

THE FIRST ENGLISH TRANSLATION
OF THE 1768 BESTSELLER

"Le Voyageur Français"

TRANSLATION AND COMMENTARY
by WILLIAM D. GAIRDNER, PhD

Copyright © 2019 by William D. Gairdner

All rights reserved. No part of this publication may be reproduced
or transmitted in any form or by any means, electronic or mechanical,
including photocopying, recording, or any information storage and retrieval system,
without permission in writing from the author.

Published in 2019 by Kinetics Design, KDbooks.ca

ISBN 978-1-988360-27-0 (paperback)
ISBN 978-1-988360-28-7 (ebook)

Cover and interior design, typesetting and printing:
Daniel Crack, Kinetics Design, KDbooks.ca
https://www.linkedin.com/in/kdbooks/

———————

Cover image: Canoes in a Fog, Lake Superior, 1873
Etching on India paper engraved by Charles Mottram (1807–1876)
Published by Goupil et Compagnie, Paris and London
Toronto Public Library Call Number: 967-9 Cab III
Public Domain

———————

The original oil painting "Canoes in a Fog, Lake Superior", 1869,
by Hopkins, Frances Anne (1838–1918) is owned by the Glenbow-Alberta Institute.

For All Those Curious About The History of Canada

TABLE OF CONTENTS

	ACKNOWLEDGEMENTS	12
	INTRODUCTION	14
	What Kind of Book Was This?	15
	The Role of Reason	19
	A Word About Imitation and Plagiarism	20
	The Rise of Romance	21
	Noble, or Ignoble?	22
	About Terminology	26
	About This Translation	28
	THE FRENCH TRAVELER	**33**
LETTER 95	**HUDSON BAY**	**33**
	Ice Monsters	33
	In Search of a North-West Passage	34
	The Pitiable Death of Henry Hudson	35
	Hunting for the Northwest Passage	36
	Instructions to Explorers to Avoid Dangers	37
	A Fire On Board!	40
	First Time in Eskimo Country	41
	Shelter, Clothing, and Food in the Frozen Wilderness	43
	Spring, Plants, Minerals, and Wonders of Nature	45
	Keeping Warm in Bitter, Cold Canada	47
LETTER 96	**HUDSON BAY ~ CONTINUED**	**49**
	An Eskimo to the Rescue! And How They Live	49
	Sex With Foreigners — and Why	50
	The Force and Majesty of Nature	51
	An Encounter with Helpful Indians	52
	Testing for Salt Water	53
	Geographical & Botanical Proofs of a Passage	53
	Eskimo Evidence of a Passage	54
	Tide Action as Evidence of a Passage	54
	Opening to the Far East	56
	The Nelson River	56
	People of the Area, Their Clothing, Customs, and Ways	58

The Caribou, the Hunt, and the Waste	58
Alcohol, Hardiness, and Foolishness	59
Cannibalism	60
Love and Self-Sacrifice	61
Euthanasia	62
The Sweat Cure	62
Social and Political Organization — The "Noble Savage"	63
Murder Unpunished	64
A Confused Religion of Good and Evil	65
Mistreatment of Women, and Indian Abortions	66
A Strange Way to Urinate / Their Language	66
Fur Pelts the Principal Currency	66
The Life of the Beaver	67
The Fable of the Beaver's "Ransom"	68
The Amazing Industry of the Beaver	69
Their Living Spaces	70
Beaver Babies	71
The Beaver Hunt	71
The Beaver Pelts	72
Last Effort to Prove French Sovereignty	73

LETTER 97 — THE ISLAND OF NEWFOUNDLAND & ITS ENVIRONS — 75

English Domination	75
A First French Settlement — and War With the English	77
A Hard Life in Newfoundland	78
Law and Order in the Wilderness	78
Fabulous Fishing Off Newfoundland	79
A Strange Habit of the Cod	80
How to Prepare the Cod for Eating and for Trade	80
The Life of Cod-Fishermen — Alcohol, Begging, and Piracy	81
What Newfoundland is Like	81
The Value of Cape Breton	82
The Indians of Cape Breton, the King, their life, & their Missionaries	84
The Climate and Way of Life at Cape Breton	85
The Fall of Louisbourg	85
The Neighbouring Islands	86

	A Horrific Abandonment!	86
	Labrador — A Forbidding Place	87
LETTER 98	**ACADIA**	**88**
	The Extraordinary Life of Charles Latour	90
	Latour Attacks His Own Son	90
	Latour the Younger Betrayed, and His Wife to the Ramparts!	91
	A French vs English Battle Over Words	92
	The Beginnings of Halifax	95
	The French Loyalty of the Indians	96
	The Life and Customs of the Indians in Acadia	96
	The Indians Adopt Some French Children	98
	A Young Boy Saves the Day, With Food — and a Guitar	98
	A Mystic Tree	99
	A Mysterious Fountain of Water, and the Origin of the Name "Canada"	99
LETTER 101	**ON CANADA**	**101**
	The Life, Divinity, and Customs of Gaspésians	101
	The Approach to Quebec, and its Character	102
	The Arrival of Champlain	104
	Quebec Seized by the English	105
	The French, the Jesuits, the St. Lawrence River	105
	The Village of Montreal	107
	The Power of Niagara Falls	108
	The Character, Language, Morals, and Manners of the Indians	108
	The Uniqueness of the Iroquois	109
	The Role of Iroquois Women, their Moral Customs, and Dress	111
	The Iroquois Character, Marriage and Childbirth	112
	The Iroquois at War	114
	Indian Tricksters	115
	More of Indians at War, and the Adoption of Enemies	115
	The Torture and Death of Enemies, and Invocation of Spirits	116
	A Story of Incredible Courage	118
	The Peace Pipe, and Honour	119
	Indian Eloquence	119
	Some Examples of Eloquence in Treaty Negotiations	120

	Aids to Memory, and Treaty Imagery	122
	Manner of Trading, Complex Personality, and Decline of the Iroquois	122
	The Gospel Not Very Effective	123
	The Manner of Living and Future of the Iroquois	123
	Admirable Qualities of the Iroquois	124
LETTER 102	**CANADA ~ CONTINUED**	**125**
	Life, War, Torture, and Ceremonies of the Hurons	125
	Indian Cruelty	127
	Indian Cannibalism and Scalping	127
	The Adoption Ritual	128
	The Duplicity of Execution	129
	The Huron War With the Iroquois, and War Customs	129
	War Preparations and Methods of Attack	131
	The War Expedition Underway	133
	Their Guardian Spirits	135
	Casualness and Skills On Route to War	136
	The Night Before Battle	137
	Treatment of Captives	138
	A Touching Love Scene	139
LETTER 103	**CANADA ~ CONTINUED**	**141**
	Courtship, Marriage, and Divorce Among the Hurons	141
	Divorce Among the Hurons ... Continued	144
	Trickery and Murder	144
	Huron Women, Their Treatment, Their Pregnancies	145
	Baby Care	146
	Growing Up	147
	The Use of Names	148
	Naming As Bonding	149
	A Story of Unusual Friendships	149
	Indian Appearance, Clothing, Tatooing, and More	151
	Their Character	156
	Filial Disrespect	157
	Their Compensating Virtues	157
	Their Nobility of Soul	158
	Character and Climate	158

LETTER 104	**CANADA** – CONTINUED	**160**
	Animal Symbols	160
	Power, Succession, and the Role of Women	161
	The Role of the Warriors	162
	The Orator of the Tribe, and its Deliberations	163
	Their Way of Dealing With Criminals	164
	The Criminal as a Slave	165
	Executing a Criminal, and Keeping the Law	165
	The Huron Religion	167
	Their Notion of the Soul	169
	The Role of Dreams	170
	The Feast of Dreams	171
	Their Art of Medicine	173
	The Sweating Cure	173
	European Diseases Unknown Here	174
LETTER 105	**CANADA** – CONTINUED	**176**
	Funerals and Burial Customs	176
	Their Mourning Laws	179
	Gathering Up the Bones of the Dead	180
	Mother's Milk on the Grave, and Feeding the Dead	181
	The Dance of the Calumet Pipe	181
	The Discovery Dance	183
	Many Reasons for Feasting	185
	Their Gambling Games	187
	The Bear Hunt	188
	The Hunt for Moose	190
	How the Wolverine Kills a Moose	191
LETTER 106	**CANADA** – CONTINUED	**193**
	More on Life, and War Among the Hurons	193
	Disaster If the Meeting Fails	194
	Barter Trade Among Them	195
	Their Notion of Money	195
	Trading by Canoe	196
	The Missionary's Aggravations Traveling With Indians	198
	The Wilderness as a New Eden	198

The French Government Meets With Indians	199
Their Knowledge of Astronomy and Time	200
A Winter Hunt	201
The Indians' Dogs	201
The Mosquitoes and Gnats	202
A Successful Buffalo Hunt — How They Do It	202
Other Animals They Trap	204
Ingenuity of the Black Fox	205
The Work of Those Who Stay Home, and Their Settlements	205
Their Land Use, Vegetable Gardens, and More	207
Their Porridge, Eating Customs, and Starvation	209
A Culture Shock for the Missionary	210
Of Plants, Threads, and the Grapevine	211
Indian Maple Syrup	211
Poison Ivy	212

LETTER 107   **CANADA** ~ CONTINUED   **213**

Christians Among the Huron	214
Huron Intelligence and Craftiness	216
Christianity at Quebec	217
A Christian Tribe!	219
On the Way to Trois-Rivieres	220
The Assault on Madame de Verchères	221
Bravery of the Master's Daughter	221
Wealth and Poverty in the New World	222
The Creoles	223
Creole Laziness and Dissipation	224
The Abuses of Military Authority	225
Finance, and Bankruptcy of the Colony	225
The English to Conquer Quebec	228

APPENDIX   **229**

Note to Readers: Delaporte published more than two dozen books on travel in various countries, numbering all his "letters" consecutively. For his writings on Canada they begin with letter #95, then skip from #98 to #101, etc.

ACKNOWLEDGEMENTS

THE journey from the discovery and first reading of this forgotten eighteenth-century work on Canada, to the decision to translate it into English with notes and commentary, has been a most pleasurable undertaking, made all the more so by the insightful comments, helpful corrections, and research suggestions so generously offered by friends and colleagues along the way.

The first person from whom I received help and encouragement was Professor Charles Batten, author of the delightful classic *Pleasurable Instruction: Form and Convention in Eighteenth Century Travel Literature* (Berkeley: University of California Press, 1978), who offered early advice and encouragement, and sent me a charming photograph of Joseph Delaporte he found in an archive. Then I was most fortunate to make contact with Professor Pierre Berthiaume, of the University of Ottawa, the author of many fine books on life in Early Canada, some of which arrived at my doorstep as a gift from him, including the one most pertinent to my effort: *L'Aventure Américaine au XVIIIeme Siècle* [The American Adventure in the 18th Century] (Ottawa: Les Presses de L'université d'Ottawa, 1990). This is a most interesting work, broad in scope and deeply insightful. Professor Berthiaume also read my entire translation, graciously offered encouragement in saying "it flows like spring water," and sent many detailed notes and suggestions, for which I am most grateful.

Two more colleagues, Professors Ian Gentles, of York University and Tyndale College, and Tom Flanagan of the University of Calgary, also offered immediate assistance. Ian is a distinguished scholar of British history, as well as a Canadianist and fellow-contributor to a book of which I was the Managing Editor: *Canada's Founding Debates* (Stoddart Publishing, 1999, and University of Toronto Press, 2000). Ian read my translation, and sent back many helpful suggestions, corrections, and points of historical interest. Professor Tom Flanagan has written much surrounding Indian history and life in Canada, and his *First Nations, Second Thoughts* (Montreal/Kingston: McGill-Queen's University Press, 2000) was especially incisive and clarifying on many heads. He also provided a handful of references to important books on Indian life, past and present, which were of great help in my commentary on Delaporte's book. Finally, I received helpful suggestions for additions and adjustments to my comments on cannibalism from Professor Cecil Chabot, for which — especially in view of the incendiary nature of that topic — I am also most grateful.

As for the process of translation? It was a pleasurable one, made all the more so by the kind assistance of my colleague Richard Bastien, of Ottawa, a francophone and professional translator, who kindly served as back-up for this undertaking. Each week, for many months, I would email Richard a handful of odd or now-defunct French words or phrases I wanted to query, and he would patiently send back suggestions, corrections, and encouragements, and for this I remain grateful.

Finally, my wife Jean has read every word, offered much comment, and encouraged the production of this book enthusiastically from the start. She becomes especially animated in her conviction that it ought to be read by every young Canadian, and finds no argument from me.

INTRODUCTION

THIS is such a fascinating book about adventure and exploration in Early Canada that some readers may wish to leave my Introduction for later, jump ahead, and get into the story right away. If so, I am pretty certain they will find much immediate delight. However, I would be remiss if I failed to say that the Introduction — and the footnotes, which I have intentionally left on the page rather than placed at the end of the book — will almost certainly enrich that experience because they lay out the intellectual and historical framework of ideas and controversies in which the book first appeared and became an instant bestseller in Eighteenth-century France. What follows is the story of how I got interested in translating and commenting on this book.

Forty years ago, during a trip to the south of France, I happened upon a small antiquarian book of travel entitled *Le Voyageur François*, composed in 1748 and published twenty years later by a Jesuit priest named Joseph Delaporte. It seemed to be a collection of letters written to a mysterious woman in France, describing travels in various parts of the world.

Leafing through, I saw with delight there were letters on *La Baye d'Hudson* (Hudson Bay), *L'Isle de Terre Neuve* (Newfoundland), and *L'Acadie* (Nova Scotia). What kind of book was this, and who was this man, of whom neither I, nor anyone I knew had ever heard?[1] Little did I know that this was to be the start of my own travels through the early days of my country.

---

1 What I had in my hands was Volume VIII of a twenty-six volume series published by L'abbé Joseph Delaporte (1714–1779). *Français* was written *François* in the eighteenth century, and the full title was *Le Voyageur François, ou La Connoissance de l'ancien et du nouveau monde* ("The French Traveler, or Knowledge of the Old and the New World"). After his death, the series was extended by other editors to forty-two volumes. The letters in my volume were dated 1748 (though they may have been back-dated to create an effect of age), and the book published in 1768 by Chez Vincent, Paris. Each volume in the series was in a small 3.75 x 6.50-inch format, rather like what we call a pocket book today, and copies are still available from some antiquarian booksellers.

Over the years, I dipped into the book on occasion for the pleasures of a trip into the past, but recently decided to read it from cover to cover, and was immediately captured by lively descriptions of Arctic beauty, Eskimo life, and the search for a Northwest Passage. This was all the more enticing because in the summer of 1957 my brother and I worked as sailors on the S.S. Kingsbridge, a British tramp-steamer on contract taking supplies to Resolute Bay (in Inuktitut: "The Place With No Dawn") in Canada's high arctic. We were going to a place just 1,000 miles from the North Pole. Once there, we hiked under the midnight sun over a faraway ridge to find a remote Eskimo settlement nestling in a bay of magical opalescent icebergs, animal-hide shelters with smoke skirling aloft, barking husky dogs, and little children with curious eyes peering at us warily through their furry hoods. Delaporte's little book woke that up again, and much more, as he described intriguing visits to the frenzy of cod-fishing off the Grand Banks, and dramatic struggles between English and French colonists to claim Nova Scotia. I was hooked.

But soon I found myself wondering: If he began his narrative with adventures in the far north, and ended in Nova Scotia, might he have written more about what was then called *New France*? I found a copy of Volume IX online in a Parisian bookstore, and sent for it. Almost the entire book was devoted to describing Indian customs, religion, culture, and war, in "*Le Canada*."[2] There would be more wild and wonderful adventures to discover!

Before long I began to wonder if *Le Voyageur François* had ever been translated into English in the two and a half centuries since it first appeared? But nothing turned up. This meant that all those without any French were never going to have access to these fascinating accounts. And I thought they should. So I decided to translate it myself.

What Kind of Book Was This?

I was enjoying what the French call a *récit de voyage* — a travel narrative. Eighteenth-century Europeans had developed an unprecedented hunger for exotic literature of all kinds, and Delaporte, a Jesuit and a man of letters, clearly had a keen sense of the publishing opportunities this presented. Much of that hunger was already being satisfied by the consumption of fictitious

---

The entire set can be seen at the Bibliothèque Nationale de France, at http://data.bnf.fr/14480403/le_voyageur_francais/#allmanifs. Delaporte was at various intervals a practicing priest, a scholar, dramatist, philosopher, essayist, and literary critic, who wrote and published on a whole range of topics, including essays on theatre, women's literature, the social and political philosophy of Jean-Jacques Rousseau, and general commentaries on French literary and social life.

2 The letters in Volume IX are dated 1749, but the book was published in 1769 by Chez Vincent, Paris; then republished in an updated edition in 1774, by L. Cellot, Paris. The latter is the edition translated for this book.

experiences in the form of the novel, which at the time was outselling every other form of literature. But the eighteenth century "was by all accounts the age of travel, and the traveler tended to be one of the century's cultural heroes."[3] So a very close runner-up to the novel in sales, was the travel narrative, which came in two flavours: the true, and the untrue.

There were authentic exploration records, letters, journals, and diaries about travel in Canada by sailors and explorers, and books by historical figures of whom many in the public were aware, such as the Frenchmen Samuel Champlain and Pierre Charlevoix, and the English arctic explorers Henry Hudson and Henry Ellis. Throughout the preceding century, serious travel literature had been much relied upon for general learning and worldly knowledge, even by such as the philosopher John Locke, who "recommended reading of travel reports as the best way to approach the study of human understanding."[4] It was he who, in his popular *Second Treatise*, imagining the Indian as Man in his natural primitive state, wrote that "in the beginning, all the world was America."

But by the early eighteenth century there was a rash of authors attempting to cash in by selling wildly fanciful and blatantly false travel books about things like nine-foot Patagonian giants, imaginary North American rivers and exotic Indian tribes, and other deceits they hoped would sell well (which they often did). Indeed, the eighteenth century was "unique in the wholesale production of this kind of travel literature."[5]

About the same time, travel to faraway places like North America was coming within reach for adventurous and daring souls. But it was costly, and still very dangerous. Sea travel was conceived by many as it was by Samuel

---

3 For an engaging summary of this phenomenon, see Charles L. Batten Jr., "Literary Responses to the Eighteenth-Century Voyages," at: http://publishing.cdlib.org/ucpressebooks/view?docId=ft3489n8kn&chunk.id=d0e3403&toc.id=d0e3403&brand=ucpress. Batten is author of *Pleasurable Instruction: Form and Convention in Eighteenth-Century Travel Literature* (Berkeley: University of California Press, 1978). He cites Peter Gay, *The Enlightenment: An Interpretation* (New York: 1969), to great effect: "Whether realistic, embroidered, or imaginary, whether on ship or in the libraries, travel was the school of comparison, and traveller's reports were the ancestors of treatises on cultural anthropology and political sociology. *It led to the attempt on the part of Western man to discover the position of his own civilization and the nature of humanity by pitting his own against other cultures*" [my emphasis]. This is precisely the context in which *Le Voyageur François* must be situated.

4 Jorge Cañizares-Esguerra, *How to Write the History of the New World* (Stanford: Stanford University Press, 2001), p.23.

5 See, for example, Percy G. Adams, *Travels, and Travel Liars, 1660–1800* (Berkeley: University of California Press, 1962), who notes that "the eighteenth-century ... was a period in which collections of voyages were very popular. From 1660 to 1800, over a hundred such collections were made, many in several editions, many translated into more than one language, and some that included twenty, thirty, even one hundred volumes ... [and] by 1750, the method had been almost universally adopted of summarizing, combining, rearranging, and rewriting the [travel] books selected" (p.88).

Johnson, who quipped that being on a ship is like "being in jail, with the chance of being drowned." If the voyage contemplated was to North America, there was also the possibility of being slaughtered by fearsome "savages" (a word to which we will return). So for honest book marketers who sensed that few had the time or patience to wade through the various, and often unreliable eyewitness accounts available, the question was: How, without the risks, expense, and dangers of actual travel, was the public appetite for authentic and exotic adventure to be satisfied?

As a means of countering the growing trend of deceptive travel narratives, Delaporte resolved to edit and *compile* the most authentic accounts available, and offer them to the French reading public as a new and improved kind of literature.[6] He would eliminate all false curiosities, of course, but also all overly-detailed material describing things like the variety of rocks and plants, would clean up awkward writing, and in particular would switch the focus typical of other authors from the thoughts and feelings of the traveler himself, to a more objective rendering of the experiences, people, and customs at hand.[7] As promised in his "Notice to Readers," he would achieve this by incorporating "the flame of philosophy and scientific observation," into every episode, and these would be narrated in the voice of a "philosophical traveler."[8] Readers would not have to search out an array of disparate

---

6 Delaporte, and popular predecessors such as John Green and Antoine-François Prévost (upon the latter of whose efforts Delaporte was determined to improve) did not travel themselves, but instead compiled all the most reliable accounts into an accessible format for the reading public. Jorge Cañizares-Esguerra, *How to Write the History of the New World*, explains that "scores of old, new, and forged accounts of exotic lands," and even many eyewitness accounts that "contradicted many of the laws of social development," had lost credibility by the eighteenth century, and so a new generation of travel editors and compilers arose, determined to rely only on more "philosophical" travelers. They were not satisfied with collecting tales of wonder, and consciously sought "to avoid the perceptual distortions that besieged untrained witnesses" (pp.1-2). They were looking for texts that had a logic of internal consistency and were not self-contradictory.

7 This motive may have been inspired by Note 10 of Rousseau's *Second Discourse* (1755), where he called for travelers who would study, "not always rocks and plants, but, for once, men and mores, and who, after so many centuries used to measure and examine the house, would finally be of a mind to want to know its inhabitants." Delaporte was familiar with Rousseau's entire corpus of thought, and published a book of his work entitled *Esprit, maximes et principes de M. Jean-Jacques Rousseau de Genève*, in 1764.

8 In Delaporte's "Notice to Readers," (see the Appendix for this book), he outlines his intention to present a more engaging and objective kind of travel narrative than found in the *Histoire générale des voyages* (General History of Travel) by his influential predecessor, the Abbé Prévost, declaring that "It is not important to know the history of the traveler, but rather, of the countries where he has traveled." By mid-eighteenth-century, there were frequent demands to include actual philosophers on voyages of exploration, as well as artists tasked with recording important scenes in their paintings as proof of objective observation. Our age is now merely the age of tourism. But the eighteenth-century was the age of discovery, and "To know how to travel well," declared the

and often unreliable accounts to find what interested them; they would find the very best accounts already selected, edited, and transformed into a single seamless objective narrative between the covers of every volume of *Le Voyageur François*. From a variety of imperfect accounts, he was preparing a new, more perfect history of world travel.

To add to the appeal, he decided that instead of the typical third-person account, he would publish each volume as a collection of first-person letters written in the personal voice of a fictitious traveler/narrator, to a very curious, educated (and fictitious) "Madame" back home in France.[9] The material to be narrated would be reproduced, often word for word, from a selection of authentic travel accounts, but to heighten the effect of authenticity, he would introduce ostensible eyewitness speakers into his text — a missionary, a sailor, or a social figure — who would speak to readers directly, thus lending the whole production a heightened sense of objectivity and personal voice. Comfortably ensconced in his armchair by the fire, he wanted to delight the public with narratives fresher and more lively than those offered by any previous travel writer.

Of this, he did a superb job.[10] Newspapers of the time record that he often sold out each newly-completed volume while preparing the next.[11]

Chevalier de Coetlogon, "is the Source of all other Sciences" (cited in Batten, "Literary responses", note 3, above).

9 French intellectual life in Paris during the Eighteenth-century was centered around the "salon" experience. Salons were gatherings of educated, aristocratic citizens who often met in the private home of an inspiring host or hostess. These continued to be centers of high culture in France until the Second World War. Delaporte's "Madame" — whose voice we never hear — we are intended to presume was a "*salonnière*", a woman of high culture around whom an intellectual circle would gather for pleasurable discussion and self-education. There was immediate precedent for this format. Delaporte incorporated and adapted a great deal of his material on Canada from Pierre François-Xavier de Charlevoix (1682–1761), whose extensive travel journals on Canada were written as a collection of actual letters sent from New France to a real woman, the Duchess of Lesdiguières. In retrospect, Delporte's travel series, in which he combines a professed reliance on objective reason, with a narrative technique of reporting to a mysterious woman, embodies the two main trends of his time: one toward a greater reliance on reason (the ostensible male virtue), another the popular appetite for feeling (the ostensible female virtue). In what may be the finest study of its kind, Pierre Berthiaume, in *L'Aventure Américaine au XVIIIeme Siècle* (Ottawa: Les Presses Universitaire d'Ottawa, 1990), explains that the classical epistolary form, in continuous use during this period, served as a kind of ordering and authenticating armature for many other types of writing, such as the journal, the memoir, the personal letter, and the diary, all of which communicate sincerity through familiarity, and hence truthfulness (p.211-212).

10 Jorge Cañizares-Esguerra, *How to Write the History*: "La Porte's remained a synthesis of all available authoritative, albeit conflicting, reports about different parts of the world," p.25. [Translator's Note: Delaporte's name was sometimes spelled De La Porte, or De Laporte. I have kept it throughout as Delaporte, as he published it this way on the title pages of all his books].

11 Adams, *Travels*, p.38, citing the evidence of a report in the French newspaper, *Mercure de France*, December, 1766, writes that "the Abbé Delaporte's *Le Voyageur François* was so much in

So successful was he in this endeavour, that he left behind his duties as the parish priest of Saint-Sulpice in Paris "to become one of the leading editors of travel compilations in Europe."[12]

This book is a translation by a fascinated citizen-reader, with added commentary, rather than an academic study attempting to resolve contested points of view about European explorers and exploiters, or whether the Indians of Canada were noble or ignoble. Nevertheless, it is the case that in any age, we tend to see others and the world around us through the lens of the ideas current in our own time. In Delaporte's day there were two main ideas, or trends of thought in serious tension, which for convenience I label "Reason and Romance." Both trends exerted a powerful influence over eighteenth century social and intellectual life, and are visible in this book. I comment on them here only to assist readers who may not be familiar with this background.

The Role of Reason

In retrospect, the eighteenth century has been called the "Age of Reason," or "the "Enlightenment," because European thinkers of the time yearned to escape what they considered the darkness of religion, corruption, and moral and class prejudice, and on principles of irrefutable reason, to create a perfect society. They strove to analyze everything according to strictly rational and scientific method, and when they put European civilization in the docket, they found it to be unjust, artificial, and undemocratic (among a host of other complaints).

At the time, to publish a book in France about Indians in a place like Canada, was to offer a very curious public a kind of literary looking-glass through which to peer at a very strange and exotic people, and by comparison, to see themselves more clearly, for better or worse. How sobering it must have been to think that these people they considered so primitive were just an earlier version of themselves. For "it is in their present condition [in the customs of the American tribes]," wrote the Scottish historian Adam Ferguson (a contemporary of Delaporte) "that we are to behold as in a mirror, the features of our own progenitors."[13] Some went farther, and through travel literature "became deeply interested in studying contemporary savages as forms of frozen classical polities," comparing the Hurons and Iroquois of

---

demand in 1766 that before volumes three and four could be printed, volumes one and two were sold out, forcing an immediate reprinting."

12 Cañizares-Esguerra, *How to Write*, p.35.

13 Cited in Cañizares-Esguerra, *How to Write*, p.50-1.

Canada to ancient Romans and Greeks.[14] Delaporte does precisely this in an admiring scene describing a Chief who stands proudly in his windblown robes, reasoning wisely before an entire tribe gathered at his feet, as Pericles of Athens, or the Roman Cicero might have done.[15]

A Word About Imitation and Plagiarism

In addition to a profound interest in rational and factual observation, however, the eighteenth century was also heir to a very long aesthetic and philosophical tradition espousing the idea that what is most real and true — perhaps even perfect — is generally to be found outside ourselves, either in nature, in a shared human nature, or in the works of the greatest philosophers, writers, and artists of the past. It made rational sense that as a lot of the very best has already been said and done, we must seek it out. Accordingly, the method to be used in the search for truth was *imitation*, and the most common metaphor employed was a *mirror*.[16] In short, if you want to know objective truth, to see it in perfect clarity, you have to avoid all the distortions caused by your own personal perceptions and feelings, hold a mirror up to nature, to human nature, and to the greatest works of the ages, and imitate them in whatever you do.

Accordingly, young artists, thinkers, and writers were taught that to strive for personal expression and "originality", as we think proper today, was highly impudent and egotistical. For reason dictates that imitation of greatness in all walks of life is the only logical pathway to excellence. Accordingly, dramatists such as Shakespeare and Racine drew their finest stories from great predecessors; the best sculptors copied the models of Michelangelo; students of rhetoric were expected to include arguments and flourishes borrowed directly from the works of men like Cicero, and without attribution (which was considered unnecessary, as everyone knew who the experts were).

Delaporte and other compilers of travel books made this the operating convention of their work, constructing accounts for an adventure-hungry public by borrowing copiously, and without attribution from the most authentic eyewitness documents available, and also from well-known moral treatises about primitive societies by philosophers like Rousseau (who, because he never visited any such society, had to borrow his own widely-influential

---

14 Cañizares-Esguerra, *How to Write*, p. 39.

15 Such Indian-Classical equations were part of the Enlightenment faith in the universality of human life and intelligence; but they were later criticized as historical conceits that obscured some of the stark realities of Indian life.

16 See especially the seminal work on this theme by Meyer H. Abrams, *The Mirror and the Lamp: Romantic Theory and the Critical Tradition* (Oxford: Oxford University Press, 1953).

ideas about Indians from other writers).[17] In mid eighteenth-century Europe, texts published — made public — were not yet considered personal property. On the contrary; they were considered goods that had been made freely available in the public domain (much like information offered freely to the public on countless websites today). So for a European author of the eighteenth century to copy and reproduce the influential works of others word for word, was not considered plagiarism, an ethical sin, or a crime.[18] It was widely understood and expected, and only an unimaginative travel writer would neglect to use every such source available.[19]

THE RISE OF ROMANCE

In a mounting tension with the idea of holding up a mirror to nature and imitating it, however, there was by mid-century a new social and aesthetic trend that differed in every respect, and was made especially attractive in France by the compelling novels and essays of Jean-Jacques Rousseau. This new movement was soon to turn an entire European public away from its former preference for cold reasoning as the best means for understanding reality, and toward an embrace of sincere emotion and "feeling" as the most

---

17 Many of Rousseau's ideas in praise of "natural man" and the symbolic "noble savage," were in the air at the time, and could be found in the writings of people like Montaigne, and in the plays of dramatists in Rousseau's own day. But most of them he took liberally from his readings in travel literature, especially those by the German writer Peter Kolben, some of whose *Description of the Cape of Good Hope* (1741) was republished in Prévost's *General History of Travel*, which is where Rousseau found it. He relied on Kolben's comments to defend what he thought was the physical superiority of South African Hottentot natives, in his influential "Discourse on Inequality" (known today as the *Second Discourse*). Rousseau worked hard to make his case, relying on some examples that he took without criticism from Kolben. One of these was a description of Hottentots "swimming" with their bodies upright and hands entirely out of the water, in waves the size of "mountains," somehow "dancing" on the crests of the waves. But no one can "swim" in this way. It is more likely they were bodysurfing, something few Europeans would ever have seen. Another was a description of a native hitting a half-penny with a stone thrown from a hundred paces (three or four hundred feet). A modern sniper with an infallibly accurate sighting scope on a high-powered rifle will be able to hit such a small target. But could a human throwing a stone do this? Only by chance. Rousseau was so keen to reverse assumptions about the superiority of European "civilization," however, that he didn't mind exaggerating native abilities to make his case.

18 For an engaging overview of how copying the great writers and artists was considered the road to success, and how "originality" of authorship only became a new, and at first a very discouraged ideal in the middle of the eighteenth century, see Jack Lynch: "The Perfectly Acceptable Practice of Literary Theft: Plagiarism, Copyright, and the Eighteenth Century," at: http://www.writing-world.com/rights/lynch.shtml

19 Cañizares-Esguerra, *How to Write the History*, p.50. This attitude that all published material in the public domain is free of access continued until late in the eighteenth century. Two decades after Delaporte's death, a gentleman named F. Pages, published a book entitled *Nouveau Voyage au tour du monde, en Asie, en Amérique, et en Afrique* (Paris: Chez H. J. Jansen, 1797), which included a great deal of unattributed material taken word for word ... from Delaporte's *Le Voyageur François*.

authentic and truthful human experience. One of the first English essays to argue that to express personal feeling and authorial *originality* is far preferable to "slavish" *imitation*, was published around the same time Le Voyageur François series was being released.[20]

The key metaphor for this new "Romantic" trend, as it came to be called, was not the *mirror*, but the *lamp*. If you want to know the truth, look within to the burning flame of your own natural light. As did every other thinker of his time (and ours), it is very likely that Delaporte wrestled with this tension between outer and inner reality and truth. This can be seen in the sometimes conflicting narratives he presents about Canadian Indians, and in the many comparisons — some very critical, some very admiring — of their natural way of life, with the moral corruption, materialism, inequality, and artificiality of European life. But in general, his "Notice to Readers," as well as the selections from his source texts suggest that with his travel publications he tended to resist the new trend of feeling, bowing to it only occasionally, and instead favoured a more objective reporting.

Noble, or Ignoble?

One example of the rising romantic trend that Delaporte took directly, word for word from Rousseau, will illustrate its influence. And the reader can imagine the shock when I realized at a certain point that I was not translating something Delaporte had written, but rather a piece of Rousseau's own moral reasoning, word for word, that Delaporte had imported.[21] In this passage, the Indian is presented as what we today would call a "Noble Savage,"[22] who is

---

20 Edward Young, "Conjectures Concerning Original Composition," 1759.

21 The piece was from "Letter" No. XVIII, of Jean-Jacques Rousseau's *Lettres Morales* (*Letters on Morality*, 1757–1758). But it was Rousseau's earlier "Discourse on the Origin and Basis of Inequality Among Men," now known simply as his "Second Discourse," an essay he submitted to a contest mounted by the Academy of Dijon, France, in 1754, that was so influential throughout European society. The basis of his argument was that European people once existed in a state of nature — much as he imagined all aboriginal people to live still — but became corrupted and artificial (that is, became "civil") through institutions he considered vicious, such as private property. The most famous sentence in his Discourse was: "The first man who enclosed a plot of ground and thought of saying, 'This is mine,' and found others stupid enough to believe him, was the true founder of civil society." He was voicing a very ancient complaint that it was *meum* and *tuum* (dividing the world into *mine* and *thine* — personal private property) that originally corrupted mankind. This new, envy-based public philosophy fed the fires of revolution in France for a hundred years, and is present today in complaints about "the one per cent".

22 This phrase has been applied to Rousseau's ideas about native people, but he never used the phrase himself. It's first use in French was likely by the French ethnographer Marc Lescarbot in 1609, when he encountered Mi'kmaq Indians in Nova Scotia engaged in a daily hunt. In Europe, only nobles had the leisure to hunt; hence, Lescarbot's solely practical description of them as "noble" savages. The first literary use of the term in English was by the poet John Dryden in

naturally good, and who lives under a natural moral law that operates like an inner light, a lamp lighting his way and guiding his behaviour so surely that he has no need for a written constitution, law courts, or a police force. The natives of Canada, as the admiring French explorer Samuel Champlain observed a century and a half before this book was published, live "*ni foi, ni loi, ni Roi*" — with neither Christian faith, nor a Rule of Law, nor a King to command them. How astonishing was that?

In reproducing this example from Rousseau, Delaporte was presenting his readers with a powerful criticism of the widely-accepted belief that to be "civilized" is to be superior to natural, less-civilized human beings. Indeed, Rousseau's most influential opinion — one that undergirded the French Revolution of 1789 — was that we are all born good in a state of nature, but modern civilization, with the advent of concepts like private property, materialism, and class divisions of rich and poor, corrupts our morals, and brings about the necessity for the whole tangled apparatus of the modern state with its burdensome laws and policing powers.[23] But these things

---

his play *Conquest of Granada*, of 1672, but now, more in the sense of a nobility of character. There is much ancient precedent in Western history for the notion of once-perfect and natural human beings, such as the pre-lapsarian Garden of Eden story, Homer's vision of the Indigenous "Pelasgians," Virgil's description of Scythians, and Tacitus' view of primitive Germans. And from America we have such as the *Journal* of Christopher Columbus of 1493, with its rendering of naked and peace-loving Arawak Indians. But the greatest influence on Rousseau came from the feast of travel narratives published in the eighteenth century — a debt he does not conceal. The historian Gilbert Chinard, in his article, "*Influence des récits de voyages sur la philosophie de J.J. Rousseau*" (Journal of *The Modern Language Association of America*, 1911), ends by stating that Rousseau should not be considered some obscure isolated genius, because "he simply lent his passionate eloquence to ideas for which *the public had been prepared for many long years by the stories of travellers.*" [My translation of Chinard's French text, and my emphasis].

23 I am grateful for the reminder from my friend and colleague, Professor Harley Price, that the Enlightenment myth of an original, pre-civilized epoch of innocence goes back to the classical theme of the Golden Age, for a demonstration of which he sent me Ovid's rendering (*Met*. I): "Golden was that first age, which, with no one to compel, without a law, of its own will, kept faith and did the right. There was no fear of punishment, no threatening words to be read on brazen tablets; no suppliant throng gazed fearfully upon its judge's face; but without defenders lived secure. Not yet had the pine-tree ... descended thence into the watery plain to visit other lands ... Not yet were cities begirt with steep moats; there were no trumpets of straight, no horns of curving brass, no swords or helmets. There was no need at all of armed men, for nations, secure from war's alarms, passed the years in gentle ease ... And men, content with food which came with no one's seeking, gathered the arbute fruit, strawberries ..., cornel cherries, berries hanging thick upon the prickly bramble, and acorns fallen from the spreading tree of Jove ...." Professor Price adds that the "authentic" Romantic "inner lamp" seems, similarly, to be related to the Heracleitean and Stoic motives of the *scintilla dei* and the *Logos spermatikos*, that is, the inner (natural) law that relativizes all merely man-made political constitutions, positive legal codes, and social conventions. Stoic natural law is in turn related to other Stoic beliefs according to which all morality is universal and innate, laid down in certain psychic predispositions (*prolepseis*) that are implanted before birth in all members of the human species, and give rise to the "common conceptions" (*koinoi*

were mysteriously absent among the Indians of Canada, who seemed to self-govern with far less crime and corruption — a reality that astonished Europeans. The conclusion argued by reformers like Rousseau (over whose writings admiring crowds often fell into hysteria) was that European society as it exists must be destroyed, and rebuilt on a more natural footing. As the high priest of this anti-establishment movement, he did not want us to return to the past, which at any rate he considered impossible. Rather, he wanted to overthrow the present in order to construct the politically and morally perfect society of the future by incorporating into modern life something akin to the natural social piety of … the Indian. Delaporte includes many instances of this thinking, as when he writes of a few primitive Indian dwellings that "they are made in the perfect image of man in the infancy of the world." The implied criticism is that a grandiose French structure like the Palace of Versailles, with all that a lavish absolute monarchy implies, was made in the image of imperfect Man.

In this sense, many travel narratives of the eighteenth century, including this one, even without this explicit intent, were dangerously subversive, as they primed commoners and social theorists to yearn imaginatively for true liberty and a political equality of condition and social justice they simply did not enjoy in Europe. In short, travel narratives such as this one about equality, liberty, and communal life in the New World, regardless of how factually true, or untrue, were used by many readers to shine a prosecutor's light on the evils of their own society.[24]

However — and herein lies the tension of which I speak — just prior to reading this passage about the innate goodness of natural man, there is

---

ennoiai) about God, right and wrong, etc., observable in peoples of every region, nation, and culture. It was the penumbra of such conceptions that Delaporte sensed in the Indians of Canada.

24 Readers interested in the ongoing controversies as to whether or not North American Indians were a naturally good, spiritual, nature-loving, animal-conservationist, democratic, communal and non-materialistic people (i.e., were noble); or, were a primitive, politically and legally backward people plagued with superstition, war, revenge, violence, cannibalism, waste of animal resources, and more (i.e., ignoble), will find a lot of bracing material in James Clifton, ed., *The Invented Indian* (New Brunswick, New Jersey, USA: Transaction Publishers, 1990). There is a veritable industry of controversial scholarship on such topics, which it is not my purpose to pursue here. But I cannot resist a judgement. I believe the vision of the natural and perfect Indian as imagined in the past — especially when described categorically as everything the detested and imperfect Whiteman was not, and is not today — amounts to a litany of historical exaggerations. The constructed images of both the Indian (as mostly good) and the Whiteman (as mostly evil) are both historical conceits constructed for various moral and political purposes, then and now. In short, "the Indian", as condemned by himself and by his real as well as literary sympathizers to an allegorical jail, ought to be rescued. That is, freed from allegory altogether, and recognized as a real live human being, with all the perfections and imperfections pertaining thereto, past, present, and future. As readers will see, by way of the segments he includes in this book, Delaporte has done a very good job of balancing the vices and virtues of all parties.

a gruesome and pitiful passage about a starving Indian who, in order to survive … kills and eats his own children! This is a behaviour people have always found shockingly repugnant and ignoble. But it is followed by a scene in which an Indian woman, after debating passionately with her husband in a sinking canoe about which of them should die to save their only child, throws herself into the river to drown. It is the juxtaposition of such scenes that serves to illustrate the conflict of worldviews that runs through *Le Voyageur François*, between the idea that human beings are naturally good, and the many accounts of human evil Delaporte includes, such as slavery, grotesquely cruel instances of torture, tribal genocides, and cannibalism.[25] Throughout this book, the Indians of Canada are presented in their most noble, and most ignoble manifestations.

To sum up, reason vs. romance, and the noble vs. ignoble savage are the main underlying, if unspoken, themes of this book, and I suspect they generated an intellectual and moral struggle in the mind of Delaporte himself. As a Jesuit Christian he was certainly thoroughly imbued with a belief in original sin, and that God and redemption can be found through faith. But he also lived in the Age of Reason, and by virtue of his Notice to Readers, and the accounts he has compiled and contrasted in the spirit of objectivity, we can see that he was just as imbued with the belief that other kinds of truth can be found through reason and science.[26] A good example of the latter is the segment he includes describing a search for the Northwest Passage

---

25 The topic of Indian Cannibalism — was it fact or fiction? — will be addressed further in notes to the translated text. For now, it suffices to say that almost all Europeans who made first contact with Canada's Indians shared a worldview shaped by the Christian religion, and many were practicing missionaries, some of whom may have had a vested interest in unfairly portraying Indians as barbaric cannibals badly in need of conversion. On the other hand, sufficient research into this morbid phenomenon will convince most readers that throughout human history cannibalism has been practiced by many different peoples for various reasons, including: starvation, sacred ritual, to terrorize enemies, for revenge, for ingestion of virtues and powers, and certainly by some Indians of Canada, and even by some starving British Sailors. An oft-cited book skeptical of all cannibalism is by William Arens, *The Man-Eating Myth: Anthropology and Anthropophagy* (Oxford: Oxford University Press, 1980). The best rebuttal of Arens' book is a scolding article by anthropologist Thomas Abler, "Iroquois Cannibalism: Fact not Fiction," published in *Ethnohistory* (1980), vol. 27, (4), pp. 309-316. The article cites references to many reports of Indian Cannibalism, including James V. Wright, "The Ontario Iroquois Tradition," *National Museum of Canada, Bulletin 210*, who attests that the practice of cannibalism made its appearance in Ontario in the 14th. century, and peaked in the mid-16th. century. Professor Cecil Chabot has produced a nuanced examination of Indian (and some Whiteman) Cannibalism with his PhD dissertation: "Cannibal *Wihtiko*: Finding Native-Newcomer Common Ground" (University of Ottawa, 2016), which is available online here: http://www.ruor.uottawa.ca/bitstream/10393/33452/1/Chabot_Cecil_2016_thesis.pdf

26 The metaphysics of St. Thomas Aquinas, which is a synthesis of reason and faith, has been central to the theology of Catholicism since the fifteenth century, and his "five ways" of knowing God via reason alone remain an important element of the Catholic tradition.

by using deep fresh-water sampling, and deductive calculations about ocean currents and land forms.

About Terminology

Sensitivities abound today around words like "savages", and "nation", as used with respect to native people. But a translation must be a translation, and not a misrepresentation, just as historical events must be revealed as they were, and not bowdlerized, sanitized, or subjected to political correctness — all forms of censorship that convert history into a lie.

The word "savage" is derived from Latin "*Silva*", meaning "forest", or "wild", and many authors suggest that prior to Delaporte's time it was simply used in a bemused or admiring way to describe those who live freely in nature.[27] But by mid-eighteenth century the many stark contrasts between the "savage" and the "civilized" that were being revealed in various kinds of travel literature were so well known as to raise a host of questions and judgements.[28]

It seems pretty clear that when using the term "savage", Delaporte often echoed the meaning of his day, which definitely connoted the lack of a highly-developed civilization, and hence, an inferiority to European society. This is underscored by the fact that after a sentence about "savages," he often began the next sentence with a phrase such as, "These barbarians ...", or something similar. He was making sure we knew what he meant. But this was not always so, and Delaporte was careful to include many praiseworthy scenes in which his savages and their customs and morals are admired and presented as clearly superior to those of Europeans. At any rate, a brief mind-experiment may help understand the realities of the time in which he lived, as in the following contrast.

Educated Europeans coming to Canada by the eighteenth century knew of all the great Greek and Roman philosophers; knew of the poetry and plays

---

27 See, for example, David Hackett Fischer, *Champlain's Dream* (Toronto: Vintage Canada, 2008), pp. 142-154. This distinguished historian explains that as a French Humanist thinker travelling to Canada in 1603, a core aspect of Champlain's dream was to convert the Indians to Christianity and to co-exist with them, for he "respected the Humanity of the Indians, even in their 'savage state' " (p.154). Fischer writes that in using the term "savages" Champlain did not mean an inferior race of people. However, he adds that Champlain "thought that some of their customs were inferior to the practices of civilized nations," and that "they lived like brute beasts," and deeply believed "the Indians were lost souls, with no hope of redemption until they were taught the true faith" (p.144). It would appear that Champlain believed the Indians were noble and ignoble at the same time — as did Delaporte.

28 Much of the discussion had to do with the idea that just as every child progresses from simple to more complex stages of development, so do civilizations: the Indians of Canada were simply at an earlier stage than Europeans and so had a "younger" mentality.

of Dante, Racine, Rabelais, and Shakespeare; knew the music of Handel and Bach; knew of the theories of great mathematicians, chemists, and physicists like Newton; and knew of philosophers like Descartes, Locke, and Hobbes. They also had complex tools, horse-drawn wheeled vehicles, and massive warships, complex systems of government and laws, and worshipped in some of the greatest architectural structures ever built. To meet up with Canada's Indians must have been quite a shock.

In stark contrast, the Indian tribes of Eastern Canada (upon which this book centers), were migratory hunters and gatherers, some of whom practiced limited agriculture;[29] but they had no wheel, and so no roads, and no horses or other beasts of burden except dogs; no complex music or instruments beyond the drum and a simple flute, no system of writing beyond some hieroglyphs or signs, and so no written literature, poetry, prose, or philosophy; no mathematics beyond simple counting, or physics or chemistry; no fixed dwellings except the semi-permanent longhouse, otherwise only very practical but flimsy tents of bark and animal hides; so no monumental architecture; no fixed system of laws or general government;[30] no firearms, no efficient agricultural tools, very little durable pottery, and no metal weapons, machinery, or cooking pots of any kind. In addition, many tribes engaged in ceaseless wars of revenge, practiced total slaughter of enemies, took many slaves (or adopted captives by force), and delighted in horribly cruel tortures, human sacrifice, and often ritual cannibalism.

Yet, to some extent, Europeans and Indians pitied each others' way of life. Imagine yourself as an Indian warrior who lives freely with his family, but under no ruler, very fit, muscular, and agile, with white teeth and almost hairless tanned skin, standing on the shore awaiting the landing of a few European explorers. What would you have seen? Mainly strangely-clad, short, capped and straggly-bearded men with discoloured teeth. You would

---

[29] The Iroquois and the Hurons practiced more extensive agriculture than most Indian nations, but they had no effective notions of fallowing, manuring, irrigation, or crop rotation, and so after about a decade, they had to move their semi-permanent villages to new ground once the local land, game, and available firewood were exhausted (see Diamond Jenness, *Indians of Canada* (Ottawa, National Museum of Canada, Bulletin 65, Anthropological Series No. 15, 1932. Also published by Minister of Supply and Services Canada, 1977), p.30: "Outside the Lowlands of Eastern Canada, there was no agriculture ..."). The Longhouses of the Huron were more durable than tipis, and housed many families at once, but had to be rebuilt when they migrated to virgin land. And some nations had impressive stockaded villages that, as Samuel Champlain discovered, were difficult to breach. The Kwakiutl and other West Coast tribes were more stationary and had fixed and impressive wooden buildings. But the Plains, Eastern, and Northern nations of Canada were all migratory or semi-migratory.

[30] The Iroquois Confederacy was an organization established mostly to control and direct matters of war and military alliances, not for establishing general laws of social and political life, commerce, equity, or criminal justice.

have considered them your inferior as ugly and barbaric savages. Especially when you learned that they lived in smelly cities, without clean running rivers or ample forests, were oppressed under countless laws, and ruled over by a single person — sometimes a child King — who could lock them up arbitrarily, in societies with a few astonishingly rich, bewigged, powdered and effeminate nobles who walked without conscience past poor people lying in rags on their streets. We can see how each party would regard the other as their inferior. These are the underlying, if often unspoken tensions and two-way contrasts laid out in the narrative of this book.

In view of such crosscurrents of feeling, and in order to preserve the sense of Indian nobility that is clearly communicated in this book, yet while staying true to the implications of a want of civilization among them and the explicit critiques of barbarism expressed — also, to preserve the honesty of what Delaporte published — I have kept the word "savages," but capitalized it as "Savages" throughout.

As for the word "Nation" — it is used throughout this text when describing the Indians of Canada. And I have kept it, too. But readers should be aware that Europeans of that time used this word in the context of the common ethnic or blood lineage of a "'people", or a "tribe", rather than to indicate a legally-bounded territory of land governed and defended by a common central authority, and recognized as inviolable by other similar nations, regardless of the blood lineage or ethnicity of those who lived within those boundaries. In this sense, "nation" as used loosely in this book, refers to an ethnic "people" of common blood, including the traditional customs of those people, rather than to a permanent place or territory.

I say "loosely", because along with the word *nation*, Delaporte used the French terms *tribu* (tribe), *troupe* (troop, band), *peuple* (people), and *patrie* (native land, homeland), and sometimes all of them in the same paragraph! In general, he seemed to be discerning an irregular hierarchical distinction between different blood *nations* — Iroquois, Huron, etc; — and *tribes*, or smaller divisions of a single nation living in groups, or in villages.

About This Translation

To translate a book about Canada that has never before been available to English-speaking readers, has been a very special personal satisfaction, and it is a pleasure to share the result with fellow citizens — especially with young adults who stand to gain a great deal of lively insight into the beginnings of their own nation.

I have been reading complex political and philosophical writings in French for many decades. But a translation, especially from a somewhat archaic French into English, is a different sort of challenge. When I taught comparative literature at York University in the early 1970s I assigned what I thought was the very best translation of Flaubert's novel *Madame Bovary* to the class. But some students brought other translations, which meant we couldn't discuss even the very first sentence, because each translated French sentence produced a slightly different English sentence. So I wrote the first sentence of this novel on the blackboard, first in Flaubert's French, then in three different English translations, and we spent the most illuminating class I can remember comparing the meanings of each of them to the original French.

What that exercise made very clear, is that a translation can never be a strict and direct rendering of the original. Rather, it is a creative act that strives to produce a new and faithful rendering of the spirit of the text that the translator hopes will be just as enjoyable as the original. But in the process, this act raises many questions. Should I translate the French strictly, even if it sounds a little odd in modern English? Or find a better word to capture the original sense? Any good dictionary shows a small feast of options for the meaning of each word given. So which one should it be? What about words that have gone out of use altogether? Should I smooth over any stylistic infelicities in the original? Join abrupt sentences? Break up overly-long paragraphs? In the end, it became pretty clear that a good translation is an art, and not a science.

I have produced what I would call a very close, but free translation of Delaporte's book, striving to preserve the original lively voice and sharp sense of observation throughout, without losing any of the feeling of first-hand experiences he presents on every page.

The original *Le Voyageur François* is divided into "Letters," as mentioned, and I have preserved this convention in my translation. But Delaporte often changed subjects abruptly, sometimes right in the middle of a paragraph. So as a convenience for the reader, I have added my own subject headings throughout his text to indicate these changes, which I hope will help the reader to enjoy the result as much as I have enjoyed producing it.

LE
VOYAGEUR
FRANÇOIS,
OU
LA CONNOISSANCE
DE L'ANCIEN
ET DU NOUVEAU MONDE,

Mis au jour par M. l'abbé DELAPORTE.

TOME HUITIEME.

A PARIS

Chez VINCENT, Imprimeur-Libraire,
rue S. Severin.

M DCC LXVIII.

Avec Approbation, & Privilége du Roi.

1768

The title page from the original 1768 Edition.

LETTRE XCV.

LA BAYE D'HUDSON.

EN traversant le détroit de Davis, pour nous rendre à celui d'Hudson, nous découvrîmes plusieurs de ces montagnes de glaces flottantes, dont quelques-unes paroissoient avoir plus de quinze cens pieds d'épaisseur. Ces masses entassées les unes sur les autres, sont d'une figure monstrueuse ; & la principale attention du pilote doit être de les éviter. Ces mers offrent très-fréquemment des débris de vaisseaux fracassés par la force des glaces. Rien n'est si dangereux que d'aller se heurter contre quelqu'un de ces glaçons : s'il ne se brise pas par le choc, il fait, sur le navire, le même effet, que le contre-coup d'un rocher. C'est pour cette raison, que tous les bâtimens destinés aux mers Glaciales, sont extrêmement forts en bois, principalement sur le devant. Quand un bâtiment se trouve pris entre deux de ces

LE
VOYAGEUR
FRANÇOIS.

THE FRENCH TRAVELER

LETTER 95

HUDSON BAY

Ice Monsters

WHILE crossing Davis Strait in order to get to Hudson Strait, we discovered a great many of those mountains of floating ice, some of which seemed to be more than fifteen-hundred feet in thickness. These massive objects, all jammed together, are really a monstrous sight, and the aim of any navigator should be to avoid them at all costs. These waters quite frequently offer up the wreckages of ships crushed by the force of this ice, and nothing is as dangerous as to allow one's ship to crash into one of these icebergs. If the ship is not damaged by the mere shock of contact, it nevertheless incurs the same damage as if it had run straight onto a rock. That's why all the ships bound for such frozen seas are constructed of very thick timbers, especially on the bow. When a vessel finds itself stuck between two of these ice-mountains, it is almost impossible for it to avoid total destruction. We have on our ship an Englishman, who made this very same voyage last year on a British ship, and who told us a story about how a long-boat became stuck in this way between two heaps of ice, was lifted completely out of the water, and ended up dry-stranded on one of them. As it was not damaged in any way, the crew simply manoeuvred the boat back into the water as soon as the two masses of ice became separated ... and the boat continued on its way! It is very easy to sense the proximity of these ice-giants, because the temperature of the air surrounding them changes so suddenly, becoming colder the closer we approach them. Even then, they announce their presence by way of a lot of low and thick fog, and although it is often dangerous to approach these moving ice-monsters, they also have their usefulness: the crews gather up fresh water from the hollows in the ice and fill their empty barrels.

You have asked, Madam, how these enormous masses of ice are formed? That is a question in the minds of everyone. According to the most common opinion, these are chunks that break off from the from the mountains of ice that dominate the coasts. They break off in due course due to their own weight, fall into the sea, and are carried off by the currents. After that, these icebergs increase, rather than diminish in size. The smaller chunks, which fill the straits, the bays, and every part of the ocean here, tend to attach themselves to the larger floating islands of ice, either through the action of the waves that wash over them constantly and as instantly turn to ice, or, by the effects of the frequent damp mists that descend like minute raindrops and coat them, yet again with more ice.

In Search of a North-West Passage

The Englishman whom I have mentioned to you, was once engaged by an English company to undertake the discovery of a Northwest passage to the East Indies. The story of this famous passage, and the various efforts made over the last few centuries to discover it, were familiar to him, and he spoke of it with all the more pleasure because he considered it essential to the growth of commerce and shipping.

"It was not in the present," he told us, "that this great undertaking was first conceived. As far back as the 15th century, Jean Cabot,[31] a very capable Venetian sailor, offered his services to Henry VII, the King of England,[32] for the discovery of this passage. The King listened with interest, and gave him Letters Patent authorising him to make this voyage at the expense of the government for the discovery and settlement of unknown lands. Cabot did not discover any Northwest passage; but we nevertheless attribute to him the discovery of North America, and it is based on this fact of history that we stake our claim to sovereignty of this country. So it is to the search for this passage," continued the Englishman, "that we owe the origin of

---

31 Giovanni Caboto (c. 1450?–1498?) Italian explorer, leader of voyages of discovery from Bristol to North America in 1497 and 1498. See Dictionary of Canadian Biography (hereafter, DCB), for further details. The online version is here: http://www.biographi.ca/en/index.php

32 Henry VII of England (1457–1509).

our settlements, and consequently, our business success and our maritime powers. Sebastien Cabot,[33] the son of Jean, above, had accompanied his father on that expedition. But in despair over the prospect of succeeding, he gave up the notion of searching for the passage to the West, and began searching to the North-East. It is true that he had no more success with his attempt. However, continued our Englishman, "it is to his efforts that we owe our business dealings with Russia, and our Greenland fishing industry — both so important to England — and from which we have gained so much commercial advantage. And so, even though the effort to find a shorter route to India has been so costly, without leading us to the objective for which we had hoped, the results have nevertheless been so fruitful that there is no reason to be discouraged, nor to cease searching.

"After the death of Sebastien Cabot, another sailor named *Frobisher*[34] undertook this by now famous adventure, during the reign of Queen Elizabeth.[35] He sailed by way of a strait between two islands neighbouring Greenland, which he named after himself. It's remarkable that he came back from all three consecutive expeditions, without success. Captain Davis[36] undertook the same expedition as Frobisher, but he, too, gained from it no greater glory than to give his name to the lands he discovered. He believed, however, that he had pinned down the possibility of discovering the Northwest passage with such a degree of certitude that he named the exact locations where he thought it ought to be found. And he added that in future this could be attempted without much expense in view of the fact that the fishing there is more than sufficient to defray the costs of the expedition. Ever since that time we have had positive expectations for this discovery, which we consider will come to pass sooner or later.

The Pitiable Death of Henry Hudson

"Someone who extended this search farther than anyone else, is the celebrated and most unfortunate explorer, Henry Hudson,[37] whose efforts were

---

33 Sebastiani Caboto (1484-1587), son of Jean Cabot. See DCB for further details.

34 Sir Martin Frobisher (c. 1535 or 1539-1594) was an English seaman and privateer (licensed pirate) who made three voyages to the New World to look for the Northwest Passage.

35 Queen Elizabeth I (1533-1603) acceded to the English throne at the age of 25 and held it for 44 years.

36 John Davis or Davys (c. 1550 - December 1605) was one of the chief English navigators and explorers under Elizabeth I. He led several voyages to discover the Northwest Passage, served as pilot and captain on both Dutch and English voyages to the East Indies. He discovered the Falkland Islands (today a Crown Dependency of the United Kingdom) in August 1592.

37 Sir Henry Hudson (b.,? - d. 1611), an English sea explorer and navigator, made two attempts on

tireless, and his courage a match for every circumstance he encountered. He entered the strait since called the Strait of Hudson, and thence into the bay that today still bears his name. Then, a vicious fellow whose life Hudson had once saved, along with a few other crew members, conspired against him. Just when the ship was ready to hoist sail and return to England, they forced Hudson, his son John, and a few others into a long-boat and cut them loose, with no provisions or weapons whatsoever. They were abandoned thus in the most terrible part of the bay, where no doubt they perished in great misery, for no one has ever learned what became of them.

Hunting for the Northwest Passage

"Captains Button,[38] Baffin,[39] Bristol,[40] and many others after Hudson made new attempts, but none of them was successful at finding this most sought-after passage — though all of them agreed in their telling of these things that we would eventually succeed in discovering it. Bristol's Journal gave a list of such frightening calamities and miseries suffered in Hudson Bay, that ever since the publication of his voyage, no one dared to think of these sorts of undertaking, which were abandoned for about thirty years. But finally, in 1746, there was a last expedition, in command of which were Captains Moore,[41] and Smith,[42] who very much wanted to employ me. I have in my pocket a copy of the instructions given to them: perhaps you will not be inconvenienced to see what precautions are taken to ensure the success

---

behalf of English merchants to find a prospective Northwest Passage to Cathay (today's China) via a route above the Arctic Circle. Hudson discovered a strait, and an immense bay (now named after him) on his final expedition, while searching for a Northwest Passage. See DCB for further details.

38 Thomas Button (b? – d. 1634). In April 1612, Button sailed in command of the *Resolution* and the *Discovery*. The "Company of the Merchants Discoverers of the North-West Passage" (known as The Northwest Company) was granted its charter on 26 July 1612. See DCB for further details.

39 William Baffin, arctic explorer (b. 1584?; d. 1622 — from a cannonball wound to the stomach during an Anglo-Persian assault on a Portuguese fort in the Persian Gulf.). In 1612, Baffin was made chief pilot on Captain James Hall's ship *Patience*, and was present when Hall was killed by an Inuk off the coast of western Greenland, where Hall had previously taken Inuit captives. Baffin is primarily known as an arctic explorer who went in search of a Northwest passage. Baffin Land and Baffin Bay are named after him.

40 Thus far I have been unable to find a reference for an arctic explorer with surname Bristol. This is possibly a reference to Captain Thomas James of Bristol, who ventured in the Arctic in 1631–1632.

41 Several men by the name of Thomas Moore were active exploring the Hudson Bay Area. See DCB for details.

42 Francis Smith first appears in the records of the Hudson's Bay Company as a second mate on its ship *Seahorse*, which sailed to Hudson Bay in 1737. See DCB for further details.

of this undertaking? At the same time, these may serve to guide us in the various expeditions we are going to take.

"Here, Madam, are the terms of the instructions":

Instructions to Explorers to Avoid Dangers[43]

You will put to sail to the south of Cape Farewell,[44] while avoiding the icebergs, steering your course toward the entrance to Hudson Bay, between Button[45] and Resolution Islands.[46] In the event that the ice is not sufficiently dispersed, your first meeting will be to the East of these first islands so that you can enter the strait with safety. If the passage is open, you will remain there only one or two days — at least insofar as it is not near the time for high tide — for then the currents are too fast. In this latter case, you would be better off to wait a few days until the tides and the currents weaken. In passing through the strait, stick as close as possible to the north side, while keeping a reasonable distance from both, such that you are able to hear each others' cannons, and render each other assistance in the event that there are any accidents while among the ice-floes.

If you get separated in the strait, your closest rendezvous point will be Digges' Island.[47] The one who gets there first will await the other for no more than two days, and if the latter does not show up, the former will build a lookout or a rock cairn beside the main cape, with a Letter to alert the other that he has continued on and has left for the next closest rendezvous.

When you have found Digges Island, and if you have a headwind, drop anchor for a couple of tides, and observe with great care the direction, the speed, the height, the time of each tide. But if the wind is favourable, and you are both together, make your rendezvous Marble Island.[48] Wherever you happen upon

---

43 Instructions to explorers were often issued by their governments, or by private investor groups that authorized and financed their explorations. Laurence Rooke, for example, published a three-page "Directions for Seamen, Bound for Far Voyages," in the *Philosophical Transactions* of The Royal Society of England, 1665-1666.

44 Cape Farewell is the southernmost tip of Greenland.

45 Sir Thomas Button (b.? - d.1634). Button was selected in 1612 to command an expedition to find out what had become of Henry Hudson, who was set adrift by a mutinous crew in the previous spring, and to complete "ye full and perfect discovery of the North-west Passage." See DCB for further details.

46 Resolution Island is one of the many uninhabited Canadian Arctic islands in what is now Qikiqtaaluk Region, Nunavut, and is located in Hudson Strait.

47 The Digges Islands are part of the Canadian Arctic Archipelago in the present territory of Nunavut. The two islands, West Digges and East Digges, are located in Digges Sound, an arm of Hudson Bay, where the strong currents of the bay meet Hudson Strait. In *Le Voyageur François*, Delaporte spells this as "Diggs", rather than Digges, and speaks of one island, rather than two.

48 Marble Island is one of several uninhabited Canadian arctic islands in Nunavut, located within

land, make exact observations on all the rivers, bays, and promontories, and the like. You must draw maps on which you will mark the details of each location, and the sights such as they appear from your ships.

Also mark the marshes, the depths, and all compass variations. If you happen to spot any currents coming from the West, and you see any advantageous openings without any ice, you should enter, albeit with a great deal of precaution, and only after sending your long-boat in advance. You must trace the latitude of every cape, and the orientation of the countryside, and take care to locate several good ports where you can take cover in the case of storms or bad winds.

If you encounter the tide, and after having passed the strait of Wager, you stumble upon an open sea, and without ice, you can be assured of a safe passage, for it is almost certain that you are not far from the ocean. You will then push on southward, where you will find a warmer and more agreeable climate to pass the winter. At this point, you may be persuaded all the more of the reality of your discovery. If, after having travelled past the intervening lands, you see whales who steer their course to the southwest, that will be yet more evidence of a navigable passage to a Western Ocean, to which these whales are attempting to return. In this event you ought to choose some navigable rivers for your trip, and a good port if you believe there is nothing to fear from the local inhabitants, and they appear to be humane and civilized. If, on the other hand, you have reason to fear trouble from them — which you must take great care to avoid — then you must go to the trouble of passing the winter on some island, at a safe distance from the mainland, where you can find shelter from any kind of surprise. For this purpose you must set up bodyguards and lookouts just as if you were in enemy country. If the island is fertile, then when spring arrives you must busy yourself and your crew with converting some of the land into a garden. There, you can sow various vegetable seeds, and plant whatever trees and plants you may have brought from England, be it for the use of the local inhabitants, for the future needs of your own compatriots, or for those who may come there in future. You must also leave there any domestic fowl such as chickens, or pigeons, if you have such on board. And you must take special care to note the different kinds of produce from those we have in Europe.

In the event you encounter a few Savages as you pass Hudson strait, you will not take time to engage with them. But you will offer them a few gifts of tools, or other things they may prefer. If after having crossed the Bay, you come into contact with Eskimos, you must be sure to win their friendship, and do not refuse to trade with them. You must do your best to leave them with a good

---

western Hudson Bay. The closest community is Rankin Inlet. During the age of sail, this island was valued as a harbour for overwintering in the Arctic Ocean.

impression of yourselves by giving them something more than they are used to receiving for their furs from the Company [Hudson Bay Company], and by letting them choose from among your goods, such as to win their confidence in the future. But don't linger there any longer than is necessary to make your observations of the tide.

If you come across other nations more civilized than the Eskimos, don't get involved with them except for casual negotiations, for fear that you may be forced into some port. You should lead them to believe that when you return next spring, you will be most pleased to open trade with them, which they will find most advantageous, and that will bind you with them in a long-lasting friendship. But do not stop there for any reason if the weather and the wind allow you to push ahead. At every place you come across, if they are uninhabited, you will take possession of the place in the name of British Sovereignty, as the first owner, while raising a monument of wood or stone, with an inscription, and giving English names to every port, river, cape, island, etc. But if you find civilized inhabitants there, be careful not to create distrust while seeking to appropriate their domain for yourself, so that at the least, on your return, they do not willingly surrender the possession of some land to you just to secure your commerce afterwards. You are not to capture anyone by force to take with you; but if anyone voluntarily asks to follow you, you can take them back to England.

In the event that you leave some of our own people in this country, you must take care to leave them a good supply of the sorts of trinkets most pleasing to the local inhabitants, so that they can get close to them by giving small gifts. You must also leave them paper, pens, ink, grains, and root-stock and other things having to do with gardening. If you get near any ports or rivers where there are civilized people living in towns or villages, you must behave with a great deal of prudence with respect to them. If they are friendly with you, you will be able to curry their favour by offering gifts; but without submitting to their authority, nor yielding to their wariness. If, on the other hand, they express any hostility — you are not to put up with that, and must get away from the coast, without, however, letting them see any sign of fear. If they start to attack you, you will begin by scaring them off with your large artillery, but without killing anyone — something you should never do unless forced to do so for your own defence. Rather, you will move away from the coast altogether until you encounter more civilized people. Then you must make alliances with them; and set up commercial relations that are profitable for Britain, and equitable for them by regulating the value of our merchandise according to the value of theirs.

If it so happens that the ships are separated after their last rendezvous, each one must try by himself to find the passage, without waiting for the other, and the place decided for meeting up again will be whatever island or port suits you both. If, by some unforeseen accident, the ships cannot make progress, whether beyond the strait of Wager[49] *or to the south, and they find neither an opening nor a passage to the West, or the Southwest, you must press on without delay to London, so you won't have to winter over anywhere, and can thus avoid useless expenditures.*

The council, which in whatever difficulty ought to decide how to undertake the discovery [of the Northwest passage] will be composed of the two captains and the chief officers of the two ships — if they happen to be together. If, on the other hand, the two ships become separated, the officers of each vessel will form the council, and the majority of votes will carry the day. If any differences of opinion arise as to how to undertake the discovery, those who may have had an opinion opposed to the majority can set this down in writing and put a signature to their reasoning in order to defend themselves if necessary. You will keep exact minutes of all your deliberations, and they must be signed by three persons, or more, before the council disbands. Upon your return you must then send them by mail from a few locations that you reach in Great Britain or Ireland, and more particularly, if the occasion presents itself, by a few ships from Hudson Bay.

"These," continues our Englishman, "are the instructions we were given on our departure. One can discern from these the nature of this expedition, and the steps taken to ensure its success. And we can sense the sincerity of intention in those who, after having conceived of their plan with such wisdom, wanted to take advantage of every possible means to have it work out for the benefit of the public, and for the furtherance of commerce and shipping.

A Fire On Board!

"Our ships set sail May 31, 1748, and nothing of any account took place until the night of the second of July, when a terrible fire started in the stern chamber of the ship I was on. The fire raged out of control so fast that it reached the ship's powder-magazine directly below, where there were twenty or thirty barrels of gunpowder, along with candles, alcoholic spirits, matches, and other combustible materials. It is not possible to express the consternation and confusion that spread amongst the whole crew. Each one of them feared that this very moment, or the next, would be their last of their lives. And for this reason we heard every possible variation of sea-going eloquence: cries, lamentations, prayers, insults, curses — succeeded each other in turn.

---

49 Wager Bay (previously: Wager River) is a long narrow inlet in Kivalliq Region, Nunavut, Canada which opens east into Roes Welcome Sound at the northwest end of Hudson Bay. Wager Bay was first charted by Christopher Middleton during his Arctic explorations of 1742. He named it after Sir Charles Wager and was trapped in the bay for three weeks until the ice cleared.

It is astonishing to witness the number of expedients that the fear of death provokes; all were ready to try any one of them without forethought, and a moment later, to abandon them due to some distraction, or to despair. In the midst of all this tumult, when he suddenly realized that the fire and the gunpowder were directly underneath him, the one who held the tiller lost his head completely and was no longer in any condition to carry out his duties. Some wanted to put to sea in the long-boats, and had as soon cut their lines, but no one had the sense of order needed to lower them. The sails were flapping with the rumble of thunder, and everyone assembled on the Bridge was awaiting the fatal moment that was going to end their sad lot, with a sort of agony etched upon their faces. Happily, despite the frightful situation in which we found ourselves, a small number of persons had managed to maintain their composure. So we soon began to draw water, and it was so well applied that the fire was quickly extinguished, and everyone recovered from their state of perplexity. The entire accident came about due to the negligence of a cabin boy who failed to keep watch over a candle!

First Time in Eskimo Country

"The rest of our trip held nothing of interest until we got to Hudson Strait, where Eskimo country begins. It is said that this name comes from the words *abenaqui esquimantsic*, which means "eaters of raw meat,"[50] because as a matter of fact they have no other means of nourishment. There is a distinction between *Eskimo-Indians*, and the *Northern Eskimos*. The latter are above the Strait, the former are in the middle of Hudson Bay. But the similarity that we notice in their language, their person, and their dress leads us to believe they were originally one people.

"We soon saw many small canoes filled with these Indians approaching us, asking to trade. They brought us whale ribs and seal skins, and in exchange we gave them axes, saws, and trinkets. They were so appreciative that the men and women stripped until almost completely naked, and sold us their leather clothing, for knives and pieces of iron. They have a strange custom of licking everything they buy before putting it in their canoe. As for their bodies? They are of middling size, fairly chubby, with swarthy faces, large heads, small and

---

50 There are conflicting opinions as to the true origin of the word "Eskimo". Cree people today associate the name with the Cree word *askâwa*, which means raw meat or eggs. Others suggest the original word that became corrupted to "Eskimo," might have been *askamiciw* (which means "he eats it raw,"). Some linguists have recently suggested that this might be a 'folk etymology' — an origin for a word which, though believed by many speakers of the language, isn't historically true. The Cree word *askimew* means "he laces snowshoes," and this may have been the original name the Crees used to refer to their Inuit neighbors. At any rate, the word *Eskimo* has recently been replaced by the term *Inuit*.

sparkling black eyes, flat noses, thick lips, long black hair, large shoulders, and extremely small feet. They are happy, sprightly, subtle, wily, and clever. Nothing can match their skill in hunting whales. One might think that they are part of the same race as the Greenlanders — and that is more or less reasonable, as they are separated from them only by the Davis Strait.

"These Savages are easily enraged, at which point they assume an air of injured dignity, but it is not difficult to frighten them. They are extremely attached to their way of life. Many of them, having been made prisoners by other Savages and brought into our settlements, always longed for their own country, even after having lived among us for a long time. One among them, having always eaten the way we do, happened to be present when an Englishman was slaughtering a seal. He virtually threw himself on the copious oil that spurted out, and swallowed all that he could scoop up with his hands with an astonishing avidity, while crying out: 'Why am I not in my own country, where I can eat as much of this oil as I want?'

"The clothing of these people is made of seal-skin, and sometimes of land and sea birds, all sewn together, and having a hood like the monks. They are closed in front from the stomach, like a shirt, and only go down to mid-calf. Their breeches are closed tightly in front and behind, like a purse, with a cord that is knotted around the waist. They have many pairs of boots and socks layered one over the other to protect them from cold and wet. The women's clothing differs from the men's, in that behind their jackets they have a kind of band that hangs down to their heels. Their hoods are also more ample, and more open around the shoulders, and are used to help them carry their babies on their backs. Their boots are likewise a lot larger than the men's, and commonly decorated with whale figures. Whenever they have to lift up their child in their arms for a short time, they stuff them in one of their boots, and leave them there until they are able to pick them up. Generally speaking, their clothes are very well sewn with ivory needles and very fine thread made from the nerves of wild animals, and split with great skill. These people display very good taste in decorating themselves with skins banded with many colours, which they wear in the form of stripes, ribbons, and cuffs, all of which lends them an air of decency and gallantry.

"Their snow-eyes, as they call them for good reason, are a novel proof of the sagacity of the Eskimo. Snow-eyes are made of small pieces of wood or ivory, of the same shape, finely worked, with which they cover their eyes, and secure them around the back of the head. They each have two slits the exact length of the eye, but narrow, and through them, one is able to see quite distinctly. This invention protects them from snow-blindness — a serious and painful illness — caused by the brightness of the light reflected on this planet. These devices improve the power of one's eyesight, and are used so habitually that when they want to see something very distant they use them like a telescope.

"We discover the same inventive spirit in the devices they use for fishing and hunting. Their darts and harpoons are very well made, as are their bows and arrows, and are perfectly suited for the uses to which they are put. They are also extremely skilled at handling their canoes, in which they carry everything they find necessary. These kayaks are ribbed with wood or whale-bone, and covered with the skin of harbour seals, and they have them both for men and for women. The men's are pointed at both ends, and are about twenty feet long, and about two feet wide. The women's, which can carry about twenty people are made of the same materials as the others, and they propel them by themselves with oars. These Savages use the sling with great skill, and can throw stones a very long way.

"We pass Hudson Strait, which is about one hundred and twenty leagues[51] long, and about eighteen wide, and goes from Resolution Island[52] to Cape Digges. From there, we enter into the Bay, and arrive at Marble Island.[53] The land is just one continuous rock cliff of a kind of white stone, very hard, and cut in some places by diversely-coloured veins of rock, white, black, and green. The tops of the peaks are very irregular and pointed and there are great quantities of enormous rock all jumbled together in confusion and piled one on top of the other, as if they had been tumbled there by some enormous flood. Beneath these rocks are very deep caves from which we can hear a kind of noise like the rumbling of angry waves; and judging by the water that falls from the crevasses, it would appear that these rocks may contain mines of copper and other minerals. In certain spots the waters have the taste of verdigris,[54] in others, they are perfectly red and tint everything they touch with this colour.

Shelter, Clothing, and Food in the Frozen Wilderness

"As our plan is to winter over at Port Nelson, we did not stay long at Marble Island. We entered Hayes River,[55] and immediately turned our thoughts to what needed to be done to set up our shelter. Some of our crew busy

---

51 A league is about three miles

52 Resolution Island in Qikiqtaaluk Region, Nunavut, is an offshore island located in Hudson Strait. Cape Digges is the easternmost point of East Digges Island.

53 Marble Island is one of several uninhabited Canadian arctic islands in Nunavut, with a history of intrigue and death. See: http://www.marbleisland.ca/history03.html for the full story.

54 Verdigris is the common name for the natural patina formed when copper, brass or bronze is weathered and exposed to air or seawater over a period of time.

55 The Hayes River flows from Molson Lake in northern Manitoba to Hudson Bay at York Factory.

themselves cutting wood for fires, and for building cabins in the style of the local inhabitants. We made them with trees about sixteen feet long, which we mounted very closely to each other, in such a way that the ends touched at the top, and spread out at the bottom. The gaps between we stuffed with moss, and on the outside we put a layer of clay. We made the doors low and narrow, and we made a space in the middle of each hut for a fireplace with a hole above to allow the smoke to escape.

"We needed to make a somewhat larger one to house the Captain and his Officers. We chose a handy and pleasant spot on a height surrounded with trees about a half-league from the river, and an equal distance from the ship. We took down a large number of pine trees, and put them to work, and sawed planks. The walls were made of large beams lined up alongside each other, with moss stuffed into the spaces between. We made the building twenty-eight feet long, and eighteen wide, with two floors, one six feet high, the other seven. A stove was placed in the middle to give off heat everywhere equally. In a word, this house was built, covered, and in a condition to be inhabited by the first day of November; which is to say, about five months after our departure from England. Winter had already announced itself as of the end of September, and one month later, the river was entirely frozen. So we soon took good measure of the cold of Hudson Bay. Our writing ink froze even when near the stove, and our beer froze in its bottles, even when covered with oakum stuffing and kept in a warm place. As the cold became unbearable outside, the sailors were set up in their cabins, and the Officers took possession of their lodging. This house was baptized, in the tradition of sailors, *The Hotel Montague*. We felt we owed this honour to the Duke of this name,[56] who expressed interest in the success of this enterprise, and was one of the main underwriters of the expedition.

"Around the same time we put on our winter clothing, which consisted of a beaver-pelt robe that fell all the way to our heels, with two vests underneath that, caps, and mittens lined with the same fur, and also with flannel. Covering the wool socks, we had boots fashioned in the style of the country, made of thick cloth, or of leather, that came up to mid-calf in length. Our boots were made of prepared elk-hide, in which we wore two or three more

---

It was an historically important river in the development of Canada, and is today a Canadian Heritage River and the longest naturally flowing river in Manitoba.

56 This reference is possibly to Montagu Wilmot, British army officer, Governor of Nova Scotia (d. at Halifax 23 May 1766). An officer from 1730, Wilmot served almost exclusively in Nova Scotia 1746–1766 and was at the siege of Louisburg, in 1758 as a regimental commander. Appointed Lieutenant-Governor of Nova Scotia March of 1763, he was advanced to governor May 1764, both appointments won by patronage. See *The Canadian Encyclopedia* for further details: http://www.thecanadianencyclopedia.ca/en/article/montagu-wilmot

pairs of large slippers. Finally, to complete our winter-wear, we had what are called "snowshoes", which are about five feet long, and eighteen inches wide, so that we don't sink into the snow when walking. Equipped in this way, we were prepared for even the worst rigours of winter. After having provided for our clothing, we started thinking about how we were going to get food. We made every effort to fashion traps for rabbits, and to shoot partridge, which are so numerous here that a hunter can kill sixty or eighty in a day, which means there is not much of a story to tell when it comes to things to eat.

"The bitter frosts grew worse as winter advanced, and became far worse when the wind came from the north, or Northwest. Often they arrived with a kind of tiny snowflake, fine like sand, that the wind drove like a wave from one open space to another. It is dangerous to find oneself exposed in such places, because this snow is usually so thick that it is almost impossible to make out anything even twenty feet away, and there is no trace left of one's own tracks. It has often happened that some people, finding themselves suddenly immersed in this sort of weather, have wandered for many hours in danger of freezing to death because they could not locate their own cabin. However, it must be admitted that this terrible cold is only felt four or five days each month, and particularly during periods of a new or a full moon which, in this country, always has a strong influence on the temperature of the air. At other times, as the cold is still really bitter, we don't find our visit so agreeable.

"Near the end of December, the crew-members start to take various provisions from our ships, which we have not made much use of up to that point, having lived mostly on the success of the hunt. The usual conveyances we used to transport these provisions, were small sleds pulled by dogs, the only beasts of burden of this country. They quite resemble our watchdogs, but they never bark, and only make a growling sound when we upset them. They carry much heavier burdens, much farther than men are able to do. They are naturally docile, and the English who get a lot of use out of them, feed them on the same footing as their servants, whereas the inhabitants of this country make them fend for themselves. On their outings, the drivers ordinarily walk in front of the sled so as to tramp down the snow with snowshoes.

Spring, Plants, Minerals, and Wonders of Nature

"With the first warmth of spring, we began once again to visit the coasts of the bay, in the hope of finding the passage that has been the object of our research. The Eskimos in these regions sometimes appear in groups along the heights of land around us, making signs as if they were calling out to us; but as we were not interested in trading, we kept going without responding to them. We studied the soil, which seemed quite fertile to us. Out in the countryside we saw a great variety of shrubs and plants, most of which are common in Europe, such as Currants, Grocer's Currants, Crane-beak, Strawberries, Angelica, Serviceberry, and so on. The banks of the lakes and rivers produce a kind of wild rice, many grasses, and really good hay. The English people who have houses there to make their trading posts profitable, have quite lovely gardens, especially at Fort York,[57] from where the bulk of our vegetables, such as beans, peas, cabbage, parsnips, and many kinds of lettuce come in abundance.

"There is no doubt that this country also supplies many kinds of minerals. I have seen an iron mine there; I have heard that we can also find lots of lead there, near Cape Churchill,[58] and the Eskimos often bring pieces of copper to our merchants. We also see a lot of talc there and a lot of differently coloured rock crystals. In the northern parts of the region we can gather a substance that resembles charcoal and burns just like it. Asbestos stone is very common, as is another sort of black stone, smooth and shiny, which flakes apart easily in thin, transparent sheets that the locals use as mirrors. Even marble is not unknown here, and one can find it perfectly white, and other veins of red, green, and blue.

"The sky in this country is hardly ever serene. In spring and autumn, one is constantly besieged by thick fog and humidity. In winter, the air is filled with an infinity of tiny shards of ice, visible to the naked eye, which form over the rivers that are not yet frozen solid. Wherever there is still unfrozen water, there arises a really thick vapour that as soon as it freezes, is carried by the winds in the form of these little darts. Then, as soon as the rivers are covered with ice, all these particles disappear. Solar haloes, or mock-suns, are quite frequent here, and we notice even more frequently, around the sun and the moon, vivid and luminous rings replete with all the colours of the rainbow. We have seen such haloes, sometimes six at a time, which made a sight as pleasant as it was surprising for Europeans. At the rising and setting of the sun, a large cone of light appears right above the sun, and this cone has no sooner disappeared with this star than the Aurora Borealis replaces it, and scatters a thousand rays of light across the hemisphere. The brightness is such that one can read by it in clear detail.

"There is rarely thunder in this country, even though the heat is quite intense for about six weeks or even for two months. But then, whenever there is a storm it is usually really violent. One can see large areas where the

---

57 York Factory was a Hudson's Bay Company fur trade post. Established in 1684 and briefly managed by the French from 1697 to1714. It became the most important fur trading post on Hudson Bay by 1730, and the major storage, manufacturing and distribution centre for the company's many other posts in the northwest by the end of the 18th century.

58 Cape Churchill is located on the Western coast of Hudson Bay.

branches and the bark of trees have been scorched by lightning; which ought to seem all the less strange, given that the lower part of these trees is covered with a white moss that catches fire as fast as hemp. This light flame spreads quickly, in the direction of the wind, and sets fire to all the bark and moss in its path. These events have at the least one advantage: they dry out the wood and make it good firewood for warming ourselves.

Keeping Warm in Bitter, Cold Canada

We would ordinarily put a cart-load of it in our stove. It was made of brick, and six feet long, two wide, and three high. When the wood was all burnt we would spread the hot coals and close the chimney; this produced a suffocating heat, along with a sulfurous smell, and despite the harshness of the weather, we were often sweating. Then, when we opened the door or the window, the cold air rushed in with a kind of fury, and suddenly transformed the humidity in that closed space into a fine snow. However, even that heat could not prevent the windows, walls and ceilings from getting covered with ice, and each night, our own breath fell like white frost on our blankets. The fire barely went out, when we as suddenly felt the real bitterness of the season. The sap from the wood framework of our cabin, which the heat of the stove had melted, began to freeze once again even harder than before, and the beams of the house made continuous noises as they cracked — often as loud as a gunshot. There was nothing liquid whatsoever that could resist the excessive cold of that country. Even wine-spirits looked like frozen oil, and other liquids even more alcoholic, became completely solid, and shattered their containers, no matter what they were made of. There is no need of salt in this country to preserve food. Wild animals, the rabbits, partridge, and pheasant, freeze as soon as they are killed, and stay that way for six months, without rotting. These animals, which ordinarily are brown or grey, become white in winter; but it is only the tips of their hair or their feathers that whiten; the rest, being less exposed to the air, keeps its natural colour.

"If, during these spells of great cold we are of a mind to handle iron, or any other hard body of a single material, the fingers will get stuck there due to the severity of the cold. One must be very careful when drinking, that the glass does not touch one's tongue or lips, or you will tear some skin off when pulling the glass away. One of our sailors, not having anything with which to close up a bottle of liquor he was taking to his cabin, used his finger, which got stuck frozen in the bottle, such that he had to sacrifice a piece of it to save the rest.

"Who wouldn't imagine that the inhabitants of such a vicious climate would not be the most unhappy of all men? But they are a long way from having such an opinion of their condition. The excellent furs in which they cover themselves, and the pelts with which their cabins are covered, puts them, in a certain sense, at the same level as those who live under more temperate skies. What ought especially to seem extraordinary, is that there are some Europeans who prefer this kind of life to all others.

"But, while I am speaking to you of the extreme cold in this country," said our Englishman, "I have almost lost sight of the goal of our discovery and the researches to which we are dedicated for part of the summer of 1746. That will be the topic of a second discussion; and, if you find it agreeable, I will add some observations on the customs and the morals of the locals."

You have wished, Madam, that I gather all these details. Having no doubt they may be of interest to you, I have the greatest eagerness to please you, and these will be the subject of the next letter.

I remain, etc.

From the area around the island of Newfoundland, July 13, 1747.

Letter 96

HUDSON BAY ~ continued

THE fond hope we all shared to know a country where we counted on spending some time was not long in being fulfilled, for that very evening our Englishman took up his narrative once again.

An Eskimo to the Rescue! And How They Live

"We resolved to visit the north coast, but were tossed by the tide on a series of rocks, where we thought our end was certain. In this extreme danger we owed our salvation to some Eskimos who came to our rescue. They approached us in their canoes, and far from taking any advantage of our misfortune, they rendered us crucial assistance. Not only did they not leave us until we were out of danger; but an old man, who seemed familiar with the pitfalls of our situation, went in front of us with his canoe and guided us to safety. So everything we read about the character of these people in many Relations,[59] do not at all square with the witness I am obliged to render as to their humanity.[60]

"We had no less admiration for their industry. Without any iron, their bows, arrows, and harpoons were fitted out with teeth made of bone, or the horns of marine animals, with which they made even hatchets, knives, and other tools. It is difficult to conceive of the dexterity with which they manage to use materials which seem so inappropriate for such purposes. They use the same dexterity to fashion their needles, and their clothing is not at all badly sewn. From the similarity of their language, their customs, and their physical shape, I believe they must originally have been of the same stock

---

59 As a capitalized word, this is likely a reference to the *Jesuit Relations*, which were eyewitness diaries kept by Catholic missionaries to North America, and published in France in 71 volumes between 1610 and 1791. They are among the most valuable records of the period, and may be accessed online here: http://puffin.creighton.edu/jesuit/relations/relations_11.html

60 Delaporte reminds the reader that his intent is to improve upon all predecessor travel accounts by rendering the true character of native people through his fictional "witness" narrator.

as the Eskimos that we encountered at the entry to Hudson Strait. If there is any difference between them, it is entirely to the advantage of those who live in the southern part of the Bay. They are generally more industrious, more affable, and more refined. Their clothing, for the ordinary person, is bordered with strips of leather, cut in fringes, and decorated with the teeth of young fawns. Their caps are made of wood-buffalo tails, and the fur covers their faces like hair that will fall over their eyes. This hairstyle gives them a terrifying and barbaric appearance. But it is very useful to them as protection against mosquitoes and other gnats that they don't know how to protect against except in this way. The women do not trim their boots with whale ribs to use them as a kind of baby-cradle, like other Eskimos: they carry their infants on their backs, in a cap which is a part of their tunic, and the infants, like their mothers, have a fur cap for warding off insect bites.

"When these people go to sea to fish, they take a container of fish-oil in their canoes, which they drink with the same great relish as our sailors drink a bottle of brandy. After they have emptied the container, they suck on it and press it into their mouths with a kind of sensuous pleasure. They use the same oil for their lamps, which are made of stone and as cleverly hollowed out as is possible with the tools I have described. Instead of a wick or cotton, they use dried goose droppings. Their way of starting a fire struck me as rather unusual. They take two pieces of dry wood, pierce a hole in each one, introduce another piece of wood in a cylinder shape between them, around which they wrap a cord. By pulling on the ends of this cord they make the cylinder spin with such rapidity that the friction starts the wood burning, with which they light the moss that serves them as a wick.

Sex With Foreigners — and Why

"I don't know whether or not Eskimos are jealous over their women, but it is a certainty that they willingly offer their sexual services to foreigners, in the belief that the children that will be born will be superior to those of their own nation. Their simplicity extends to believing that each man reproduces an exact copy of himself, in the most literal sense; which is to say, that the son of a captain will, according to them, become a captain, and so on. This ridiculous idea is not at all peculiar to them: we see that in the civilized culture of Europe, we think in the same sort of fashion. Without this, would there be as much in the way of hereditary employments and responsibilities? A magistrate makes his son a magistrate; the son of a poet believes he is called to poetry, and so on.

"In continuing our research of the northern coast, we discovered an opening which, at the entry point, was only three or four leagues wide. It became all the more so as we penetrated further; then it got more narrow little by little, and then got wider again. But we were apprehensive about going any farther, because we found the water to be flowing less freely, colder, and not very deep. It is quite possible that this opening connects with some large lake in the interior of these lands, and that this lake in turn has a connection with the ocean.[61] This conjecture rests upon the fact[62] that the flow of the tide there goes faster by half than the tide in the Thames River. It would nevertheless seem that the greater freshness [less salinity] of the water would count against the probability of its being a passage. But if by chance this water had such freshness only at the surface, this conclusion would be less persuasive. For as this was then the season for the snows to melt and run into the sea from all the surrounding lands, it was not so extraordinary to find the water sweeter, just as this happens after the rainy season in the Baltic Sea.

The Force and Majesty of Nature[63]

"The place where we had the highest hope of finding this famous passage, was named the *Strait of Wager*.[64] The narrowest spot is between the Montagu[65] headland and Cape d' Obs.[66] The flow of the tide there has all the force of a

---

61 This is again an expression of the hope to find a passage to the ocean presumed to lie on the Western side of Canada and leading to the Orient.

62 This is one of many examples of the explorer's use of pure reason to solve a problem. This book was written in the mid-eighteenth-century "age of reason," and we sense in this passage, as in many others in this book, the attempt to understand experience via logical deduction, or induction, as would a student of Euclid's proofs in geometry.

63 In this passage we sense the rising Romantic sensibility that co-existed for a time with, but was gradually supplanting, the penchant for pure reason that was all the rage among European scientists and political thinkers, and is evident in the previous passage. Romantics, especially in their evocations of nature in the New World, laid the emphasis on expressions of emotional, rather than coldly analytical reactions to the grandeurs of nature. This was especially true for travel literature about North America, where towering mountains, arctic wonders, and enormous primeval forests evoked a sense of the rawness and power of the world as it must have been at creation, as seen for the very first time by human beings. The persistent questions underlying travel literature were something like: What was nature like in its untamed state? What was Man? What were these Savages like before exposure to civilization, and to the Christian religion? Travel literature was among other things, a means of examining the state of European life both in its advanced, and corrupted aspects, by contrasting it with the rawness of nature and the "natural" lives of Indians and Eskimos. Above all, it provided European critics a standard with which to scold their own society for its imperfections.

64 Probably what is now called Wager Bay, at the northwest end of Hudson Bay, named after Sir Charles Wager, (1666–1743) First Lord of the British Admiralty between 1733 and 1742.

65 Likely John Montagu, 4th Earl of Sandwich (1718–1792)

66 Cap d'Obs, as Delaporte spelled it, is Cape Dobbs, named after Arctic explorer Arthur Dobbs, (1689–1765). The ship used by explorer Henry Ellis for descriptions of the arctic voyage on which Delaporte relied was named the Dobbs Galley.

sluice. When we got there, we were no longer masters of our vessel, and the speed of the flow made it spin around four or five times, despite all the efforts of our crew. Just try to imagine a furious sea, smoking, boiling, foaming, and spinning, like an impetuous torrent, split everywhere by a multitude of rocks; all of which nevertheless seemed to have no cause but the narrowness of the channel, in relation to the enormous quantity of water that runs through there. A quantity of huge ice-floes came in to this narrows right after us, and even though we had already made a lot of progress, the power and the speed of the current often pushed them right up against our bow, and swept them afterward to the stern. We were more than three hours in this situation, but as soon as the channel became larger things got a lot safer.

"Having found a favourable spot to put our vessel, we continued our researches from the safety of our long-boats. This strait, which continued to narrow, was soon only a league in width, and we became alarmed by a frightful noise, which sounded like a huge waterfall. The sides of the strait were bristling with rocks, and very steep. We disembarked from the long-boat, and after mounting the heights, we had the most majestic, and yet also the most terrifying and frightening spectacle by which any mortal has perhaps ever been struck. The sharp rocks seemed ready to detach from the cliffs and fall upon our heads; the cascades of water rolled from precipice to precipice; enormous ice-formations suspended one behind the other appeared like organ pipes of a monstrous size. But what gave us the greatest terror in this theatre of nature's rubble, were the huge heaps of broken rock that we saw at our feet, and that, detached from their peaks by the force of the cold had rolled from hillside to hillside until the spot where they came to a stop.

"We went down to the shore, and were not long in discovering that the amazing noise which had assaulted our ears, came from the fact that the flood of the tide found itself squeezed by a passage that was not more than thirty fathoms in width. The mass of water was prodigious, and its speed surprising. We could see that beyond this cataract, the strait got larger by five or six leagues — which made us entertain great hopes for the passage.

An Encounter with Helpful Indians

"While we were in this place, three Indians approached us in their canoes, and we figured from their behaviour that these were the same people that we had seen in other parts of this coast. But they were a lot smaller. We remarked with astonishment that to the extent that we advanced to the North, everything got smaller. Even the trees, became, in the end, like shrubs. And above sixty-seven degrees north, we did not encounter any more human beings. These Savages seemed at first a little timid, and we were probably the first

Europeans they had ever seen. But, encouraged by our attentions, they became more bold, and began trading with us. We made them understand that we had need of game. So they promptly went ashore, and brought us a good supply of it. There were many kinds of smoked meats, and a few pieces of fresh wood-buffalo meat. We got everything they brought us at a good price, and they left very pleased with the trade.

Testing for Salt Water

"We continued to follow the Strait, and would frequently come across whales and seals. But most of our people were very upset because they found that the water was almost entirely fresh, which seemed to indicate that this far end of the channel did not connect with any sea, and consequently that we had to give up the prospect of discovering a passage by way of the strait of Wager. As I thought that perhaps this fresh water was only at the surface, I lowered a tightly-corked bottle to the depth of thirty fathoms; then, once the cork was pulled out, it filled with water, which we found to be as salty as any at mid-ocean.[67] My experiment renewed our hopes. But this promise of a happy success soon evaporated, for that same evening we were crestfallen to see that what we had assumed until then was a strait, came to an end in two non-navigable rivers, one of which came from a large lake that was only a few leagues away.

Geographical & Botanical Proofs of a Passage

"So it was necessary to abandon our adventure, and from then on we dreamed of nothing more than to get back to our ships to return to England. It was not that we thought it was impossible to find a passage to some other ocean — for in my opinion, I have never doubted its existence, and the proofs[68] on which I have relied seem so convincing that we could only hope for such certitude in other matters. First, it is an undisputed fact that in countries of small extent, be they islands or peninsulas, there are hardly ever large trees, and we see there only low forests, and shrubs, whereas in continents situated at the same degree of latitude, there are large and beautiful trees. We can conclude from this, that all countries that lack large trees in a climate where

---

67 Hudson Bay has a lower average level of salinity than does open ocean water. The main causes are the low rate of evaporation (the bay is ice-covered for much of the year); the large volume of terrestrial runoff entering the bay (about 700 km3 annually); and the limited connection with the Atlantic Ocean and its higher salinity.

68 Once again, the narrator is relying on logical and deductive "proofs" as would a geometer solving an equation. In what follows, he proceeds to set up major and minor premises, as for a syllogism, to reach conclusions as to the possible existence of a Northwest passage.

we know they ordinarily grow in abundance, necessarily have a sea on both coasts. But, as I have already observed on this matter, in the regions that border on Hudson Bay, as we move northward, all plant matter gets visibly smaller by degrees, such that in the end, instead of trees, we find nothing more than shrubs. We know, however — and there can be no doubt of this — that at more northerly latitudes, there are very extended forests. Can we explain such a marked difference other than by the proximity of some sea?

"In the second place, I mentioned that the Northwest winds bring with them a lot of snow consisting of tiny flakes which the cold changes into what we call *frozen smoke*. Can we not infer from this, with sufficient credibility, that in the Northwest of this region there is a large mass of water — which is to say, an ocean of some kind?

"Thirdly, even the shape of the land supplies us with new conjectures. No one denies that most countries situated between two seas have, in their centre, a chain of high mountains, or hills, and on both coasts, a slope. Well, this country fits that case. It is low at the entrance to the Bay, and to the extent that we continue along, we see mountains arise, one behind the other. Once we are farther along in the Bay, we see a lowering of land toward the other side.

Eskimo Evidence of a Passage

"Finally, the report of the Eskimos supports my opinion. All of them unanimously confirm that there is a great sea not far from their country, toward the setting of the sun, on which they say they have seen ships manned by men with long beards, and wearing bonnets. Even some of these Savages who had never seen ships like ours, were able to draw pictures of them in their own way.

Tide Action as Evidence of a Passage

"But that is not sufficient," says our Englishman, "to prove that this land has a sea on both sides. We shall still need to see if these two seas connect with each other and that there is a passage leading from one to the other. I would say even more: such a passage must be short, open, and serviceable. In effect, tides originate in great oceans or from large masses of water. They enter into specific seas more or less according to whether these have a greater or lesser opening at the place where they connect with the ocean whence the tides have come. But seas surrounded by land that have no visible connection with the ocean, or which connect only by means of a single passage, like the Mediterranean Sea and the Baltic Sea, have almost no tides at all. Or, I should say — which amounts to the same thing — the rise and fall of the tides there are barely noticeable. It is also incontestable that the tides are higher, and come sooner in places near the ocean than on places farther away; and on the contrary, they are lower and come later in places farther away. Just so, if we suppose Hudson Bay has no connection with another sea by a northwest passage, we would have to consider it a sea enclosed within the country that only connects with the ocean by the Strait of Hudson. In this case, the tides would have to be higher at the beginning of the Bay, and would diminish in the measure that we advance to the northwest.

"However," continues our Englishman, "it is precisely the contrary that we observe. In measuring the tide we found that it mounted ten feet at the sixtieth degree of latitude, and thirteen feet at the sixty-fifth, and always getting higher thus, which shows, obviously, that this tide cannot come from the ocean by way of Hudson Strait. Nor can it come from any other northern sea by Davis Strait, because in that strait, the tide rises barely to eight feet. Furthermore, the flow there comes from the south, whereas in Hudson Bay it comes from the north. So this means that on that side, there must be an opening, a connection, a passage to another sea. But where is this passage situated? That is what I don't dare decide," resumes our Englishman. "However, if I indulge my own conjectures, I would situate it either in the Gulf of Chesterfield,[69] or in what we call *Rebut Bay*.[70] The depth, the saltiness, and the clarity of the water, combined with the height of the tides, would seem to confirm this opinion.

"If, after a long stretch of years, we have searched for this famous passage, and have undertaken so many expeditions to find it, at the least there have been no discoveries that oppose, with any force, the reasoning that proves the reality of its existence. All the knowledge that we have managed to pull together through so many attempts serves, on the contrary, increasingly to prove its existence. It is therefore appropriate not to abandon a plan, in the name of which we have spent so much, which has always deserved all possible support and encouragement of government, and for which it will not take much more to succeed. It will perhaps take nor more than one more expedition to see all this work crowned with a happy success. Once the passage is found it will open commerce with the countries situated on both sides, for sure. It is likely that to the Northwest of the sea, where it ends, there must be many great regions of more than thirteen hundred leagues. These countries are no doubt unknown, and we don't know if there is a great continent, or if there are only islands; but if we rely on the stories of the Eskimos, we must

---

[69] The Gulf of Chesterfield, today's Chesterfield Inlet, was named about 1749, after Philip Dormer (Stanhope), 4th Earl of Chesterfield (1694–1773) who was the British Secretary of State from 1746–1748 and is the well known author of "Chesterfield's Letters" and other works.

[70] The French word *rebut* means "repulse" in English. Repulse Bay (*Naujaat*, in Inuktitut), is on the northwestern coast of Hudson Bay, and lies right on the Arctic Circle. It was named Repulse Bay by explorer Christopher Middleton in 1742 because he was disappointed that this was a closed bay, and not the Northwest Passage he had been seeking.

conclude on this matter that these countries are populated; that the inhabitants are civilized, and that as a consequence their trade will become very useful to us, even if we don't take into consideration what sort of merchandise we will be trading with them. It would only take a few trips to get a clear understanding of the needs and productions of these unknown countries.

Opening to the Far East

"Other than the immediate advantages associated with this discovery, there are unanticipated ones that are quite considerable. Among them, for example, are the opening of a new and easy route to the South sea,[71] as well as to that vast ocean that lies between America and Asia, in which there are certainly many very lush islands that have never been in contact with Europeans. We would have another much shorter and more certain route to the islands situated to the east of Japan, to Japan itself, to the countries situated beyond there, and even to Korea, and to China, and so on.

"In spite of all the reasons that seem to prove the usefulness of this passage, many people still doubt that it makes the possession of Hudson Bay a lot more important. Very skillful sailors believe that this discovery, about which the English get so excited, may well prove not to have all the advantages they anticipate. We are obliged to construct ships bound for the navigation of the Bay in a special way, on account of the ice they will encounter there. And so, in assuming we are going to find this passage, it will possibly serve no purpose for establishing an easy and profitable connection between the Northern Ocean and the South Sea.

"But I see that this dissertation of mine, which has made me lose sight of the rest of my voyage, has not amused you much; and so I will get back to my story about the Strait of Wager. We directed our course toward the South, keeping Cape Fry, Marble Island, and Button Bay to our right, and went on to land at Fort York, situated on the Nelson River, about five or six leagues from its mouth.

The Nelson River

"This river, the largest in all of Hudson Bay, is navigable for a lot of its course, and connects with the lakes that are on the other side of Canada. We could do a very advantageous business there by setting up our establishments thirty or forty leagues from the mouth, where the climate is more temperate. The river is divided into two arms that are shaped like two separate streams; the southern branch is called Hayes River, and is not less than two leagues wide before it enters the Bay. These banks are low, and are covered with fir,

---

71 "South Sea" in this period was a reference to what is now called the South Pacific Ocean.

poplar, birch, and willow trees. We find there great numbers of deer, hare, rabbits, geese, ducks swans, partridge, pheasant, plovers, and many other kinds of bird, in the season proper for them, with a great abundance of fish of various species.

"Fort York is itself surrounded by forests on all sides, except by the shore, which is an exposed frontage. To the southwest there is a shipyard for building and repairing long-boats and rowboats. The fort is a square building made of wood, and flanked by four small bastions that serve as lodgings and storehouses. In one is the Governor's apartment, made of many wood-clad rooms. Each facade has three cannons, and the whole place is finished with stockades. The battery which defends the river is defended by a parapet, and when all the inhabitants are gathered together they are but thirty or thirty-six in number. This Fort is nevertheless the most important of the English Company that goes by the name of The Hudson Bay Company.[72] It is the true centre of its commerce and each year its handles between forty and fifty thousand pelts of different kinds of animals, but mainly of beaver. The forts at Churchill,[73] St. Alban,[74] and Moose River,[75] which belong to

---

[72] Two centuries before Confederation a pair of resourceful Frenchmen named Radisson and des Groseilliers discovered a wealth of fur in the interior of the continent — north and west of the Great Lakes — accessible via the great inland sea that is Hudson Bay. However, despite their success, neither French nor American interests would finance them. It took the vision and connections of Prince Rupert, cousin of King Charles II, to acquire the Royal Charter which, in May, 1670 granted the lands of the Hudson Bay watershed to "the Governor and Company of Adventurers of England trading into Hudson Bay." Its first century of operation found the Hudson Bay Company (HBC) firmly ensconced in a few forts and posts around the shores of James and Hudson Bays. Natives brought furs annually to these locations to barter for manufactured goods such as knives, kettles, beads, needles, and blankets. By the late 18th century, competition forced HBC to expand into the interior. A string of posts grew up along the great river networks of the west foreshadowing the modern cities that would succeed them: Winnipeg, Calgary, Edmonton. This stimulated competition from the Montreal-based North West Company, that culminated in the "Battle of Seven Oaks" of June 19, 1816 between mounted forces of the Métis fighting for the North West Company attacking a smaller HBC troop, that resulted in the deaths of 21 HBC men. These two companies soon realized joining was better than fighting, and they merged in 1821. The resulting commercial enterprise now spanned the continent — all the way to the Pacific Northwest (modern-day Oregon, Washington and British Columbia) and the North (Alaska, the Yukon, Northwest Territories and Nunavut). More at the Hudson's Bay Company website, at: http://hbcheritage.ca/hbcheritage/history/overview

[73] The Hudson Bay Company built the first permanent settlement, Churchill River Post, in 1717. The trading post and river were named after John Churchill, 1st Duke of Marlborough (an ancestor of Winston Churchill), who was governor of the Hudson Bay Company in the late seventeenth century.

[74] Delaporte may be referring to Fort Albany, which was one of the three original Hudson's Bay Company posts on James Bay, the others being Moose Factory on the south shore, and Rupert House on the east.

[75] Moose River, is today Moose Factory, a community in the Cochrane District, Ontario. It is

this same company, are nothing remarkable. They each have at most twenty inhabitants which, when combined with those at Fort York, don't come to a hundred English people in the entire country.

People of the Area, Their Clothing, Customs, and Ways

"During the brief period that I have lived among them I have had the opportunity on many occasions to see the Eskimos who live in the southwest part of Hudson Bay, between the Hayes River and Canada. They have black eyes, and loose hair of the same colour, are happy, affable and friendly, and are of upright character. In summer, the men wear a large robe made of a cloth like our bed-covers, which they buy from the nearby French or the English. They have leather boots so long that they function as knickers, with soles made of the same material. The women's clothing doesn't differ from the men's, except that they usually wear a petticoat that in winter descends a little below the knee. All these clothes are usually made of deer, otter, or beaver skin. The sleeves are attached to the shoulder with cords such that their armpits are exposed to the air, even in times of the greatest cold — which they regard as essential to maintaining good health.

"They live in cabins covered with moss and the skins of wild animals. As they are mostly occupied in hunting and fishing, they change habitations according to where they find conditions more or less favourable. It is for this same reason that they never live in large bands because they would then find it difficult to clothe and feed themselves. They do not rely at all on the fruits of the earth for their subsistence, and only live on the flesh of animals.

The Caribou, the Hunt, and the Waste

"There are some seasons when they kill more wild animals than they can eat, and they are of the absurd opinion that the more of them they destroy, the more they will multiply. Sometimes they leave three or four hundred dead animals out in the open, taking only their tongues. The rest rots on the ground or is devoured by birds of prey and carnivorous animals.[76] At other

---

located on Moose Factory Island, near the mouth of the Moose River, which is at the southern end of James Bay. The term "Factory" refers to the jurisdiction of a "factor" (a business agent or merchant in charge of buying or selling) of the Hudson's Bay Company. Just as a rector presides over a rectory, a factor holds authority over a factory.

76 It is not the purpose of this book to sort out the conflicting evidence with respect to whether or not beaver, caribou, deer, and other animals were killed conservatively by Indians only for essential need, or often wantonly and wastefully over-killed for choice parts such as tasty caribou or buffalo tongues only (with whole carcasses often left to rot). Jenness, *Indians of Canada* (p. 300) reports that the Neutral Indians "had the strange custom, unknown elsewhere in Canada, of killing every animal they encountered, whether or not they needed it for food, lest it should carry a

times, they attack them in the water and kill prodigious numbers, which they bring on rafts to our dwellings. In spring, these wild animals travel over an immense area of the country, from south to north to have their young in safe places, which is to say in a more northerly climate, almost entirely uninhabited. They are tormented along the way by large flies, and to avoid them they take refuge in rivers and lakes, where the Savages kill them more easily.

"Among these migrating animals the most significant and greatest in number are the caribou, who are of the same species as the deer and the reindeer. They are extremely light and have flat and very large cloven hooves, with rough hair between them that prevents them from plunging deep into the snow, over which they run almost as quickly as on land; and the pathways they make in the snow have more intersections than the streets of London. The way to capture them is to cut down trees that the Savages pile one on top of the other, between which they leave openings to set traps. In the months of July and August these same herds return from south to north,[77] and when they come back across the rivers, they attack them easily from their canoes with spears. They also nourish themselves with birds and fish. They boil their meat without seasoning, and they drink the sauce.

Alcohol, Hardiness, and Foolishness

"When they are able to get brandy, they drink it with delight, and then get carried away with all sorts of excesses. They fight among themselves like madmen, burn down their cabins, mutually abuse their wives, and in the drowsiness of drunkenness, they sleep around a big fire and burn themselves horribly, or in a like manner freeze themselves, according to how they get too close or too far from the hearth.[78]

---

warning to other animals of its kind ...." In the end, both Indians and whites engaged in a massive trade in animal pelts and parts for money, liquor, and other European goods. Shephard Krech III, *The Ecological Indian* (New York: W.W. Norton, 1999), gives a full and balanced picture of many disturbing practices, including some Indian taboos, and animal-reincarnation beliefs dictating (as attested in this passage) that because more killing would produce more animals infinitely, waste was not considered a problem. It is a study that provides much detailed historical evidence from both sides of the animal *conservation* vs. *waste* debate, but in the end casts into very serious doubt self-congratulatory statements such as voiced by a former Canadian Chief, that "we have hunted and fished, in balance with nature, for more than 300 generations" (p.199). If anything, the opposite may be true: European hunters may have taught Indians about animal husbandry and conservation, and that hunting and eating the female of a species such as the buffalo by preference, as they often did indiscriminately, is counter-productive.

77 Delaporte wrote *du sud au nord* (from south to north), when he must have meant the opposite direction, as the caribou are returning from the north.

78 In the DCB entry for "Frontenac", we read: "The clergy, and particularly the Jesuits since they were mainly concerned with missionary activities among the Indians, were adamant in their oppo-

"Although the greatest part of their life is spent getting what they need to live, they don't have the foresight to take precautions against times of famine. They copiously consume their provisions when they are abundant, without ever thinking of conserving them for winter. It often happens that those who come to trade at the trading posts of the bay, and who have depended upon help that never arrives, have to cook while on route the very pelts they came to sell, to feed themselves. But when they find themselves reduced to such cruel extremities, they suffer it with an admirable resoluteness and patience. It is quite routine, even in the heart of winter, for them to travel two or three hundred leagues without ever raising a tent or a hut to shelter themselves. When night falls, they pick out a small spot, remove the snow, surround it with undergrowth, light a fire, and sleep between the fire and the brush on the side opposite the wind. If they find themselves in a place without wood, they dig a hole in the snow and sleep there. This bed feels less cold to them than the outside air, from which the snow protects them.

Cannibalism

"The excesses to which these Savages will go whenever they lack provisions, seem incredible — if a story well known in all European establishments were not proof enough. One of them, who went with his family to trade in a place really far away, had the misfortune to find neither fish nor fowl there, and saw himself, his wife, and his children reduced to extreme famine. First, they ate the furs they had brought to trade, and then the ones they wore for clothing. This last resort gone, the parents had recourse to eating their own children, with which they nourished themselves for the rest of the trip. When they arrived at the English settlement, the unhappy Indian, whose heart appeared to be filled with sadness, told his lamentable story, with all the most moving details, to the Governor of the fort. But this officer, to the shame of our nation and of all humanity, only responded to it with a great burst of laughter. Upon which the astonished Savage said in broken English that there was, after all, nothing to laugh about in this matter, and he left, utterly shocked.

"'These horrible meals are so common for them,' the governor told me (without doubt in an attempt to justify his lack of sensitivity), 'that even though we have not lived among them for long, we have to get used to these kinds of stories. Whenever they are threatened by starvation, the fathers and mothers begin by killing their own children, eating them, and in the end, the

---

sition to the use of brandy in the fur trade, claiming, with good cause, that the Indians were cheated out of their furs by unscrupulous traders who first got them so drunk that they became utterly debauched, and committed the most heinous crimes when brandy was brought into their villages."

strongest of them eats the other. I knew one who, after having devoured his wife and the six children he had with her, swore that this heart only melted over the last child, because he loved him more than the others, and that when opening his head to pull out the brains, he felt so moved he did not have the strength to break his bones and suck the marrow from them.'"[79]

Love and Self-Sacrifice

"These examples of cruelty do not square well with another story that came in around the same time, and which illustrates the heroic nature of paternal love. Two canoes travelling on the Hayes River got to the middle, and one of them, carrying an Indian, his wife and his child, was overturned in the rapids. The other canoe was quite small, and at most could save only one of the two adults and the child. So an argument began. It was not a dispute between the man and the woman as to who should die for the other, but only about saving the life of the object of their common affections. They took just

---

[79] There are many modern accounts from various cultures of survivors who have had to eat the bodies of their dead friends or family members in order to survive. Survival, or famine cannibalism is always horrifying, but understandable. A notorious account of Indian parents conniving to kill and eat their own children, from which Delaporte may have adapted this narrative, is found in a French account published in Paris in 1691 by the Jesuit missionary Chrestien le Clercq, and available today in an English translation as *New Relations of Gaspesia, with the Customs and Religion of the Gaspesian Indians*, William F. Ganong, ed., (Toronto: The Champlain Society, 1910). The gruesome logic of killing and eating your own children would be that either both parents and all children die, or the parents survive by cannibalism of some of their children (as in the le Clercq case, to enable them to survive and look after the very youngest); or, all of their children if necessary, in order to produce more children in happier circumstances. Delaporte balances this story by describing the compassionate nature of the Indian in the drowning story that follows. For more on cannibalism among Canada's Indians, see, for example, Diamond Jenness, *Indians of Canada* (National Museum of Canada, Bulletin 65, Anthropological Series No. 15, 1932. Also, by Minister of Supply and Services Canada, 1977), who writes that "shortage of food caused many natives to die of starvation and sometimes led to cannibalism ... which inspired no less horror among the natives than among us ... [It] must have occurred fairly frequently, however, for the early fur traders and explorers mention several instances," (p.285), which Jenness cites. The Mohawks (he translates this name as "flesh-eaters") were especially vicious and in the seventeenth century conducted wars of extermination against the Ojibwa, Cree and Montagnais of Ontario and Quebec as far north as James Bay. He adds that "although the rules of the [Iroquois] Confederacy strictly prohibited cannibalism, we find records of several cases in which the Mohawk cruelly sacrificed a prisoner to their war-god Aireskoi and divided up the body to be devoured in the different villages" (p.305). He also describes the secret "Cannibal Society" of the West Coast Tsimshian nation, "whose members tore to pieces human corpses and devoured portions of the flesh" (p.339). For some U.S. accounts, see George Franklin Feldman, *Cannibalism, Headhunting and Human Sacrifice in North America: A History Forgotten* (Chambersburg, Pennsylvania: Alan C. Hood and Co., 2008), who presents atrocities of both the Indian and the Whiteman. Recent discoveries of "coprolites" — human "dung stones" — containing traces of digested human flesh, give what looks like irrefutable evidence of cannibalism among the Anasazi peoples of Colorado. See: "Biological evidence of Cannibalism at a Prehistoric Puebloan Site in Southwestern Colorado," *Nature* 407, 74-78 (7 September 2000).

a few moments to ask which of the two would be the most useful for the care of the child. The man insisted that at such a tender age a child has the most need of his mother's care. She protested to the contrary; that in being the same sex as his father, he would learn from his father all the skills of hunting and fishing. And then, after having counselled her husband never to neglect his paternal care, and after exchanging vows of mutual tenderness, she threw herself in the river, where she soon drowned.

Euthanasia

"To finish my contrast between humanity and barbarity that illustrates the character of these people,[80] I will report a cruel custom that has been seen with respect to old people. As soon as they become senile, their children have an obligation to strangle them, and here is how they acquit themselves of this horrible duty. The old person gets into a hole dug expressly to serve as his grave. He chats for a while quite calmly, with his helpers, while smoking a pipe, and drinking spirits. When he signals that the time has come, two of his children loop a rope around his neck, and pull with all their strength in opposite directions, until he is dead. Then they fill his grave with earth, and put a marker of stones on top. Those who have no children ask their best friends to perform this horrible ministry. But as it is not a duty for them, they often refuse.

The Sweat Cure

"The inhabitants of this coast are seldom subject to sicknesses, and heal themselves almost entirely by sweating. They have a large stone, on which they build a fire until the stone gets red hot. Then they build around it a small closed hut, and get in naked with a full jug of water which they sprinkle on the stone. The water becomes a hot wet steam that soon fills the hut, and makes the sick person sweat very quickly. Once the stone begins to cool, they hasten to get out before their pores close over, and leap into cold water on the spot, or else roll in snow. This is the generally accepted method and it is considered an infallible remedy for all sorts of illnesses. The method they use for colic and for all sorts of intestinal disorders is no less unique: it's the smoke of tobacco, which they inhale in very great quantities.

"Most of their sicknesses come from the cold they catch after having consumed strong alcohol. It's up to the rest of us Englishmen, who have this obligation, because the French are prudent and do not sell any intoxicating drinks to these Savages, for fear of harming their character, and subsequently

---

80 Here Delaporte reveals the tension discussed earlier between humanity and barbarity — between the noble and the ignoble — felt throughout this book.

their business with them, the success of which has always depended on the energy of these people and their skill in hunting. We also see that the Savages who live among us become thin, small, weak, and lazy; whereas those who live among the French are tough, active, and vigorous. There is no comparison as to the numbers of furs the one group and the other brings to trade.

Social and Political Organization — The "Noble Savage"

"These people are guided in their conduct by a natural rectitude that prevents them from committing any act of violence or injustice.[81] They choose the chiefs of each tribe from among the elders of their nation, and give precedence to those who have distinguished themselves by their skill in the hunt, by their experience in trading, and by their warrior status in the frequent wars they have with their neighbours. These chiefs govern the entire band, and organize the different domestic jobs. But their opinions are followed more by deference than by any obligation. For these people are among the freest on earth. In general, this is the form of government of most of the Savages of Canada — pure naturalism.[82] In war, they choose captains who

---

[81] The inference is that the natives do not require any imposed law or religious doctrine to control or guide them to correct behaviour; they are guided by an inherent goodness of nature, by what many today think of as "natural law." This view follows the immediately previous view in which the natives are presented as performing various unnatural acts such as cannibalism, and killing their elders, without compunction or conscience. These two contradictory views: the Savage as angel, and the Savage as devil, persist in tension in much of the literature of the period, as well as today. Christian missionaries considered it their sacred duty to convert the latter into the former — the wandering, den-bound wild man, into the settled, property-owning civilized man — through the grace of baptism. There are some historical reports that "reverse" conversion sometimes occurred: Europeans — even some missionaries — so enraptured by a romantic conception of natural man as he must have existed before the Fall in the Garden of Eden, that they abandoned the corruptions of modernity and of Christianity to adopt a natural Indian way of life. Sometimes these were whites captured and adopted by force who, when offered the possibility of escape or rescue long afterward, chose to continue living the Indian life (such people were described as "white savages"). The habit of portraying barbarian races as either inferior, or superior to Europeans, has been traced back to the *Histories* of Herodotus (440 B.C.). See Anthony Grafton, *New Worlds, Ancient Texts* (Cambridge, Mass.: Harvard University Press, 1992), pp. 37-40. Pierre Berthiaume, in *L'Aventure Américaine*, pp. 250 ff, offers a deep analysis of the theological role of the Savage in the mind of the Missionary, who oft-imagined the former, with his dancing, nudity, sexual licence, and superstition as possessed of the devil and needing Christian deliverance, and North America as the scene of a final struggle between good and evil.

[82] Much of this section is imported directly from Jean-Jacques Rousseau's *Letter XVIII of his "Lettres Morales"(Letters on Morality)* of 1757-1758. Rousseau famously argued that all men are good by nature, but got corrupted by a divisive and unequal society rooted in the evils of private property. For him, even the Savages he read about, because already organized into social groups ("*en état de troupeau*"), were far removed from his hypothetical natural Man roaming as an individual in the "state of nature." Later, in his famous *Social Contract* (1762) he rationalized an entire political theory for unifying the separate and divided wills of all the people, under the

have only rallying rights, being the first into battle, and above all, the first rights to the booty. They have neither Ministers, nor a council of state; but the wisest, most experienced, the most illustrious according to their heroic deeds, and above all the oldest, gather together and judge in common both the good and the bad of all things. There are no other laws but those of reason, honor, and conscience, and a certain tradition of morality and custom from which they are not parted easily.[83] Nevertheless, one may ignore these things at will, and the same for all the other duties of society, for they really have no means of constraint, whether to punish wrong-doers, or to control them. A young girl will bring someone she loves to the cabin one night. The father, the mother, and her brothers, will say to her: 'My daughter, my sister, you are wrong; you dishonour us; you will never make a husband of him.' We will tell her these things, but we will only tell her. And if she makes fun of our advice, no one will take offence over it. They have lots of high honours, of booty, and of food; but no sort of corporal punishment, even for children. They instruct them; but never punish them. The missionaries take them through the catechisms, exhort them, and give sermons; but there are no classes or schools. There are Preachers — all one could want of them — but no rulers. They cherish these missionaries as if they were their fathers, but never as lawmakers, or chiefs.

Murder Unpunished

"When they have a bad person, someone gets drunk and goes off to kill him, and the slayer is never punished. One nation comes to make an orderly peace with another nation. This treaty, of the most solemn kind, is executed along with speeches, pledges, hostages, and gifts, does not please everyone — be it only a scatterbrained twenty-year old. So this fellow tells the ones who made the treaty that it is worthless, and he is going to break it. 'You are wrong my

---

pseudo-mystical conception of a General Will (a "*Volonté Générale*"). It is interesting that during World War II, many Germans were crestfallen to discover that many American Indians, whom they had idealized as among the most natural of all human beings — *naturvölker* — had joined in the fight against them. This perplexed them, as the main thrust of German National Socialism was its "anti-civilization" appeal to the naturalness of "*Blüt und Boden*" (blood/race, and soil/ patrimony), of which North American Indians were the ultimate symbol. See Christian F. Feest, "Europe's Indians," in *The Invented Indian*, pp. 313-332. This peppy essay explains the Indian as an imaginary European construct, an *Indian of the mind*, invented and relied upon as a timeless and incorruptible, and wholly imagined reference figure used mostly to expose the perceived evils of European society.

83 The inference by contrast, latent in this statement, is that these natural people are noble because they guide their conduct according to high moral standards of reason, honour, and conscience, unlike their European contemporaries who have lost these natural faculties and so must resort to unreason, dishonour, and evil acts.

brother,' he is told; 'you will make things worse between us.' He is definitely told these things, but is nevertheless allowed to do it. So he goes off to get an enemy scalp,[84] and brings his trophy back home, all the while mocking his elders. He gets blamed for this, for sure, but no more so than before; and everyone gets ready to wage a new war.

A Confused Religion of Good and Evil

"Such is the national character of most of the Savages of the new world. When it comes to religion, those who live around the Hayes River acknowledge a Being of an infinite goodness, whom they consider as the author of all good. They only speak of this being with respect, and chant, in his honour, a kind of hymn in very grave and reasonably harmonious tones. But their opinions concerning all this are so mixed up that it is not possible to understand anything of this sort of cult. They acknowledge another Being also, whom they represent as the source and instrument of all sorts of evils, but I have never seen them render this being any sort of homage.

"Whenever these people run across a grave in their travels, they consider it an omen of some evil event. To foil it, they place a stone on the grave and continue on their journey. Among them, there are groups of charlatans who buy all sorts of stuff from the English, like sugar, ginger, licorice, spices, seeds for gardening, powdered tobacco, and they sell it all in small portions as remedies or as specifically useful for fishing, hunting, or fighting, and so on. These are the English of Hudson Bay who, to advance their interests, have attributed these virtues to their merchandise, and I cannot conceal the fact that a third of the trade of that country today comes from these charlatans. They deceive even their own friends, and abuse the artlessness of these good

---

84 There is frequent reference to the gruesome custom of "scalping" in this book, and ongoing debate in Indian studies concerning the origins of this custom. Was it invented by Indians, or by the Whiteman, both of whom practiced it? Readers will find a history of all this in James Axtell, and William C. Sturtevant, "The Unkindest Cut, or Who Invented Scalping," in *William and Mary Quarterly* (July, 1980), 37, no. 3, pp.451-472. It can be read here: http://www.amstudy.hku.hk/staff/kjohnson/PDF/engl56_kj_axtell_unkindestcut.pdf. The evidence from eyewitnesses, documents, and the scalping cuts left on prehistoric skulls, leaves no doubt that scalping was a pre-Columbian practice of North American Indians subsequently taken up by white soldiers and bounty hunters. Evidence for this is still "on the books" of what became the province of Nova Scotia. First Nations chiefs there asked the Premier to remove the Province's 250 year old "scalping law" in 1999. This was an official Proclamation of 1759 that commanded settlers "to annoy, distress, take and destroy the Indians," and offered a bounty — by 1750 the bounty-per-scalp was raised from ten to fifty pounds — for the scalps of Mi'kmaq Indians. This scalping war went in both directions. In Acadia and Nova Scotia, both the British and the Wabanaki Confederacy engaged in frontier warfare. The British paid the New England Rangers for Mi'kmaq scalps, and the French paid members of the Iroquois Confederacy for British scalps.

people by trading their false remedies for good furs, that these imposters then come among us to trade.

Mistreatment of Women, and Indian Abortions

"These Savages have very little regard for the fair sex (if the women of this country can be described thus). They are very offended whenever one of the women dares to cross her legs in front of them, and think it is beneath them to drink from the same vessel. Often, when they fear they may have more children than they can feed, they make their women abort their children by means of a certain herb. Yet this custom is no more barbarous than in China, where the law permits the killing of babies as soon as they come into the world. In our civilized European states, we have recourse to more gentle expedients, if the truth be known (even though, without doubt, just as criminal) for preventing an excessive burden on a family already too numerous. In all countries of the world, it is only ease and affluence that adopt the views of nature in good faith.

A Strange Way to Urinate / Their Language

"Our Savages differ from all other peoples in their peculiar manner of urinating: the men squat, and the women stand up.[85] The language of these people is guttural, without being rough or disagreeable. They have very few words, but they signify a lot, and a happy way of rendering new ideas with composite terms which express the qualities of the things to which they want to give names.

Fur Pelts the Principal Currency

"What principally attracts Europeans to this country, where nature presents so many obstacles, is the multitude of beaver, black fox, and other animals that provide them with the most beautiful furs and the certainty that they may be procured by them with very little cost. That is what we can see in the exchange rate for merchandise of the [Hudson Bay] company: ten beautiful beaver pelts for a rifle; one pelt for a half-pound of powder; two pelts for a

---

85 The first example in history of this counter-intuitive practice is found in the *Histories* of Herodotus written in 440 BC, who says of the Egyptians that their women who urinate standing "seem to have reversed the ordinary practices of mankind." A little checking on anthropology sites suggests that indeed in some cultures of the world, women have, or may today, urinate standing, for reasons such as reluctance to use a dirty toilet. And there are cultures and cases where men who wear long tunics and are accustomed to urinating in public, may squat such that the tunic will not be fouled, as it forms a kind of privacy tent around them. I have not found any documents verifying that Huron women urinated standing.

comb and a mirror; five beaver pelts for a red cloak; six for a woman's dress, and so on. We can see from these prices what an immense profit the English company would be able to make at Hudson Bay if this business were well carried out. Right off the mark one would not make less than four hundred per cent. But laziness, or any number of other obstacles would halt progress so much that costs would very soon become higher than the returns. Moreover, the locals have more of a tendency to trade with the French than with us, because they pay better, and are more polite. By being more just and honest in our dealings, the consumption of our goods would be ten times greater, and soon we would gain the upper hand in the places where the French have displaced us. I have myself been a witness many times to the knavery of our merchants and our employees. One put his thumb in the weigh-scale while he was selling gunpowder to Savages. Another mixed water in with the spirits he was selling them. Furthermore, there is no difficulty in selling things for more than the price set by the company, and by such underhanded methods, combined with the gifts they extort from the locals, they get what they call *the surplus*, which is to say — more than a third of their profit.

The Life of the Beaver[86]

"From the nature of the business in this bay, you can see that it consists mostly of beaver pelts, which are said to be better than the Canadian[87] ones. These amphibious quadrupeds, which, in open country gather together to live in society, display as much industry in building their homes as they do in their manner of governing themselves. The largest beavers are a little less than four feet long, and seldom weigh more than sixty pounds. Their colour differs according to the various climates in which they live. In the most northerly and out of the way places, they are usually completely black, and they become more brown as they move south. There are some white

---

86 The Iroquois Wars, also known as "the Beaver Wars," or the French and Iroquois Wars, were a series of 17th-century conflicts involving the Iroquois, or Five Nations (then including the Mohawk, Oneida, Onondaga, Cayuga and Seneca), and numerous other Iroquoian groups and French colonial forces. The wars represented the intense struggle for control over resources in the early colonial period and resulted in the permanent dispersal or destruction of several First Nations in the Eastern Woodlands.

87 "Canada" was the name of the French colony that once stretched along the St. Lawrence River; the other colonies of New France were Acadia, Louisiana, and the south shore of Newfoundland. Canada, the most developed colony of New France, was divided into three districts, each with its own government: Quebec, Trois-Rivières, and Montreal. The governor of the District of Quebec was also the governor-general of all New France. Because of the level of development of Canada compared to the other colonies, the terms "Canada" and "New France" were often used interchangeably. After the Treaty of Paris of 1763, when France ceded Canada and its dependencies to Great Britain, the colony was renamed the Province of Quebec.

ones, too, but they are rare. The more black they are, the less of a coat they have, and as a result their pelts are less sought after. Their coat is of two kinds everywhere on their bodies: long hair, and down. The latter, which is extremely fine, compact, and an inch thick, serves to preserve the animals warmth. It is also the one we use in the clothing factories. We don't use the other for anything; it merely protects the down from mud and moisture — and perhaps also helps him to swim.

"The head of this amphibian is almost square. His ears are round and very small, hairy on the outside, and hairless inside. His eyes are small, the muzzle elongated, and the forefront of his mouth armed with four strong cutting incisors — two above and two below — like squirrels. In addition, he has eight molars on each jaw which, along with the four others, are the only tools he has for cutting, felling, and pulling trees. The upper incisors are about two and a half inches long; the lower ones more than three inches, and the upper ones cross over the lower like the two blades of a pair of scissors. His legs are short, especially those in front, which he uses like a pair of hands with the skill of a squirrel. The fingers of his hands are well separated and divided and have long and pointed nails. The back feet are flat and have webs which serve as flippers, as for a goose, and the beaver has the same gait when he is on land; but he swims perfectly. His tail is above all quite remarkable, and very adapted to the uses he makes of it: it is long, a bit flat, all covered with scales, equipped with strong muscles, and always moistened with oil and fat which prevents water from penetrating.

"I have been told that the doctors in Paris had categorized this quadruped in the class of fish, and the theologians in the class of animals whose flesh may be eaten on days when meat is forbidden. It has a gamey taste that it only loses after being boiled in water. With this preparation it takes on such a fine quality that there is no meat more light, more delicate, or more healthy. The habit this animal has of always keeping his tail and the rear parts of his body under the water, seems to have altered the nature of his flesh. The flesh of his forward parts, up to his loins has the taste and consistency of a land animal or a bird, while the flesh of the hips and the tail have all the flavours of fish. When it is boiled it calls for something to offset the taste; but spit-roasted, it can be eaten as it is.

The Fable of the Beaver's "Ransom"

"The reproductive parts of the beaver are not visible from outside; they are closed up inside his body. We once believed that these contained *castoreum*, a kind of oil made use of in medicine. This substance — which seems like a mixture of wax and honey, of a brown colour, with a strong and fetid smell and a bitter and disgusting taste[88] — is found in four sacs placed below the intestines of this quadruped. There is reason to believe that he makes use of this smooth oil to grease his body hair and protect himself from water. When it is fresh it flows, but as it ages it gets harder, brown coloured, and brittle, and all the more valued when it has the most disagreeable smell. It has proven successful when used to treat hypochondriacs, and it is said that a sponge soaked in vinegar, in which some *castoreum* has been dissolved, gets rid of lethargy and the drowsiness caused by coal fumes. Those who have said that this drug comes from the reproductive parts of the beaver, have added that this animal, when he senses that he is being pursued by hunters, tears out these parts and leaves them behind for his ransom.[89] Others, who reject this story, have maintained that the beaver has these parts attached to the spine of his back, where it is impossible for him to tear them off. But all these opinions are equally false. It is not true, either that these parts are placed where they say, nor that he tears them off when he sees that he is being hunted.

The Amazing Industry of the Beaver

"Beavers live for about fifteen or twenty years; the females carry their young for about four months; and the litter is usually about four babies. Sometimes we can find three or four hundred of these animals together, who live in a kind of village. They know how to select a place well-suited to them, which is to say, where there are abundant foodstuffs, and especially water. If these waters always stay at the same height, like a lake, they don't need to build dikes or dams. But if the waters are flowing, and raise and lower in height, they build a raised causeway which keeps them always at the same level. This dam is often eighty or a hundred feet in length, and is built with admirable industry. Their first concern is to go find some wood above the spot where they have chosen to build. Many of them sit around a tree and gnaw at the bark until they manage to cut down the tree with their teeth. Their judgements of distance are made with such exactitude that to spare themselves any more work than necessary, they know how to make the tree fall towards the water. Then it is just a matter of rolling it to the place where it has to

---

88 *Castoreum* is an oily substance found in castor-sac scent glands located just inside the anus of both the male and female beaver. The beaver marks a territory by excreting castoreum, and hunters extract it from the beavers they kill and use it to bait beaver traps. Humans have used castoreum as a food flavouring because it has a sweet vanilla scent. Health agencies label it GRAS: "generally regarded as safe." It is also used extensively in women's perfumes, but in perfumes and foods is labelled only as a "natural additive," or "flavouring". The sweet smell of castoreum is thought to be due to the bark, sap, and leaf diet of the beaver.

89 This fable began with Pliny the Elder (23 AD–79 AD), *Natural History*, Book VIII, chap XLVII.

be placed. It is more or less long, or large, according to the nature and the specifics of the spot chosen. Once it is knocked down, these animals busy themselves with removing its branches, so that they can take it anywhere they want. During this time, other beavers run along the banks of the river looking for pieces of wood of different sizes, and cut them to the necessary height to make piles, and after having dragged them along the bank of the water, they take them, with their teeth, to their intended destination. While some of them hold them perpendicular, others dive to the bottom to dig a hole with their front feet in which to set the pile. Then they connect them by weaving branches and fill the spaces between them with a clay so well applied that not even a drop of water gets through. Beavers do all this with their paws, and their tail serves them not only as a kind of masonry trowel, but also as a trough for moving the mortar. The foundations of their dikes are usually about ten or twelve feet thick, and narrow to about thirty or thirty-six inches. One must admire the exactitude with which all these dimensions are observed. The side that has the flowing water is always an embankment, and the other side, perfectly vertical. Thus, these structures not only have all the necessary solidity, but also the most useful shape to hold water, prevent it from penetrating, and hold its weight without ruining their efforts.

Their Living Spaces

"After having worked as a group on this grand structure, of which the purpose is to keep the water always at the same level, they arrange themselves in groups to build particular living spaces. The same art is observed in the building of these huts, which are usually built on stilts in the middle of the small lakes which the dikes have formed, or on the banks of a river. Their shape is round or oval and the interior coating of clay doesn't allow any air through. They are from five to ten feet in diameter, and some have two or three floors, with the whole structure coming together in a vaulted ceiling.

"Two thirds of the structure are out of the water. The beavers have many apartments within, and each one has his own spot marked out. They don't eat in the same place where they sleep, so that they won't dirty it. There is never any garbage in there, because in addition to the common entrance, there are many other openings through which they empty waste into the water. During the day, they don't go near their beds unless they need to sleep. There are never more than eight or ten in each hut always in male-female pairs, among which there is always one who has the job of making his fellows work. If there happens to be a lazy one, the others, with brute force, make him search for his means elsewhere. These huts are always close to each other so as to have easy communication between them. They have two exits, one to get on land, the other to dive into the water. All these works are completed by the end of September, and winter never falls by surprise upon these animals during their work. Each of them gathers their foodstuff in summer. While they live in the forests, they feed themselves on fruits, bark, and leaves of trees. They also fish for crayfish and certain fish. But the provisions for winter consist only of tender wood, such as the poplar, the aspen, and others of the same quality. They put it in a pile, arranged in such a way that they can always take the wood that is soaked in water. The piles are arranged for the inhabitants of each hut, and according to whether winter will be more or less long. For the Savages, this is an indication, that is never wrong, of how long the cold will last. Each hut has a common storage spot where the wood is stored. These animals cut it in small pieces for eating, which each of them carries to his own living space.

Beaver Babies

"When the months of working are over, the beavers begin to enjoy the pleasures of domestic life. It is a time for rest, and the season for love. It seems that these quadrupeds are ready to reproduce around the age of one, which tells us that they have done most of their growing. They leave their dwellings during the spring thaw, to avoid the worst floods, but the females return as soon as the floods begin to ebb. And that is when they have their young. They are then occupied with nursing and raising their babies, who are able to follow them around at about three weeks of age. Then in time they go around on their own and pass the summer in the water and the forests. The males stay afield until the month of July, when they all gather to repair the breeches that the water may have made in their structures. If they have been destroyed, they make others — as long as the lack of foodstuffs or the frequent ravages of hunters do not force them to change the location of their home. But there are places for which they have acquired such an affection that despite the persecutions they suffer, they cannot bring themselves to leave.

The Beaver Hunt

"The beaver-hunt takes place from the end of autumn to the beginning of spring, because that's when they have the thickest coats. The Savages set traps, and seldom use arrows or rifles, because when he is dying of a wound, the animal will throw himself into the water and never surface. If the hut is close to some small river, the ice is broken across it so as to place a net. Then, the hut is smashed, and all the beavers try to save themselves by rushing into the river — only to find themselves trapped in the net. In some spots they make do with a hole in the dikes, whereupon these animals soon find themselves on dry land, and because they don't walk very well, they have no defence.

The Beaver Pelts

"The use made of beaver down is mostly for hats and fur coats. For white hats the down from the underside of the belly is used; for ordinary hats the black down from the back is used, and the hair on the flank, which is the longest, is spun for making stockings and bonnets. We have tried to make fabrics of it, but found them tending to harden, like felt. Besides beaver pelts, which are the main focus of commerce for the English company of Hudson Bay, their ships are filled with many sorts of furs which are taken from the same part of the country. Fish glue[90] is yet another branch of its trade. The company has established many other factories in the different forts it owns.

"Two-thirds of the beaver pelts that are sent to England are worked on by the hat-makers of the nation. The other third leaves England for Holland, and goes on from there to Germany. The best pelts, once the hair has been removed, are used to make gloves. Glue is made with the leftovers. A bale of beaver pelts, weighing one hundred and twenty pounds, consists of about one hundred and fifty pelts, but the company hardly ever manages to send more than ten thousand pelts per year to England.

"The difficulty in obtaining food and the rigors of the cold give pause to consider that the colony of Hudson Bay will never have a great number of inhabitants, because despite whatever gains may be promised from commerce there, one is obliged to transport from Europe or from New England, all the necessities of life — something that adds up to one of the greatest expenses of the company. The losses it suffered during our last wars, and the changes in style, which resulted in a loss of taste for furs, caused quite a drop in trade for quite a while. But the restitution of the places that the French had taken from the company, the peace that has since come with repossession, and the taste that has revived in London for furs, has revived trade, and extended it farther than ever. From the beginning of the war for the succession of Spain, the French had expelled us from nearly every port that we occupied in the bay. But by the peace treaty signed at Utrecht,[91] all that we possessed

---

90 This is a reference to "Isinglass", a transparent substance obtained from the dried air-bladders of fish. It is a form of collagen used mainly for the clarifying of beer and wine. It can also be cooked into a paste for specialized gluing purposes. Isinglass was originally made exclusively from sturgeon until the 1795 invention by William Murdoch of a cheap substitute using cod.

91 The Treaty of Utrecht (1713), which brought an end to the War of the Spanish Succession, broke the equilibrium that existed in North America between Great Britain and France. This treaty marked the start of the reduction of French royal authority in this region of the world. France recognized the rights of Great Britain to the Hudson Bay region and also ceded continental Acadia, Newfoundland, and Saint Pierre and Miquelon. The territory of modern New Brunswick was a source of contention between Great Britain and France for 50 years, resolved by the Treaty of Paris in 1763 with the surrender of the French.

in these districts, was restored to us, and the property of the entire bay was ceded to us."

Last Effort to Prove French Sovereignty

With these reflections, Madam, our Englishman ended his story. From the beginning of his narration I took the liberty of interrupting him whenever the topic of Jean Cabot came up, to whom, as you have seen, he mistakenly attributed the first discovery of North America. He concluded that England had acquired the sovereignty of this country, because he supposed that Cabot's expedition was undertaken by order of the British government. But I proved that the discoveries attributed to this sailor are entirely chimerical, and were thought up by the English only to dispute the ownership of French possessions in this part of the new world. It is true that Cabot began his voyage under the flag of England,[92] in order to discover a northeast passage to the east Indies. However, despite the fact that it was he alone who paid for this outfitting, he admitted on his return that he only saw a few parts of the continent of America, all distant from each other. It is, however, only on the basis of this voyage, undertaken by a foreigner at his own expense, with no ambition to make a permanent settlement, and with no undertaking to be successful there; it is, say I, based on this simple trip that the English grant themselves a property title in the entire continent — as if, merely to *perceive* the land proffers the same right as *to settle* there. Their first efforts to found a colony in America only go back to the end of the sixteenth century, and all their expeditions ended very badly until the beginning of the seventeenth century, when captain Newport built the first English village in North America.[93] It has not been difficult for me to prove, in this respect, that the French nation has rights of precedence over Britain. A long time before Cabot, people from Dieppe, St. Malo, and La Rochelle, and other French

---

92 By 1495, Cabot had moved to Bristol, England, with his family. He made a voyage in 1497 on the ship *Matthew* and claimed land in Canada — mistaking it for Asia — for King Henry VII of England.

93 Christopher Newport, (1561-1617), was a British sea captain who was one of the founders of the Jamestown Colony. Newport was elevated to the rank of principal master of the Royal Navy in 1606, the same year that he was chosen by the Virginia Company to lead a colonizing mission to the New World. He set sail from London in December 1606 in command of the *Discovery*, the *Godspeed*, and the *Susan Constant*. That small fleet entered Virginia's Chesapeake Bay on April 26, 1607. Also at the company's behest, the colonists settled inland from the coast, on a peninsula in the James River. That settlement, named Jamestown for England's King James I, was established on May 13, 1607. For further details, see: http://www.britannica.com/biography/Christopher-Newport.

sailors, had been to the Grand Banks and the coast of Newfoundland. We owe to them the beginnings of the cod fishing industry, in which other nations, over the passage of time, have shared the benefits with us. But as we are speaking now only of voyages undertaken to get established in those countries, I know that sixty years before Newport, a Frenchman named *Quartier* [Jacques Cartier[94]], being familiar with the greater part of the Gulf of St. Lawrence, made alliances with the Savages, built a fort, and took possession of the country. A few years later, he built a dwelling in Cape Breton. So, in comparing the period of the first efforts of the French to build settlements in America, with the first conceptions of a similar nature conceived by the English, I have demonstrated that we preceded them by sixty years.

Finally, this little digression was made without bad feeling from either side, but it seemed to me that each held fast to his own feelings. I have no less interest in listening to the rest of the story, and everything I learn about Hudson Bay, is all the more agreeable to me, but the season is already advanced for this part of the country, such that it no longer allows me to continue this trip. It has been decided that we will get ourselves back to Newfoundland, and from there, go to Nova Scotia, and then to the different provinces of Canada.

I remain, etc.

At Newfoundland, August 2nd., 1748.

---

94 Jacques Cartier (1491–1557) a navigator of Saint-Malo, Brittany, was the first European explorer of the Gulf of St. Lawrence in 1534, discoverer of the St. Lawrence River in 1535, and commander of the settlement of Charlesbourg-Royal in 1541–1542. See DCB for further details.

Letter 97

THE ISLAND OF NEWFOUNDLAND & ITS ENVIRONS

MANY nations of Europe fight over the glory of having discovered America, and even claim to have landed on the island of Newfoundland long before the birth of Christopher Columbus. The French and the English made settlements there only a long time after it was discovered. The former have never stopped going there for cod-fishing. We find also, in ancient accounts, some indications of English trading in this island during the reign of Henry VIII. They tried to found a colony there near the end of the sixteenth century, but with so little success that a shortage of food caused the entire crew to perish — a misfortune that certainly curbed their ambition and caused them to give up on the entire project. The French and the Portuguese benefited from this aversion and on their own continued in the cod-fishing and fur-trapping businesses. Nevertheless, they never thought either to build fortifications there, or to settle. But the benefits that accrued from their voyages became a spur to the English, and they followed this example.

English Domination

However, not content to share in the same advantages, they came, as if in triumph, to take possession of the island in the name of Queen Elizabeth. This ceremony was carried out with splendour, and they did not miss a beat in proclaiming it an offence to all the other nations of the world to come to fish off the coasts of this island without the permission of England. Nothing could match the hopes to which this so-called right of ownership gave rise in them. Budé composed a poem in Latin, where he speaks of this with enough emphasis to make it seem like it had to do with the conquest of a new world.[95]

---

[95] Stephanus Parmenius Budeius, a Hungarian scholar and traveler from Buda (now a part of Budapest) Hungary, was probably the first Hungarian to visit North America. He could not pene-

The war between the English and the Spanish interrupted their voyages. Following this the English formed a company which obtained a concession from James I for part of the island.[96] The company built several houses which were the beginning of the first settlement. The new colonists did not lack for furs to cover themselves, nor fish for nourishment. However, success did not at all match their expectations, because the company slacked off in its efforts, and resigned its rights to various private concerns. Doctor Vaugham [sic], a celebrated physician and poet,[97] purchased part of this concession, settled in his new domain, and wrote a poem entitled *"The Golden Fleece,"* which he dedicated to Charles I. The knight Calvert,[98] Secretary of State, retired there with his family, to devote his attentions more freely to the practice of the Roman [Catholic] religion, which he professed. He had a well-fortified chateau built, armories, out-buildings, and cabins for the thirty people who accompanied him.

---

trate the tangled forests around St. John's to explore further, was impressed by the fishing, but saw none of the Beothuk Indians he had hoped to find. He died by drowning on a side trip to Sable Island or Cape Breton, in August of 1583 after his ship ran aground. His poem about New Found Land, was entitled *De Navigatione Illustris et Magnanimi Equitis Aurati Humfredi Gilberti, ad Deducendam in Novum Orbem Coloniam Suscepta* (London, 1582). The poem is about thirteen pages in length, and can be seen here: https://archive.org/details/denavigationehu00budegoog. See DCB for further details.

96 No formal attempt at colonizing Newfoundland was made until early in the 17th century. Sir Francis Bacon and his associates formed the *Newfoundland Colonization Company* and in 1610 sent John Guy to found a colony in Newfoundland. Guy carried with him a Charter from James I containing explicit instructions regarding the purchase of fish and cod oil, the cutting of timber for export, the raising of sheep and other matters. He settled with his 41 colonists at Cupids (then Cuper's Cove) in Conception Bay. Houses, stores and wharves were built and a fort erected. Further inland a farm and a mill were established. In 1613 the first white child was born in Newfoundland.

97 Sir William Vaughan (1575-1641) was a well-known Royalist leader preparatory to the English Civil War, which broke out in 1642. In 1616 he bought a grant of land on the island of Newfoundland, from the London and Bristol Company. In 1617 he sent Welsh colonists to establish a permanent colony, which he called Cambriol, which eventually failed. Vaughan visited his colony in 1622, and returned to England in 1625, taking with him two works ready for publication. *The Golden Fleece*, (1626), is a long and fantastical prose allegory attempting to demonstrate "the Errours of Religion, the Vices and Decayes of the Kingdome, and lastly the wayes to get wealth, and to restore Trading" through the colonization of Newfoundland. See DCB for further details.

98 Sir George Calvert, or 1st Baron Baltimore (?1580-1632) had a successful career at the court of King James I, which reached its peak in 1619. That year he was appointed a secretary of state, and became a member of the privy council. Soon after this, his position at court crumbled, and early in 1625 he resigned as Secretary of State. At the same time he made known his conversion to Roman Catholicism. Retirement from court gave Calvert more time to devote to his interest in overseas plantations — in Newfoundland, and later, and more famously, in Maryland. He had already acquired land in Newfoundland, purchased from Sir William Vaughan in 1620, and in 1621 his colonists had set off for what is now Ferryland, on the Avalon peninsula of Newfoundland. This was to become one of the earliest permanent European settlements in northeastern North America and among the best capitalized, for Calvert was influential and wealthy.

Imperceptibly, the island became more populated, for until then, only a few Savages were seen to the north, and they were in such small numbers that it is doubtful whether they lived there permanently, or were just travelling over solid ground so they could fish and hunt.

A First French Settlement — and War With the English

The French got established there much later than the English, for the court paid very little attention to this island. Everything was abandoned to private operators, who outfitted at their own expense so they could send fishermen there. But in 1660, an officer obtained a concession for a port and the title of *Governor*. He built a fort there by the name of *St. Louis*, and the village which soon arose there under its protection was named *Plaisance*.[99] It was the first French settlement on the island of Newfoundland. The intent of the court, in founding this settlement, was to uphold the possession rights of the subjects of his Majesty in a place where they had been for such a long time — even before the English — so they could go there every year for the cod-fishing.

However, the English already possessed great wealth and power there, which made them absolute masters of cod-fishing — which is to say of the most widespread and easiest fisheries commerce in the world. The French had not taken sufficiently good measures to at least share in this with them. The colony of Plaisance, even though situated in the most beautiful and ample ports in all of America, did not equal even the most mediocre settlements of the English. There were no more ample lodgings there than one might find on a ship; each person had only a daily ration; no one was in any position to help the poor or the sick; no one even had the thought to build a hospital there. Despite this, these two nations lived more or less peacefully together until the time of the war that preceded the peace of Riswick.[100] Then they attacked each other by turns, and drove each other from various outposts. This peace put an end to hostilities, but the war that flared up in Europe at the beginning of the eighteenth century, got it all going again. The two parties became once again, by turns, conquered and conqueror. Finally, by the Treaty of Utrecht, France ceded the entire island to England, and only reserved for itself the right to fish in a limited zone, on the west coast, during a specified time of the year.

---

99 Today, this is the town of Placentia.

100 The Treaty of Ryswick was signed on 20 September 1697 and named after Ryswick (now known as Rijswijk) in the Dutch Republic. The treaty settled the War of the League of Augsburg (Nine Years' War), which pitted France against the Grand Alliance of England, Spain, the Holy Roman Empire and the United Provinces.

A Hard Life in Newfoundland

With the exception of the cod-fishing business, the English did not gain a great deal from this island, because the winter there is long and violent, and the heat of summer, while excessive, does not warm the land sufficiently long to make it fertile. It's soil — at least in those parts with which we are familiar — is sterile, and filled with rocks; but in such a vast area it is unlikely one would not find lots of variety. Around Plaisance, there are ponds and streams that attract lots of game; but in the parts of the country that are rough and mountainous, the hunt for wild animals is impossible. As far as the interior of the island is concerned, we can only speak about it by conjecture, as no one as yet has boasted of penetrating there. We are no better informed on the natives of the country: the most common opinion is that it has never been inhabited by any settled people. On its coasts, we have only seen Eskimos, who cross over to there from the great land of Labrador during the summer, to live on their fishing and hunting.

Law and Order in the Wilderness

The English, who are today the sole masters of the island of Newfoundland, amount to about six thousand inhabitants dispersed in various hamlets along the shore, and protected by a few forts, of which the most important is called Fort St. John. This colony has been without a governor for a long time. In peacetime, the master of a vessel which was the first to arrive in one of the ports of this island during fishing season, took command during that season, and was called *Harbour Master*. This custom brought about many misfortunes because of the eagerness it caused in each ship's captain to be the first. In wartime, the leader of the squadron commanded to support the English fishermen and get rid of the enemies of Great Britain, revelled in his authority. Today, the master of a ship that arrives in one of these ports ahead of others, is still the Harbour Master, but there is a Governor in Plaisance who is in charge of the island.

In the past, the military governor of Fort St. Jean, likewise appropriated all the rights, but without having been authorized to do so by any specific commission. Only with the power that belonged to his rank, he exercised the powers of Judge and Chancellor. In truth, there was not much need for laws in a country where the inhabitants owned almost nothing at all. A few nets, a few tools stolen, a bit of space encroached upon on someone else's shore — these were the main disputes. And justice was rendered with few formalities. The Harbour Master, or the military commander was familiar with all crimes except murder, and once having sent armed guards to get the guilty one, he pronounced the sentence on the spot. A murderer was sent back to England in shackles. And as it would have been too costly to send witnesses with him, the charges were ordinarily dismissed by the judges in London, who sent him back to Newfoundland with a copy of their judgement.

Fabulous Fishing Off Newfoundland

Fishing and trade are the sole occupation of the English living on this island. It is claimed that every year they sell more than four million codfish to Spain, Portugal, and Italy. This sum is all profit to them, because the sale of the scraps of this fish, which are shipped to the West Indies to feed the Negroes, and that of the oil of the cod, suffices to offset their costs. In addition to the advantages gained by private individuals from this trade, and the sums it contributes annually to national wealth, it also employs a countless multitude of men and ships, which again amounts to new profits for the state. More than five hundred ships, and three thousand sailors are employed in the cod fisheries alone. It is so fruitful, that the articles circulated daily in London ceaselessly provoke the government to seize the first opportunity that presents itself to prevent France from taking part. Without the unhappy circumstances that caused us to conclude the Treaty of Utrecht, we could blame our leaders for not having fully appreciated the importance that the island of Newfoundland held for us. The people who have sovereignty over it in times of war, can easily make themselves masters of the fisheries. They only have to have a few armed vessels to run down the ships of their enemies when they are not protected by a superior force, and they can find refuge there in the event they are not strong enough to attack.

"Ever since England has been in possession of that island," a man very informed on these matters told me recently, "the French have no longer had bountiful fishing. They are obliged to buy more than two million dried cod from English merchants — people who, at the time of the Treaty of Utrecht, sent eight hundred ships to Newfoundland every year that kept nearly forty thousand men busy, as much sailors as artisans and labourers — and every year developed three thousand new sailors."

The cod-fishing season goes from spring to the month of September, and there are two kinds of fishing. The stationary kind, which is done by the inhabitants of the colony; and fishing on the move, which is done by the ships that leave from Europe every year. The first sort has done a lot to grow the local population of the English communities, and due to the cheap prices at which they are able to supply their fish, gives them a huge advantage over the nations that can only fish on the move.

The main cod-fishing is done on the Grand Banks of Newfoundland. We refer thus to an immense mountain hidden underwater that is more than a hundred leagues in extent.[101] Its width is irregular, and the water that covers it is sometimes no more than ten or twelve fathoms in depth.[102] The one inconvenient thing about this area is that the sun hardly ever comes out, and the air there is usually thick with a dense and cold fog — which is how you can tell you are approaching the Bank. The quantity of shellfish, and fish of all sizes that is found there is unimaginable. Most of them end up as food for the cod, about which we can almost say, without exaggeration, that their number equals that of the grains of sand in this part of the ocean. Fishermen from all nations who gather in this place, are wholly occupied from morning to night throwing in their lines, and pulling them out to disembowel the cod they catch, then putting the guts on a hook, to catch more. A single fisherman can catch up to three or four hundred in a day. Each year, for nearly three centuries now, we load three or four hundred ships with them, without seeing hardly any lessening of it. It is believed that an ordinary female cod carries more than nine million eggs.[103] The ones caught in this sea are three feet long, and nine or ten inches from back to belly; the body is large and rounded, the belly well forward, and the back and the sides of a brown or olive colour.

A Strange Habit of the Cod

A singular property of this fish has been noticed, which would be the envy of any gourmand:[104] on every occasion where its eagerness has caused it to swallow a bit of wood, or some other indigestible thing, it vomits the contents of its stomach, turns it over in front of its mouth, and after having emptied it and rinsed it well in sea water, he returns it to its place, and goes back to eating again.

How to Prepare the Cod for Eating and for Trade

Cod is prepared in many different ways. I have already spoken with you, Madam, about the way the inhabitants of Iceland do this. There are two other ways in America. The first way, is to salt the fish on the ships as they are taken aboard, and make way promptly to Europe with them, without anchoring at Newfoundland. The second method is different. The fishermen

---

101 A league at sea was three nautical miles (6,076 yards; or 5.556 kilometres).

102 A fathom is six feet.

103 A 35 kg female cod indeed produces this many eggs, and smaller cod, fewer, proportional to their weight.

104 This reference is surely to some gourmands (gluttonous consumers of delicacies) who make a practice of filling themselves with fine food and drink, and sometimes self-induce vomiting so they can start eating all over again.

take the fish ashore in longboats, take off their heads, gut them, salt them, and arrange them on scaffolds they build on the coast of the island. Then they spread them out on the beach to dry them. This is what we call *hake* [dried cod], which does not differ from what we call *salt cod* or *white cod*, except in the preparation; because both are made with the same fish.

Those who take their cod unprocessed, return to Europe as soon as they have caught thirty or thirty-five thousand of them. They don't dare take more aboard, for fear that those they caught first might spoil; sometimes they don't even wait until they have caught thirty thousand. When it comes to the dried cod, called *hake*, it is the French from the coasts of Normandy who fish for them in the vicinity of the lands of Labrador; and after they have passed through several hands, they load them up again and go off to sell them in the various ports of France, Spain, and Portugal, where they may then serve as food for voyages to Africa, the Indies, and America. New England makes a private business of dried cod, which makes up at least a third of the entire English fish harvest. If we add this to their own consumption of fish, and what they sell to foreigners, and considering this business in all its aspects, I am persuaded it yields at least six million [pounds sterling] per year for Great Britain. And two thirds of this profit comes from Newfoundland. The liver of this fish produces an oil that is used in the tanneries, and is also good for burning [as lamp oil]. It is transported in barrels weighing four or five hundred pounds, and the volume of it is considerable.

The Life of Cod-Fishermen — Alcohol, Begging, and Piracy

"Cod-fishing," a sailor told me latterly, "is the nursery for pirates who from time to time plague the Western Ocean. The sailors who work there earn very low wages and in addition are obliged to pay for their transport when they return. Their taste for strong liquors — which, at bottom it is difficult for them to avoid, due to the rigors of the climate — causes them to become indebted, and to spend the winter at Newfoundland, where they work like slaves just to earn what they need to live on. It often happens that foodstuffs are hard to come by, and those who have provisions profit from the famine by selling them at an exorbitant price. So most of the seamen, finding themselves reduced to begging, decide to desert with their fishing boats, either to engage in piracy, or to get hired onto private ships, which never fail to show up at Newfoundland when they need recruits."

What Newfoundland is Like

Newfoundland could be three hundred leagues in circumference, and is no more distant than six hundred from the coasts of Normandy and Brittany.

In less than twenty days this crossing can be made — and it has been a long time, Madam, since I have found myself so close to you. It is only separated from Canada by a strait of the same width as that which separates France from England. It is called the *Strait of Belle-Isle*.[105]

The trees that grow on Newfoundland would be very good for construction, and the forest animals supply excellent pelts for fur coats, both of which would be very lucrative businesses if the cod-fishing did not take all the energies of the inhabitants. The system that causes them to neglect these productive possibilities traps them in the most binding dependence on other Englishmen. They would lack all the things most necessary for life, if the ships from Europe, or from the English colonies in America, did not bother to bring these things to them.

France, having ceded Acadia and Newfoundland to Great Britain under the Treaty of Utrecht, has been left nothing for cod-fishing except Cape Breton, otherwise known as L'Isle Royale.[106]

The Value of Cape Breton

This island which, like the island of Newfoundland, is at the entry to the Gulf of St. Lawrence, could be twenty-five leagues long, and fifteen at the widest point. Although fertile in many places, and capable of supporting all sorts of animals, and especially very convenient for fishing, the French have never had but a small number of houses there, and did not seem to attach much value to the place. But it was not the same after the Treaty of Utrecht, when they began to sense the usefulness of it, and to think about establishing a settlement there that would gain them the same advantages — or perhaps even greater — than the lands they had abandoned. They understood that Cape Breton, being in a place that served as a natural storage-house between the old and the new France, could supply to the first, cod, oils, coal, plaster, and construction lumber; and to the second, merchandise of the Kingdom more cheaply. Navigation from Quebec to this island would transform inept men, even those dependent on the colony, into good sailors. That these two countries might help each other mutually could not fail to enrich them through reciprocal trade. And they would work together in other enterprises, such as

---

105 The Strait of Belle Isle, sometimes referred to as Straits of Belle Isle or Labrador Straits is a waterway in eastern Canada that separates the Labrador Peninsula from the island of Newfoundland. Its width ranges from 60 to 15 km. The shortest distance from mainland France to England across the English Channel, is 33.1 kilometers.

106 Île-Royale was a French colony in North America that existed from 1713 to 1763, consisting of two islands, Île Royale and Île Saint-Jean. Its territory is now known as Cape Breton Island (part of the Canadian province of Nova Scotia) and Prince Edward Island.

opening iron mines, which would give relief to those of the Kingdom, which would be spared the need for wood — or, at the least, we would no longer be obliged to get iron from abroad; and finally, we would never have a retreat more secure for ships, from whatever place they may come in America. And in times of war, this would be a station from which we not only would be able to disrupt English commerce, but from which we could make ourselves masters of all the cod fishing with only a few frigates.

All these considerations, and others like them caused the Minister of France to found a new town in Cape Breton, that was called *Louisburg*, and the cape, *L'isle Royale*. We had counted on transferring all the French settled in Acadia there, but, not finding in this island anything like the same advantages they enjoyed in their old location, they decided to stay where they were. The port of Louisburg, previously *English Harbour*,[107] is one of the most beautiful in America. It is not less than forty leagues around, and everywhere there are six or seven fathoms of depth. Its entrance, which is not even two hundred fathom-measures wide, between two small islands, can be seen from twelve leagues at sea. In winter, ice closes it completely, and the water freezes so hard, you can walk across its whole width. This freeze-up, which usually begins toward the end of November, lasts until the month of May, and so ships winter over in a nearby gulf where they are sheltered from the all the winds.

Even though the island has many ports which could support a population and be fortified, the French have believed they should limit themselves to Louisbourg, persuaded that one location suffices for the preservation of a mountainous and forest-covered island that poses little fear of an attack by land. The village is of a medium size, with houses built of wood on stone foundations, and its fortifications are very modern, with all the structures that make a place commendable. A the centre of one of its bastions there is a fortified house that is called *the citadel*. This building is made up of lodgings for the Governor, barracks for the garrison, an arsenal, armament stores, and a chapel that serves as a parish church for the inhabitants. In the town there is a hospital run by the Brothers of Charity.[108]

---

107 In 1713, the Treaty of Utrecht gave the English control of mainland Nova Scotia but the French were awarded the islands in the Gulf of St. Lawrence, including Cape Breton Island. They renamed the ice-free port of "English Harbor," Louisbourg, in honor of Louis XIV, the Sun King, and proceeded to heavily fortify the area. For thirty years thereafter Louisbourg prospered, becoming the fourth busiest port in North America. Fortified against the threat of British invasion during a turbulent time of empire-building, Louisbourg was besieged twice before finally being destroyed in the 1760s. The site lay untouched until well into modern times, when archaeologists began to reconstruct the fortress as it was in the 18th century.

108 For a brief history of the *Frères de la Charité*, see: http://www.cchahistory.ca/journal/CCHA1981/Johnston.pdf

Louisbourg is populated by French families — some European, some Creole — among which are well-heeled private persons whose wealth consists of cod-fish shops. Before the English made themselves masters (in 1745), some of them owned about fifty boats, each crewed by three or four men, who received regular pay for supplying a certain quantity of fish each day. At the return of the good weather, the shops found themselves filled with fish, and then we saw the ships arrive from all the ports of France, filed with goods they exchanged for the cod. The French colonies of Saint Domingue[109] and Martinique transported foodstuffs from their country there, and returned with ample provisions. Whatever merchandise Louisbourg received in excess, went on to Canada, or those who ran businesses took pelts in exchange.

The Indians of Cape Breton, the King, their life, & their Missionaries

Cape Breton Island had natural inhabitants, to whom the Europeans gave the name *Savages*. They were neither entirely subdued by the French, nor entirely independent of them. If they recognized the King as a sovereign, it was without accepting his laws for their own government, and without changing anything in their way of life. Neither did they pay him any tribute. On the contrary, every year his Majesty sent them a certain amount of clothing and spirits, as well as gunpowder and rifles for the hunt, with the sole objective of gaining their loyalty. We deal in the same manner with the Savages of Canada. Our missionaries teach them, and these coarse people — though capable of gratitude — love and respect, as their fathers, those from whom they have received baptism and the light of religion. These Indians, even when gathered together, can pass for wanderers, for it is rare that they stop for very long in the same place. Their shelters are built very lightly because they never count on a long stay. Their first concern when they get to a place where they want to live, is to build a chapel and a house for their pastor, after which each one builds his own shelter. They live there for a long or a short time according to whether or not they find the hunting there more or less easy. If the game gets scarce, they decamp and look for another place that suits them, always accompanied by their priest. Many of them commit to serve for a time with the French, and rejoin their group at the end of an agreed period.

---

109 The Treaty of Ryswick (1697) formally ceded the western third of Hispaniola from Spain to France, which renamed it Saint-Domingue (which is now Haiti, and the Dominican Republic). The colony's population and economic output grew rapidly during the 18th century, and it became France's most prosperous New World possession, exporting sugar and smaller amounts of coffee, cacao, indigo, and cotton.

The Climate and Way of Life at Cape Breton

Although it is quite frequently foggy at Cape Breton, the air is nevertheless healthy. The land there is not all good, but it produces every variety of tree. Oak trees of a prodigious size can be seen there, pines suitable when mature, and various kinds of construction timber. This obviously contradicts the system of our Englishman, who, to prove his opinion about a Northwest passage via Hudson Bay, assumed, as you have seen, that in lands of smaller size — be they islands or peninsulas — we do not find large trees here at all, but only bushes and shrubs. Be that as it may, in addition to the species I have just mentioned, cedar, ash, maple, plane trees, and aspen are very common in Cape Breton Island. Fruits, and especially apples found there are of a pretty good quality, as are crops such as wheat, flax, and hemp. Domestic animals such as horses, cattle, pigs, goats, sheep, and poultry, find lots to live on there. Hunting and fishing serve to feed the inhabitants most of the year, but the main advantage of that island is that there is no other coast where more cod can be caught, nor a place more satisfactory for drying them. As this business is more than sufficient to enrich the people of this country, there are very few who bother to work the land. Besides, winter there is very long, and the countryside, which is covered with three or four feet of snow for a long time that only melts in summer, is not suitable for crops nor to feed animals. They have to be shut in at the first frost and fed on hay until the good weather comes again. It is true that when the snows have barely disappeared there is a rebirth of abundance in the fields, that consoles the inhabitants for the length of the winter.

The Fall of Louisbourg

"Louisbourg would never have been taken," a Frenchman told me, who had been there at the surrender of this place, "if the opinion that it was impregnable had not caused the neglect of all sorts of precautions. It's not that France didn't send money and food for the subsistence of the troops and the upkeep of the fortifications. It was the greed of those in charge of the distribution of these things that made them keep too much for themselves, causing such malcontent in the garrison that it did not bode well for the fate of the place when a squadron of Englishmen disembarked in the port. The siege was preceded by a battle between a French ship and the enemy fleet. In losing the victory, the Marquis de Maison-forte[110] achieved an enduring glory with his fine defence. Despite this disadvantage, the town withstood

---

110 The Marquis de La Maisonfort (1699–1752). See DCB for further details, where his glory is disputed.

a siege of six weeks, and the commander secured an honourable surrender such as is accorded to brave men who surrender only in unfortunate circumstances and to a superior force."

The Neighbouring Islands

The other islands neighbouring Newfoundland are St. Jean, Anticosti, and Sable Island, and so on, also situated at the mouth of the St. Lawrence. The first is the largest, where large prairies and ponds can be found. Wild game abounds, and the land is covered with forests of fir. In 1719 a company was created in Paris that undertook to populate it.[111] The Count St. Pierre,[112] first squire of Madam, the Duchess of Orleans, was at the head of this project, and acquired letters patent that gave him the islands of St. Jean and Miscou, with no obligations other than to render loyalty and homage to the fort of Louisbourg. The goal of this company was cultivation of the land, the timber trade, and especially cod-fishing. However, as the first efforts had very little success, the enterprise was abandoned.

The small island of Anticosti belongs to the descendants of a Frenchman[113] who was part of the discovery of Mississippi. He obtained it as recompense for his services — but it was not a lucrative gift. The island is sterile, and has lots of forest, but not a single harbour where even the slightest ship could find shelter. There were noises a few years ago that a silver mine was discovered there, but a silversmith was sent there from Quebec who disproved this, and removed this deception of the public.

Sable Island is about twenty-five leagues from Cape Breton Island, and we are certain that at the beginning of the sixteenth century the French undertook to establish a colony there. But no worse choice could have been made. This island, which is really small and without ports, barely produces a few herbs and bushes. In a circumference of about ten leagues, it includes a lake of no less than five leagues, and mountains can be seen from a long way away.

A Horrific Abandonment!

An adventurer named *Laroche*[114] unloaded forty miserable people that he had pulled out of the prisons of France, and who would soon have reason

---

111 This was the Company of L'Isle St. Jean (today, Prince Edward Island).

112 The Count St. Pierre was the founder of the Company of L'Isle St. Jean, and he acquired the island by concession.

113 The reference is to the descendants of Louis Jolliet, who obtained the Island of Anticosti, of which Daumont de Saint-Lusson was the first Seigneur.

114 Troilus de la Roche de Mesgouez, Founder of the Establishment of Sable Island, in 1598.

to miss their dungeons! He went off to explore the coasts of the nearest land masses, which are those of Acadia, and after having gathered knowledge sufficient for his purposes, he set out on the route to Europe without being able to land at Sable Island again, because the winds kept distancing him from it. The unhappy souls he left there discovered a few planks of a vessel on the shore from which they built shelters. It was the debris from several Spanish ships, from which a few sheep and cattle emerged, which, having multiplied on that island, supplied a resource for a while for the forty French. Then fish became their main sole source of food, and when their clothing wore out, they began to wear seal-skins. They spent almost eight years in this situation, until King Henry IV, having heard of their travail, sent a skipper to fetch them. But most of them had died of misery, and no more than a dozen were found, whom the King wanted to see in the same condition in which the skipper had found them. They showed up covered with their seal-skins with hair and beards of a hideous length, and their entire appearance in the greatest disorder. Henry IV gave a sum of money to each of them, and pardoned them all.

Labrador — A Forbidding Place

A short distance from Newfoundland is the coast of Labrador. That is the name the Spanish gave to this large peninsula of North America.[115] We only know the coasts of this country, which is rather poorly named *land of the workers*, because it is neither cultivated, nor fit for life because of the excessive cold that has it in its grip. It is inhabited by men so ferocious we have not as yet been able to humanize them. Nevertheless, they trade with the people of Canada, who exchange pelts for other goods. But both parties stay in their own boats, and this trading is done at the end of a pole. Our Bretons gave the name of their province to the eastern coast of Labrador, and built a new Brest.[116] The English occupy the western part on the bay, and toward the strait of Hudson.

I remain, etc.

Louisbourg, August 17, 1748.

---

115 "Labrador" is the Spanish word for worker, or farmer.

116 Brest is situated on the westernmost tip of France and as early as the seventeenth century became an important French naval port.

Letter 98

ACADIA

It remains for me, Madam, to tell you about another country, next to Cape Breton, and which connects with the continent by way of an isthmus that joins it with Canada. You will understand that it is Acadia about which I will be speaking, or, as the English call it, *Nova Scotia*. That province had been occupied by the French for a long time, who ceded it also to England with the Treaty of Utrecht. In changing masters, its capital, the town of Port Royal, was renamed *Annapolis*, after Queen Anne,[117] who was then reigning in Great Britain.

The French were the first to take possession of Acadia at the beginning of the seventeenth century, and laid down the foundations for a colony there. Almost all those who were part of it were Protestants, and had Pierre de Monts as their head,[118] a Saintongeois[119] gentleman whom the king had permitted the free exercise of religion for himself and his own kind in America. It is he who built the town of Port Royal — Annapolis, today — a port that would be one of the most beautiful in all of America if its entry and exit were less difficult. Only one ship at a time can land there, and even then, infinite precautions must be taken. Its length is around two leagues, while its width is one generous league. In the middle of this vast basin there is a small island called *Goat Island*, which ships can approach quite closely. It is

---

117 Anne (1665–1714), daughter of James II of England, Anne Hyde, became Queen of England, Scotland and Ireland on 8 March 1702. On 1 May 1707, under the Acts of Union, two of her realms, the kingdoms of England and Scotland, united as a single sovereign state known as Great Britain.

118 Pierre de Monts (b.1558? – d. 1628), born in Saintonge, France, was an explorer, trader, governor of Acadia, and founder of the first permanent settlement in Canada. See DCB for full details.

119 Saintonge is a former province of France located on the west central Atlantic coast. It was the birthplace of French explorer Jean Allefonsce (or Alfonse) in 1484, and of the founder of Quebec, Samuel de Champlain, in 1574. It also was one of the centers for followers of the French Huguenots.

estimated that a thousand ships could anchor in this bay, and all would be sheltered from the wind.

The town has never been any great size, even though it was situated in a way very advantageous to the French, to whom it provided the opportunity to unsettle the inhabitants of New England, and upset their trade. As long as it belonged to France, it never had any other fortifications than worthless stockades incapable of stopping even the weakest body of troops. Since the English have been in possession, they have got it in better shape. The business they conduct there is the same as always: as previously, it consists of construction wood, furs, fish, raw leather, etc., which, from the start of the time when we were in possession, had already attracted more than six thousand inhabitants. The Savages brought pelts and traded with them for European merchandise of little value, and the French recruited the Savages to resist the progress of the English colonies. In times of war, they got a lot of help from them during forays made against the English, and Port Royal provided a retreat for the privateers who pursued the ships of Great Britain. It was therefore very important for the English to secure the possession of Acadia: and they would spare nothing to make themselves masters of it. As soon as they saw it under the dominion of France, they behaved as if it were a supposed gift from France made by James I[120] to Count Sterling.[121] The Letters Patent expressly stated that the transfer should not take place until the time this country would be emptied of inhabitants or occupied by disloyal people — a condition that rendered the gift null and void because Acadia was possessed by the French, who for many years had settlements there. Also, the ship which carried Count Sterling returned to England from there without having attempted to establish a community. In what followed, the English were not shy about seizing sole title to the place, and [Oliver] Cromwell[122] ceded it to a French gentleman named *Latour*,[123] who bought the rights to the title from Count Sterling.

---

120 James VI and I (1566–1625), was King of Scotland as James VI, and King of England and King of Ireland as James I. He was the first monarch to be called King of Great Britain. He ruled in Scotland as James VI from 24 July 1567 until his death. He ruled in England and Ireland from 24 March 1603 until his death.

121 Wiliam Alexander, Earl of Stirling (b.1577(?) – d.1640), is remembered in the land of his birth as a scholar, poet, courtier, and the favourite of James I and Charles I of England in their dealings with Scotland; and on this side of the Atlantic as the putative founder of a new Scotland under the aegis of both monarchs. Delaporte misspelled his name as Sterling.

122 Oliver Cromwell (25 April 1599 – 1658), was an English military and political leader and later Lord Protector of the Commonwealth of England, Scotland and Ireland. For a short, excellent biography, see: Ian Gentles, *Oliver Cromwell: God's Warrior and the English Revolution* (Palgrave Macmillan, 2011).

123 Saint-Etienne de la Tour, Charles de, (b.1593 – d.1666), trader, colonizer, and governor of Acadia. See DCB for a fascinating short biography of this extraordinary and highly entertaining life.

The Extraordinary Life of Charles Latour

Madam, I am going to share an anecdote with you respect to this gentleman, which tradition preserves with great care among the French of Louisbourg, where it was told to me in the following way. "Latour had quit France under religious pretexts, during the siege of la Rochelle,[124] and had gone to establish himself in London. We had lost almost all of Acadia — there remained no more there for us than a single fort — and it was his son who defended it. The older Latour, in order to obtain for himself the title of *baronet*, promised to put the English in possession of this fort. On the assurance he gave to succeed in this, his demand was granted, and two ships were outfitted of which he was given command.

"Upon arriving in America, he asked to be taken to the fort where his son was, and spoke with him in the most tender and urgent way in an attempt to get him to declare himself in support of the British Crown. But the young commander, who listened to this proposition with as much astonishment as indignation, declared that he was resolved to remain loyal to his master until the last breath of his life, and the father, not expecting such a response, left extremely upset. He wrote to his son the next day to say that it was within his power to take by force what he had not been able to gain with tenderness, and begged him not to drive him to the sad necessity of treating him like an enemy. These threats had no more success than his entreaties and caresses.

Latour Attacks His Own Son

"Thus obliged to take extreme measures, he arranged his troops around the fort, and began the attack. His son defended himself with such valour that the father, seeing several of his soldiers killed, with no advantage whatsoever gained, was discouraged by his effort, and at the end of two days, he offered to lift the siege. This offer having been accepted in a council of war, he found himself in a horrific perplexity. He could no longer appear at the English court, where he had responded with such confidence about the surrender of the fort. On the other hand, he didn't dare go back to France. The only way out, which he was determined to take, was to appeal to his son, and to abandon himself entirely to the goodness of his heart.

"After having explained to his son the unhappy circumstances in which he found himself, he begged to be allowed to spend the rest of his days in Acadia. The son agreed to grant him asylum nearby, but only on the condition that

---

[124] The Siege of La Rochelle was the result of a war between the Catholic French forces of Louis XIII of France, and the Huguenots Protestants of La Rochelle in 1627–1628. The siege marked the apex of the tensions between the Catholics and the Protestants in France, and ended with a complete victory for King Louis XIII and the Catholics.

he never enter within the ramparts of his fort under any pretext whatsoever. He permitted his father to build himself a nice house at a certain distance from the place, and to procure all the charms of life by his own means. As tough as this condition may have been as between a son and a father, the latter, who had no right to complain of it, accepted it with pleasure, and submitted to it faithfully.

Latour the Younger Betrayed, and His Wife to the Ramparts!

"Latour the younger gained more extensive government after this incident as recompense for his services. He built his home in a fort situated on the St. John River, and another Frenchman, named *Charnisay*,[125] shared the command of these lands with him. The country remained tranquil for a long time because each of them applied himself to the betterment of his own domain. But they had a falling out, and their civil discord not only opened the path to their own ruin, but narrowly missed bringing about the loss of the whole country for France once again.

"But Charnisay, having become richer and more powerful, schemed to usurp all the trade for himself, and to make this happen he planned first of all to seize the fort and all the building on the St. John River. He chose a moment when Latour had gone foraging a few days distance away with a troop from his garrison, and sent his own troops in to take possession of the place. This unexpected attack at first threw the wife of the governor, who only had a few soldiers at her disposal, into a very awkward situation. But once having recovered from her first fright, she resolved to defend herself until her last breath. In the end, she defended herself so well that her attackers were beaten within three days. On the fourth day, having learned that her enemies were preparing to scale the walls of the fort, she climbed upon the ramparts and showed herself on the parapet at the head of all her forces. Her attackers, who saw a greater number of soldiers than they had expected to find there, and who were most of all astonished at the resolve of this woman, decided that the fort was much better defended than they had been told. With this in mind, they decided to offer her an honourable capitulation, and the fort was surrendered.

---

125 A rivalry between Charles Menou d'Aulnay de Charnisay and Charles de la Tour resulted in the construction of Fort Charnisay. La Tour, who had constructed Fort Sainte Marie (also known as Fort La Tour) on the east side of the Saint John Harbour in 1631, contested Charnisay's 1632 appointment as Lieutenant-Colonel to the King in Acadia. Charnisay attacked and destroyed Fort Sainte Marie in 1645 and subsequently built Fort Charnisay, a fortified trading post, on the west side of the harbour. For further details, see: http://www.historicplaces.ca/en/rep-reg/place-lieu.aspx?id=13465

"The General, once he entered the fort and saw to what a small clutch of people it was to whom he had granted such a glorious capitulation, declared that he had been surprised by such conditions, and that he could absolutely not observe them. So then, having declared the entire garrison a prisoner of war, he hanged all the soldiers except one, whom he saved to serve as the executioner of his comrades. He even made Madam Latour witness these barbarous executions with a rope around her neck."

Charnisay had found a means to place the loyalty of Latour under suspicion at the French court, and arranged to have an order given to have him arrested if he refused to return to France. Latour was deprived of all his possessions, and his rival obtained letters from the king reuniting the two governments of Acadia in his favour.

A French vs English Battle Over Words

The English benefited from these internecine struggles to seize most of our settlements. They took them, and returned them to us, many times prior to the peace of Utrecht, but they have held onto them ever since that treaty. The articles of the treaty specify that they would possess Acadia according to the old boundaries; but as those boundaries have never been regulated, it gives rise to a fear that they may someday be the subject of a war that will perhaps result in the loss of all of Canada. We will begin by disputing a lot according to the true meaning of the words, *according to the old boundaries*; and the English will give them the broadest interpretation. The French will want to restrict their meaning as strictly as possibly. We will name the commissioners on both sides; each side will support his own expectations; we will write Reports; the English will demand from the French four or five hundred leagues of the country; they will argue that not only the whole peninsula, but also the southern part of the Gulf of St. Lawrence, and also the southern bank of the river of that name up to the height of Quebec, was contained in the old borders of Acadia, and in consequence will want that vast expanse of land to be ceded to them according to the intent of the treaty.

In order to press their expectations, they will propose to show that the borders have always been the same, and therefore the British Crown has an incontestable right to all these lands, islands, gulfs, and rivers, and so on, that are contained within them. To prove this, they will say that France gave the government of Acadia to Charnisay, and that this government therefore understood the same limits that Great Britain assigned. They will add that Mr. Estrades,[126] our ambassador to London, in requesting the restitution of Acadia, which the English had seized, specified these same borders

---

126 Godefroi, Comte d'Estrades (1607–1686) was a French diplomat and marshal.

many times, and that when they were returned to France under the treaty of Breda,[127] there was the same understanding. In short, they will trot out every proof they can find to make sure that the boundaries of this province are pushed well beyond the limits ascribed to them by the French. And from there, they will move on to the treaty of Utrecht. Then, by dint of quibbling over the terms, they will believe they have proven that what they have been demanding belongs to them. They will add to all these arguments a few geographical maps that they will have taken great care to see are to their advantage.

Such, Madam, will be the main means by which the English court will exert itself to push forward its expectations; and you would be correct to assume that the French will not let these go without response. They will first of all make it clear that the government that was given to Charnisay comprised, not only Acadia, but also the *borders* of that province, and that who says *borders*, says adjoining lands, and that the adjoining lands of Acadia are not Acadia itself. In the second place, they will add that Mr. Estrades, though a capable negotiator, was not familiar with the geography of the southern borders of new France, because in his letters he gave eighty leagues as the extent of its land — which in fact, is of more than three hundred leagues. Furthermore, the sole concern of Count Estrades was to prove that the forts he sought to restore belonged to France, and that they were invaded unjustly. It is certain that in this respect he had no reason to discuss the precise names of these establishments, for the question of ownership was a completely independent matter. As soon as that ownership was established — under whatever name we may have owned them — restitution followed accordingly. And it was according to this single point of view that Mr. Estrades ought to undertake negotiations, for it was not a matter between him and the court of England to assign the true borders of Acadia.

With respect to the treaty of Breda, the French will not fail to mention also, that it did not have to do at the time with establishing the old limits of this country, but simple of putting things back in America on the same footing they were on prior to the reciprocal hostilities of these two nations. In other words, with respect to the treaty of Utrecht, when it comes down to arguing only over words, the French will not be placed in the awkward position of interpreting the exact words of the treaty in a biased fashion, as have the English, and finding therein all of Acadia circumscribed within the most restricted and most cramped borders. So it will come to pass, as in all

---

127 The Treaty of Breda, (July 31, 1667), was a treaty between England, the Dutch Republic, France, and Denmark, which brought to an inconclusive end the second Anglo-Dutch War (1665-1667), in which France and Denmark had supported the Dutch. For details, see: http://www.britannica.com/event/Treaty-of-Breda

disputes, that no one will want to concede, and that what cannot be ended by way of the written word, will be decided by the canon, and that to preserve a few acres of snow,[128] we could lose all of Canada.

Be that as it may, some call this triangular peninsula, which borders America to the south-east, *Acadia*; others restrict it to the southern coast of this peninsula. The latter divide the entire country into four provinces: the first, from the Pentagoet River[129] to the St. John River; and they called it *the country of the Etchemins*.[130] The second, from the St. John River up to Cape Sable[131] is called *French Bay*;[132] the third runs from Cape Sable to Camceau Harbour, and is what we properly call *Acadia* — and the English call *Nova Scotia*. The fourth goes from Camceau to Cape Rosier,[133] has taken the name

---

128 The famous derogatory phrase "quelques arpents de neige" used to describe Canada, was put in the mouth of Voltaire's character Martin, a friend of the character Candide, in chapter XXIII of his novel *Candide* (1758), as follows: «… vous savez que ces deux nations sont en guerre pour quelques arpents de neige vers le Canada, et qu'elles dépensent pour cette belle guerre beaucoup plus que tout le Canada ne vaut." The "letters" that comprise *Le Voyageur François* were apparently composed in 1747-1748, before *Candide* was published. But Vol. 8, which treats of Hudson Bay and its environs was first published in 1769, after *Candide* appeared. We know that Voltaire and Delaporte were well acquainted. It would be intriguing to know whether Voltaire got this phrase from reading Delaporte's work before it was published, or — perhaps more likely — if Delaporte read Voltaire's *Candide*, and subsequently revised his work to include the phrase.

129 Fort Pentagouet (alternately: Fort Pentagoet, Fort Castine, Fort Penobscot, Fort St. Pierre) was a French fort established in present-day Castine, Maine, which was the capital of Acadia (1670-1674). It is the oldest permanent settlement in New England. Castine was founded in the winter of 1613, when Claude de Saint-Etienne de la Tour (whom we met above), established a small trading post to conduct business with the Tarrantine Indians (now called the Penobscots). English colonists from the Plymouth Colony seized it in 1629, and made it an administrative outpost of their colony. The colonial Governor at Plymouth, William Bradford, personally traveled there to claim it. Bradford's settlement at Plymouth is roundly described in his journal, which is published as S.E. Morison, ed.,William Bradford, *Of Plymouth Plantation* (New York: Alfred A. Knopf, 1966)]. In 1635, it was retaken by the French and again incorporated into Acadia. In 1638, Charles de Menou d'Aulnay de *Charnisay* (whom we met above) built a more substantial fort named Fort St. Pierre. Major General Robert Sedgwick led Oliver Cromwell's soldiers on an expedition against Acadia in 1654. But before taking its capital, Port Royal, Sedgwick captured and plundered the French settlement at Pentagouet. The English occupied Acadia for the next 16 years and Fort Pentagouet saw very little use.

130 Etchemin was a language of the Algonquin language family, spoken in early colonial times on the coast of Maine. The word "Etchemin" is thought to be either a French alteration of an Algonquin word for "canoe", or a translation of "Skidijn", the native word for" people" in use by the inhabitants of the St. John, Passamaquoddy and St. Croix Rivers. "Les Etchemins" is today a regional county municipality in the Chaudière-Appalaches region of eastern Quebec, Canada. It is named for the Etchemin River which finds its source in the region, as well as Etchemin Lake.

131 Cape Sable Island, referred to locally as Cape Island, is a small Canadian island located at the southernmost point of the Nova Scotia Peninsula. Sometimes confused with Sable Island.

132 Today, the Bay of Fundy.

133 Cape Rosier overlooks Penobscot Bay, Maine.

of *Bay St. Lawrence*. Let us not say that we had this distribution of lands in mind when, in the treaty of Utrecht, we declared that the Most Christian[134] King ceded Acadia and Nova Scotia according to their old limits, as well as the town of Port Royal and its outlying communities, to the Queen of England and her successors in perpetuity. Because this treaty appends Port Royal to Acadia, it follows, it seems to me, that it did not include all the peninsula under this name.

The Beginnings of Halifax

There is much talk here of a new colony that the English must establish there as soon as the treaty of peace — which we hear is not far off — is signed by these two powers at Aix-la-Chapelle.[135] It is assured that the government of England, having benefited from the reform of its troops after the war, would increase the number of dwellings and would even build a new town in Acadia. It offered to give up a piece of land to each officer, soldier, sailor, and artisan willing to settle there. This project which, we hear, is designed by Lord Halifax,[136] will soon be announced, and the word is that a lot of English people will set sail for this country. The state will pay for the costs of transport, food, and the upkeep of the new colonists for a year after their arrival. And for ten years, they will not have to pay any taxes. They will be given weapons, provisions, utensils and tools, as much as will be deemed necessary to set them up to clear and cultivate the land, build homes, and engage in hunting and fishing, and so on. There is word that there are already four thousand people who have lined up to be part of this new population, and the town they are to build will be called *Halifax*, in honour of the founder of this initiative. It is going to be situated in the south-east of the peninsula in

---

134 This title, *Rex Christianissimus*, or *Roi Très-chrétien* owed its origins to the long, and distinctive, relationship between the Catholic Church and the Franks. The title was frequently accorded to French Kings (although on a number of occasions Kings of other realms would be addressed as such by the Church), and came into frequent use during the reign of Charles VI; under his son, Charles VII, it became recognised as a hereditary and exclusive title of the Kings of France.

135 The Treaty of Aix-la-Chapelle of 1748, sometimes called the Treaty of Aachen, ended the War of the Austrian Succession following a congress assembled on 24 April 1748 at the Free Imperial City of Aachen — called *Aix-la-Chapelle* in French, and then also in English — in the west of the Holy Roman Empire. The resulting treaty was signed on 18 October 1748 by Great Britain, France, and the Dutch Republic.

136 George Montagu Dunk, 2nd earl of Halifax, (1716–1771), English statesman, after whom the city of Halifax, Nova Scotia, is named. He was the son of George Montagu, 1st earl of Montagu, to whose title he succeeded in 1739. He assumed the name of his wealthy wife, Anne Dunk, whom he married in 1741. He became president of the Board of Trade in 1748 and took an active interest in colonial development, helping to found Halifax, N.S., and in several ways rendering good service to trade, especially with North America.

a most suitable location, and will be a lot better for fishing than the port of Annapolis. It will be large, very well built, fortified with stockades, and with wooden forts in all directions enabling it to fend off any attacks by Savages.

There are politicians who suspect that despite whatever desire may be felt to make this into a flourishing town, its surrounding areas will never yield to cultivation: they have inspected the land, which seems to them very hard to clear, and even if it were cleared, it would produce little and would cost a lot to work.

The French Loyalty of the Indians

And in any case, they add, the English will never succeed in gaining the friendship of the Savages, who are uniquely devoted to the French nation. So they are going to suffer incredibly at the hands of these Indians, and will only be able to keep them as far away as the range of a canon, and will be able to work their lands only at great danger to themselves. Also, as they will not be able to gather even a fifth of those things necessary for their upkeep, they will be obliged to procure most of their provisions from New England. And they will die of hunger if the fishing, along with the scarcity of other sea-food and the pay of the garrison only allows them to subsist. Even the garrison will not amount to much help against the Savages, even though we have heard it will comprise three regiments. These soldiers, anxious from lack of exercise, attacked, for the most part by scurvy, and weakened through use of strong liquor, will never be able to resist the energy, vigilance, patience, and skill of the Americans. If the king of England abandons this colony even for a moment, notwithstanding the enormous sums it has cost, or the incentives that will be given to it, or the assistance that will be procured for it — these politicians insist it can never sustain itself. If, with more difficulties to overcome, and less expectation of assistance from Europe, the French have multiplied and prospered there, it is because they were friendly with the Savages. And the latter, on the other hand, have declared an eternal war against the English, by whom they do not want to be controlled.

The Life and Customs of the Indians in Acadia

In the interior of Acadia there are about seven or eight Indian nations, all enemies of England. The main ones are the Etechemins, who occupy the western part, and the Souriquois[137] who live in the area around Port Royal. These people have certain customs particular to them, and others that are

---

137 The term, "Souriquois," means "salt water men" and was commonly used by early French explorers and settlers of Canada to describe the Mi'kmaq people of the Nova Scotia mainland and sea coast.

generally like the customs of other Savages. *Samago* is the title they give to their chiefs; each village has its own, who has absolute authority over the young. They are obliged to obey him until they are married. All the fruit of their labours belongs to him, and after their marriage, even if they have many children, they pay him a kind of tribute that he exacts with utmost rigour. Even though this office is elective, the one who is head of the largest family is almost always chosen. He sorts out all the squabbles that arise among his people. If the parties cannot agree, he makes a judgement on the spot according to the *lex Talionis*,[138] which is strictly observed. In matters that concern all the people, nothing is ruled upon without a general decree from the assembled chiefs.

These Savages are hard with their women to the point of cruelty, and in their fury they revile them inhumanely. They won't stand for the slightest reprimand, and if anyone who witnesses these barbaric scenes dares try it, they tell him: *I am the master in my own house, and I can beat my dog as often as it pleases me.* A woman caught in adultery is often punished with death, and in general, the women are very reserved. But if it happens that one of them secretly makes a mistake, the secret is carefully buried by the family. But if it gets out, the girl is banished from the home. These people love their children with tenderness. At the birth of a boy they put on a feast and spend the day in joyful celebration; and they have another celebration when the first tooth comes in; and a third, even more magnificent when he brings his first wild animal back from the hunt — this is the age of manhood.

Before going into combat, these Indians try out their strength in a pitched battle against their women. If they are beaten, their defeat only stirs up their courage and they no longer doubt the happy success of their expeditions. If, on the contrary, they are victorious, it is a bad sign for them. This conduct Madam, as ridiculous as it may seem at first, is not rooted in reason. In the first case, the husband, animated by despair, does not dare return home except as conqueror for fear of receiving a beating with a stick for a second time from his wife. In the opposing case, despite whatever misfortune he may have suffered in combat, he is certain to be well received on his return as soon as his wife learns he is the strongest.

The way in which these people declare war on their enemies is very expressive. The whole people assembles over this matter, and the one offended complains bitterly about the injury done to him. And then, lifting a hatchet held in his hands over his head, he swears to avenge himself for the

---

138 Talion (Latin, *lex talionis*), is the principle developed in early Babylonian law and present in both biblical and early Roman law that criminals should receive as punishment precisely those injuries and damages they had inflicted upon their victims. Many early societies applied this "eye-for-an-eye" principle literally, and some still do.

affront received. Then all the others, who never refuse to take up his cause, raise the hatchet, as he has done, and holding this posture, sing as one choir in a sombre and menacing tone accompanied by the deafening sound of the stones they shake in hollow gourds.

The Indians Adopt Some French Children

The French, from the time of their first settlements in Acadia, and in order to gain the confidence of the Savages, came up with the notion of having some of their own children adopted by some of the most powerful chiefs of these people. These adoptions were quite frequent, and had this advantage over those of the Romans: the real fathers, in taking part in a war against the adoptive fathers, did so without prejudice to the privileges of adoption.

A Young Boy Saves the Day, With Food — and a Guitar

This reminds me of a story I heard from someone of this colony. A few Frenchmen who had begun an argument with the Savages, began a little fight with each other in which the Savages were quite mistreated. When informed as to what had happened, their comrades assaulted the Frenchmen in such large numbers that there seemed to be no way they could escape. One of these adopted children, of whom I have just been speaking, seeing his compatriots on the eve of their loss, went off to find his adoptive father, who was chief of all the people. "My father," he said to him, "I have a strong desire that is really bothering me, which is to take part in one of those feasts where we are expected to eat everything that is prepared, with absolutely nothing left over. I beg you to arrange one for the whole village, and I swear I will die without fail if anything of this meal is left over." The Indian chief, who suspected no trickery in the beseeching of this young Frenchman, replied to him, "I am pierced, my son, by the troubles of your soul, and so I assure you I will give an order for the preparation of this feast." It was fixed for the day that the Frenchmen had decided to flee. The feast began in the evening, and the tables were loaded with such abundance that the guests begged for mercy. The young man, to whom the Frenchmen had given the signal to flee, came to his father to say that he was so filled with compassion for the guests of the feast, that he wanted to relieve them of the obligation to eat any more. "I beg you my father, to order them to leave the table, and to go take their repose; I will see to it that they fall into a sweet sleep." The guests immediately accepted these agreeable offers. So the young man took his guitar and played such a soporific tune, with such high art, that there was not a single Savage that did not succumb to a deep sleep. As soon as this cunning musician saw them in the condition for which he had hoped, he joined his companions and saved himself along with them, without having run the slightest risk.

A Mystic Tree

The natural history of Acadia today does not offer anything remarkable. But in the old days it was said that at the mouth of the St. John River, where there is a sandbank that opens out and forms a bay about four hundred paces around, there is a large tree floating which, despite the violence of the tides and floods, never moves, and appears, in remaining always upright, to turn on its root as if on a pivot. It seemed to be the thickness of a small barrel; but sometimes the sea would cover it for several days. The Savages developed a kind of superstitious cult around it, attached the skins of beavers and other animals to it, and regarded it as a bad sign to take no notice of it. Some Frenchmen went out there one day in a rowboat, attached a rope to it, and tried in vain to dislodge it. But the trunk, resisting all their efforts, could never be moved from its position. The St. John River is one of the largest in the country. Its banks are covered with large oaks, and with other kinds of highly valued wood. Species of walnut tree are found there with triangular fruit of a very tasty flavour, and vines that produce excellent grapes.

There is boasting also about the banks of the Pentagoet River and the fertility of its land: besides the trees common to France, such as the oak, beech, ash, and maple, you can find pines there sixty feet high. This country has a lot of bears that live on acorns, and that have flesh no less white and delicate than veal. Surrounding the islands at the mouth of the river, there is great mackerel fishing, and the English do a good trade in mackerel with the West Indies. On the northern bank of the Pentagoet, the French had a small settlement in the past called *St. Sauveur*.

A Mysterious Fountain of Water, and the Origin of the Name "Canada"

Near Acadia there is an island called *Miscou*,[139] where nature compensates for the river water lacking there, from a really extraordinary source. About two hundred paces from this island you can see coming out from the depths of the ocean a bubbling of fresh water two fists in size and that spurts up a considerable height. The water is fresh in a circle around it about twenty feet in diameter, without the incoming or outgoing tide stopping it or changing its course, such that it rises and falls with the tide. The fishermen go there in their rowboats to get drinking water, and draw from it with buckets as from a

---

139 Miscou Island is in present-day New Brunswick. See: http://www.ilemiscouisland.ca

fountain. The place where it spurts out has not less than one fathom of depth at the lowest tides, and the water all around it is just as salty as on the open sea. The island of Miscou is situated in *Spanish Bay*, so-called because some travelers from that nation came here looking for gold mines. But after quite a few useless efforts, they went back home, crying out, "*a ca nada*," which means *there is nothing here*, and that, it is said, is the origin of the name *Canada*.[140] Others say it is derived from the Iroquois word *Kannata*, which signifies *a cluster of cabins*. Be that as it may, I am now at the doorway to this grand country, and ready to head for Quebec, where I intend to spend the winter.

I remain, etc.

At Louisbourg, September 4, 1748.

END OF TOME VIII

---

140 This (false) origin for the word "Canada" was first suggested by Louis Hennepin, *Nouvelle Découverte d'un très grand pays Situé dans l'Amérique, entre Le Nouveau Mexique, et La Mer Glaciale* (Utrecht; Guillaume Broedelet, 1697), pp.56-57. In his next sentence, Delaporte reported the correct origin: the name *Canada* is now generally accepted as originating from the Iroquois word *kanata* or *canada*, meaning "village" or "settlement".

Letter 101

ON CANADA

TRAVELLING up the St. Lawrence River, from Louisburg to Quebec,[141] we leave behind to our left, a country full of rocks, mountains, and forests, that some French people have called the *Gaspésie*. It is inhabited by Savages[142] who have no other clothing than the skins of animals, and no other lodging than huts covered with bark so thin you can roll it up like paper and take it wherever you want. As these people have neither animals to feed, nor land to cultivate, they are almost always on the move, and as soon as one place no longer furnishes them with a means of living, they move along to another.

The Life, Divinity, and Customs of Gaspésians

Prior to the arrival of the French in this country, the Gaspésians made no use of either bread or wine, and lived only by means of their fishing and hunting. They didn't know of cooking pots or ovens, and cooked their food in wooden bowls filled with water into which they would throw hot rocks until the meat was half-cooked. Even today they still do not keep stocks of anything, and it is said that they are sometimes reduced to the cruel extremity of eating their own children.[143]

In former times, these people did not worship any divinity, nor follow any cult. They considered the sun to be the author of nature, because it is

---

141 Delaporte writes *Quebec* with no accent over the first *e*, throughout.

142 The Introduction to this book deals with the changing sense of the word "Savage". In Delaporte's work, we see the term used in both the admiring and critical senses, depending on context. However, when he couples it with the word "barbarian," as he often does, there is no doubt of his disapproval. But neither is there any doubt of his admiration when he includes scenes of Indian nobility, accompanied, often, with a sense of unresolved bewilderment that in certain matters such an untutored people has managed to arrive at a level of personal and group moral conduct that puts his European compatriots to shame.

143 See Note 79 of this book for my comment on starving parents said to have eaten their own children.

the main ornament of nature. At the rising of this star, the Gaspésians came out of their huts to greet the sun, and to the sunset, they rendered the same homage. In sickness, they had recourse to impostors, and in their conflicts, to referees. Among them, there are neither prisons, nor penal laws. If it so happens that a guilty person is judged deserving of death, the first person willing, smashes his head in. The chiefs of the nation are distinguished neither by their clothing, nor by any external marks of dignity. The only desire of these barbarians is to have enough to live on, and their only ambition is to be esteemed as capable hunters and warriors. If they go into battle, it is never to extend their domain, but rather, to avenge insults they have suffered. They remove the skin of the head, along with the hair, of those they conquer, carry the scalps back as a badge of honour, and hang them as trophies at the doorway of their huts.[144]

After warfare, hunting is the most honourable pursuit, and they garner no less a reputation for the number of animals they kill, than for the number of men they massacre, and the scalps they tear off them.

Marriages are undertaken without ceremony; a boy asks for a girl in marriage. If it is agreed, he gives, and receives, gifts. He lives for a year in the home of his future father-in-law, and hands over to him all the pelts he brings back from the hunt. The girl, for her part, tends to the home, and the two lovers live together with the appropriate decorum. At the end of a year they are married. But if they go a few years without children, they separate, and look elsewhere to provide for themselves.

The Approach to Quebec, and its Character

The two banks of the St. Lawrence River, from the country of the Gaspésians to Quebec, offer very pleasant vistas. We see islands of different sizes on which well-cultivated properties rise up like scenery in a theatre to form a most charming sight. The town of Quebec, although one hundred and twenty leagues from the sea, has a port capable of handling a hundred ships, and is situated on the most navigable River in the universe. This River, which is never less than four or five leagues in width from its mouth, narrows so

---

144 Scalping, as mentioned in note 84 was a widespread Indian practice, later adopted by white men, especially by bounty hunters in the American West, who took revenge for Indian raids, or who were hired by officials to reduce Indian populations — especially the troublesome Apache — as an act of extermination. The amounts paid per scalp in today's equivalent was about $200. George Franklin Feldman, *Cannibalism, Headhunting, and Human Sacrifice in North America: A History Forgotten* (Chambersburg, Pennsylvania: Alan C. Hood & Co., 2008) gives an overview of this gruesome practice. During the same time period, far across the Pacific Ocean, Samurai warriors of Japan collected the severed heads of their enemies as war trophies and badges of honour, and the English disinterred Cromwell's body and placed his head on a pike.

much just before reaching Quebec, that from this — so it is said — has come the name of this capital, which means *narrowing*. The largest ships can dock there with no trouble, and there is even a shipyard there, where a lot of them are built.

The town is divided into upper and lower, and both towns are well-constructed and well-enough fortified. There is a really beautiful cathedral, an episcopal palace, a magnificent Jesuit College, three monasteries for men, and three convents for women. It is defended by a Citadel in which the Governor makes his residence. The administrative centre is called the palace, because it serves as an assembly for the high council.

Quebec is not very substantial for the capital of such a vast country. It has no more than seven or eight thousand inhabitants. "But among this small number," a Jesuit told me, "one may nevertheless find oneself in a very pleasing society: a governor general, with staff; a nobility; officers and troops; a bursar; a superior council with lower-court judges; a supervisor of roads and bridges, and another of lakes and forests — whose jurisdiction has to be the most extensive in the world; well-off shopkeepers — or at least, they live as if they were — a bishop, and a full seminary; and brilliant circles surrounding the governess and the wife of the bursar. And that," he continued, "is enough to pass the time without boredom, and everyone does his part to contribute to the amusement of all. We play at cards, we have group outings; in summer, in bathing suits, or in small boats; in winter, in sleds on the snow, or with skates on the ice. We hunt a lot, because here, as in France, many gentlemen have nothing but this resource. The latest news does not amount to very much, because the country produces very little, and news from Europe arrives all at the same time. But it keeps us busy for part of the year: we argue about the past, and conjecture about the future. The sciences and the arts each have their turn, and conversation never lags. The Canadiens — which is to say, the Creoles[145] — breathe the air of liberty from birth, which makes them very agreeable people in the business of life, and there is nowhere that a more pure French is spoken. It is really remarkable that here, they speak without any accent. We don't see any private individuals who are rich, because each prides himself on what is his own, and no one is trying to hoard money. Everyone lives well, and dresses well, and both sexes are handsome. Cheerfulness, politeness, and gentleness, too, are of benefit to everyone, and grossness of manner and language is unknown, even in the countryside."

---

145 The term "creole" was used in the colonial period to designate a person of mixed blood; usually of European and Indian ancestry, today called a *Métis*.

I saw for myself that nothing in this picture was exaggerated. I spent the winter at Quebec, where I found, in effect, all the charms of a good society. I saw especially, well-educated people, who gave me the history of our first settlements in Canada.[146]

The Arrival of Champlain

Samuel Champlain, a gentleman and ship's captain from Saintonge, France, having arrived from the West Indies, where he made himself a reputation, became head of a commercial company formed in Dieppe, and with the consent of the king, left with a merchant fleet to found a trading post on the St. Lawrence River. After having inspected the various places where a settlement agreeable to the Court might be established, he settled upon the location where the town of Quebec is today. He arrived there in the month of July of the year 1608, built a few shacks, cleared the land, and laid the foundations of this capital.

Always most eager to ensure the progress of his new village, Champlain returned there two years later. The harvest of rye grain and wheat had been bountiful, but as the vineyards did not do as well, the people tore them up. The inhabitants became allied with the Savages of the area, who gave them assistance in their need, and who themselves found this alliance helpful in strengthening their defences against other Savages — especially the Iroquois, the most dreaded in this country.

We gave the name of New France to this part of America, and built the fort of Quebec. The Duke of Ventadour[147] was named the Viceroy of the country, and when this gentleman resigned from the Court to embrace the ecclesiastical life, he devoted the bulk of his wealth to the work of converting the Savages. The Jesuits inspired him in this aim, and offered to help him achieve it. They were sent to New France with craftsmen and workers, and their zeal, devoted both to the salvation of the Indians[148] and to the progress

---

146 Delaporte's emphasis on meeting up with a variety of "well-educated people" is a device that confers credibility on his narrator, who is now able to supply readers of *Le Voyageur François* with a more copious history of Canada than could have been supplied by any single traveler.

147 Henri de Levis, Duke de Ventadour (1596–1680), an Ecclesiastic, was made Viceroy of New France in 1625, and directed missionary work there as of 1641.

148 The Jesuits of North and South America (especially of Paraguay) were engaged in "Reductions" — a word made from the Latin *re* [back] + *ducere* [to lead] — that meant a "leading back" of the Indians, away from European influence, back to an uncorrupted Christian life in the State of Nature, as Man was imagined to have lived before the Fall in the Garden of Eden. The modern "reservation" system, at least where it was not a clear remaindering of the Indian, or a blatant theft of territory, was intended even by secularists as a reduction to protect them from the crassness, materialism, and sexual and alcohol predations of Europeans. Jean-Jacques Simard, in his article "White Ghosts, Red Shadows: The Reduction of North American Natives," in *The Invented Indian*

of the colony, kept them busy on both counts with equal success. Quebec, which one could barely consider a small village, at last took on the shape of a town.

Quebec Seized by the English

However, the English, feeling empowered by the siege of La Rochelle[149] to engage anew in hostilities against France — even though the two monarchies were at peace — seized the settlement again. So then we had to deliberate whether or not we had suffered a significant loss, and whether Quebec was worth the trouble of demanding its restitution. Sentiments were divided. One side held that the climate there was too harsh; that the costs were far greater than the returns, and that France could never populate a country so vast without enfeebling itself. Others replied that we only have to send over a small number of families to America each year; that we knew from experience that the French women there are very fertile; that children can be raised there without difficulty; that the cod-fishing alone is capable of enriching the whole kingdom; that the fur trade could become a very important factor; and finally, that the single best reason of preventing the English from becoming too powerful in this country, is more than sufficient to get the Court to demand the restitution: which it effectively did.

The French, the Jesuits, the St. Lawrence River

Once France regained all its rights, we allied ourselves with a group of Savages by means of religion, and we distanced ourselves by means of arms from those who insisted on rejecting the gospel. The college of Jesuits, founded by the house of Gamache,[150] and other religious institutions that set up there successively, contributed no less to the embellishment of the town than to the strengthening of the faith in the converted nations. New settlements were formed which became populated by degrees, and the banks of the St. Lawrence River were adorned with superb homes.

---

writes that reserves were intended as "havens against a surrounding alien, heartless 'White' world" (p.339). The Whiteman, he opines, is free to evolve as he wishes, but modern Indians on reserves (which he calls "cultural zoos"), are all but condemned to remain static and "true to their eternal ethnic essence ... forced to bear the Whiteman's burden, but upside down ... forever destined to recreate their identity vicariously, as *Our* eternal opposites" (pp. 357-8).

149 The Siege of La Rochelle was a result of a war between the French royal forces of Louis XIII of France, and the Huguenots of La Rochelle in 1627-1628.

150 The Marquis de Gamache, of the order of Jesuits, founded a college at Quebec, and also an Indian school at Sillery. Sillery was a small village located just west of the town of Quebec, that was amalgamated into an expanded Quebec City on January 1, 2002.

The source of this river is still unknown, even though it has been explored for more than seven hundred leagues. It passes through different lakes before arriving at Quebec. The first, beyond which we have not as yet penetrated, is called Lenemignon,[151] which flows into *Lake Superior*. This latter flows into the lake of the Hurons, and from there into Lake Erie, and finally, into Lake Ontario. It is from this last one that the St. Lawrence River exits, which flows at first with a certain tranquility, and then more rapidly, up to the town of Montreal. There, it joins with another large river with which it passes through all the most beautiful parts of the French settlements; and then, enlarging little by little, it ends majestically at the sea.

Lake Superior is about five hundred leagues around. This little sea of fresh water is peaceful enough from the beginning of May to the end of September. But during winter, which lasts no less than seven months, the cold there is so bitter that the water freezes for ten or twelve leagues from its shores. These places are not inhabited by settled Savages; but as is the custom of these people, a great number of them go there to hunt and to fish in summer; for this lake, which produces a lot of sturgeon, trout, and other fish, has many large islands, full of moose and caribou. And there is something very distinctive about this lake: storm warnings are noticeable there two days before they arrive. At first we can notice a little agitation on the surface of the water that lasts the whole day without any perceptible change. The next day quite large waves cover the whole lake. The third day, it's as if the lake is on fire, and the agitation of the currents becomes so furious that one can only find safety in the sheltered bays on the north coast. This lake flows into the lake of the Hurons by means of a waterfall that is two leagues long, called *Sault Sainte Marie*.

Lake Erie, also called Conti,[152] is one of the most beautiful in the world. Every part of it offers pleasing perspectives; its shores are covered with oak, elm, and chestnut trees, as well as apple and plum trees and vines, that bear their clusters of fruit to the very tops of the trees, on a very level ground. There is boasting about the multitude of wild animals and turkey-hens to be found in the forests, and in the vast fields we discover on the south side of the lake. The islands on this lake are veritable deer-parks — like so many orchards where nature has taken care to gather all sorts of trees and fruits. If travel by

---

151 Today, the Nipigon River.

152 Lake Erie was sometimes called lake Conti, but the Huron Indians called it lake *Erige*, or *Erike*, "The Lake of the Cat," a word that was softened by Europeans, to *Erie*. There is conjecture that it was so dubbed because this lake could be wild and unpredictable, due to its shallowness (about 62 ft. on average). The greater part of its southern shore was at one time occupied by a nation the Iroquois League called the "Erielhonan," or the "long-tails" — a people from which some say the lake derived its name. Some attribute the name *Lake of the Cat* to the existence of wildcats, or bobcats in the region.

water from Quebec directly to Lake Erie were possible, these charming spots could be made into the most fertile, wealthy, and beautiful kingdom in the world. The name "Erie" comes from a nation speaking the Huron language that was quite established on the borders of lake Erie, but whom the Iroquois wiped out completely. It means *cat*, and the Erians were known as the cat people, because in fact, in this region, a lot of these animals may be found. They are a lot larger than our cats, and their pelts are highly valued.

The Village of Montreal

The village of Montreal is situated between Quebec and Lake Ontario, about sixty leagues from the capital of Canada.[153] The countryside on both sides of the river, from one village to the next, is quite populated, and makes a very pleasing sight. A great number of farms and country cottages may be seen there. Montreal is situated on an island in the river, near Iroquois country. The name Ville Marie, which it took at its founding, never came into common usage, and is only preserved in public acts and among the Sulpician Priests[154] who are the lords of the island. As all the land there is very good, and as Montreal is as little populated as Quebec, this lordship is considerably productive. The town tenders a most pleasant aspect; the charm of its surroundings and of its views produce a gayness that all the inhabitants feel. But it is not properly fortified. A stockade with bastions, and not well kept up, with a poorly made inner fort, is all there is for defence. It is in the shape of a rectangle, situated on the banks of the river. The land rises unnoticeably, dividing the village lengthwise, and also into upper and lower parts. The former contains the parish, the seminary, the Jesuits, and the housing for the Governor; the latter, the town hall, the main hospital, the storehouse for the Royal supplies, the military square, and the general hospital. The main hospital is run by the nuns, and the seminary, which is at the center of the town, is known as the Manor house.

Every year in the month of June there is a fair held at Montreal which is attended by a lot of people from everywhere. It begins with a lot of

---

153 Quebec, where the Governor-General and the Intendant resided, was the capital of New France.

154 Sulpicians are a society of diocesan priests founded in Paris in 1641 by Jean-Jacques Olier de Verneuil. The first foundation was the Seminary of St Sulpice, Paris; hence, their official name, the *Company of Priests of St Sulpice*. Olier can also be considered to be one of the founders of the city of Montreal. Along with Jérôme le Royer de la Dauversière, he founded the Society of Our Lady of Montreal, in whose name Paul de Chomedey, sieur de Maisonneuve, led the expedition which founded Ville Marie (Montreal) in 1642. In 1657 the Sulpicians arrived. They were the Seigneurs of Montreal until the English Conquest in 1759. They served as missionaries and educators, and trained clergy, a role they still carry out today, among other pastoral duties. In 1996 there were 118 Canadian members (30.5% of the world total).

ceremonies: guardhouses are established, and the governor himself shows up to prevent any disorderliness that might erupt among so many different nations of Savages.

The Power of Niagara Falls

There is no point in mentioning the other settlements on the banks of this same river, for there are far more remarkable things to see, such as the famous Niagara Falls — perhaps the most beautiful in all the world. This waterfall is more than one hundred and fifty feet high; the water tumbles straight down along its entire width, and the river below receives from it such a violent impact that it is not navigable until a full three leagues downstream. This cascade has the shape of a horseshoe for about four hundred feet of circumference, and is divided in two by a small island that somewhat slows the speed of the current. This enormous sheet of water falls onto rocks where, over time, it has carved out a deep cavern, and upon falling, it makes a deafening sound like distant thunder.

The Character, Language, Morals, and Manners of the Indians

You have expressed a desire, Madam, to know about the character, morals, and manners of the different people who inhabit this vast country. The Algonquin and Huron languages are shared by almost all the Savages of Canada that trade with the French. Once these two languages are understood, you can cover more than fifteen hundred leagues of the country and make yourself understood by more than a hundred peoples, each of which has a different dialect. Here is what a missionary who has lived a long time among the Huron, and who understood both languages perfectly, had to say about them.

"The Huron has no labial letters,[155] speaks gutturally, and aspirates almost every syllable, whereas the Algonquin expresses himself more naturally. The language of the former is of a richness, a vigour, and a nobility that is unlikely to be found in any of our most beautiful languages. The Algonquin language is less vigorous, but it is sweeter and more elegant. Both languages have a richness of expression, a variety of turns of phrase, a fine quality of words, and an evenness of delivery that astonishes. And what is even more surprising, is that among these barbarians, who have never known education, and who do not even make use of writing — they use no corrupted constructions, or improper terms. Even the children, when using familiar speech, conserve the purity of the language.

---

155 A "labial" letter such as *m*, or *p*, is formed by closing the lips momentarily. The former is a voiced labial; the latter an unvoiced plosive.

"In the Huron language, a verb has as many different forms as there are things to which it applies; for example, if we wish to say that a man is eating bread, meat, or fruit, and so on, we do not always make use of the same verb, as in French. The verb changes with each type of food; as if we were to say: *to eat bread, to devour meat,* or *nourish oneself with fruit*, and the like. So the verb 'to eat' varies as often as there are different edibles. The same action is expressed differently, according to whether it refers to a person, or to an inanimate substance. One would not say: *I saw a man, I saw a tree*. The verb *to see* would be improper either with one or the other. The turns of phrase in common use in this language, have a sort of nobility that most European languages do not have. A Savage of whom we might ask: Why did God create you? Will reply: 'The Great Spirit has thought about me; such a one knows me; loves me; protects me; and I will share with him in an eternal happiness.' To say of a man that he is courageous, and of a woman that she is pretty? Here is how that ought to be expressed: *I am thinking about you; Mister is courageous. I am thinking about Madam; she has a pretty figure*, and so on."

I have been in this country for so little time, that I can't tell you much about it, except according to what I hear, and the same missionary who has traveled among all these people, will easily be able to supplement what I have not been able to learn myself.[156] Every day I converse with him about his apostolic work. These details, may not interest you very much, and are always accompanied or followed by remarks and curious observations on the morals and customs of the people he has seen. Here, for example, is what he has told me about the Iroquois.

The Uniqueness of the Iroquois

"It is the one nation in Canada that seems to hold first rank. Its military victories over most of the other Savages has given it a superiority they are not in any condition to dispute. But nothing has contributed more to making it formidable than the advantages of its situation. Finding itself situated between the settlements of the French and the English, it has well understood that both these colonies have an interest in handling it gingerly. And having figured out that if one of the two prevails over the other, it will soon be oppressed, it has long since discovered the art of balancing its chances of success. However, even with all its forces united, it has never amounted to more than five or six thousand warriors. So, of what skill has it not had need, to supplement such a small number? We have seen, in these last wars, the advantages that arise from Iroquois skill and valour. These people — whom the English call in

---

156 This imaginary "missionary" is again a literary device used by Delaporte to import and personalize information he has gleaned from various travel accounts.

general, the *five nations*, and that we French call *the Iroquois* — are, of all the Savages spread over North America, the ones that interest the French and the English the most. The neighbouring nations have become dependent[157] on them, and dare not make peace or war without their consent.

"The Iroquois — so esteemed in all the accounts of New France — occupy the southern coast of Lake Ontario. This country is very fertile, but so lacking in wild animals and fish, that the inhabitants are forced to do their hunting a long ways away, and to come to fish from the shores of the lake, from whence they transport dried fish to their village. It is apparently the necessity of having to leave their own district to procure the necessities of life, that has turned them, little by little, into the most bellicose and feared of nations in all of America. It was to mount a barrier to people so unsettled and war-like that the French built Fort Frontenac[158] at the entrance to the lake, in the name of the officer who commanded them.

"The Iroquois have a chief who acts as a judge in all their disputes. The man who makes himself known by his exploits, and his zeal for the public good, is always the most highly esteemed, and never fails to rise to the highest level of dignity. The son is respected because of the services rendered by his father; but if he has no personal merit — which happens almost as often as among our own people — he plays no role in government. So they must be astonished when we tell them that in Europe, an ignorant rascal of a son often takes over the work of an enlightened and virtuous father.

"The chiefs of these Savages gather together to deliberate their affairs in general, but they can act separately when it comes to unforeseen circumstances, and the league [of nations] only has authority if all are in agreement.

---

157 Delaporte wrote: *"sont devenues les tributaires;"* which has the sense of, "pay tribute to them." The League of the Iroquois, originally a council of fifty chiefs drawn from five Nations, was neither truly representative, nor elective. The Mohawk and Oneida had nine chiefs each, the Onondaga fourteen, the Cayuga ten, and the Seneca eight, which did not reflect population shares (the Seneca had more people than the other four nations combined). Unanimous consent was required for all decision, and succession of chiefs was often decided by clan mothers. This combination of *inequality* in representation, *unanimity* in voting, and *matriarchal* succession of leaders was not an inspiration for the American democracy, as is often claimed (See Elisabeth Tooker, "The United States Constitution and the Iroquois League," in Clifton, *The Invented Indian*, pp. 107-128). Matrilineality (succession as a hereditary right through a female line) and matriarchy (the exercise of power by females) should not be conflated. Indian women of the Five Nations had certain specified rights and powers. But they were not permitted to speak in the Council, and so did not participate directly in decision-making.

158 Louis de Buade, Comte de Frontenac et de Palluau (1622–1698), soldier, governor-general of New France; one of the more turbulent and influential figures in the history of Canada, chiefly noted as the architect of French expansion in North America, and defender of New France against attacks by the Iroquois Confederacy and the English colonies. Fort Frontenac, also called Fort Cataraqui, was located at present day Kingston, Ontario, where the Cataraqui River meets Lake Ontario. See DCB for much more on the difficult personality of this garrulous man.

There are no factions to fear among these men, who have neither wealth nor power to offer or to share, and even though the chiefs have no officers to execute their orders, no one fails to obey them, for fear of creating indignation or public scorn.

The Role of Iroquois Women, their Moral Customs, and Dress

"Like the men, the women preside in the national councils, and are no less courageous in war. Titles of honour are conferred on those who distinguish themselves through admired exploits, and these titles render them so respected that they have the power to free a criminal or a prisoner condemned to death. They release him from the stake by presenting and raising a swan's wing to him, which is how they confer their pardon.

"Their moral customs are as simple as their government. Their houses are built with piles stuck in the ground, and covered with tree bark. In the middle there is an opening for smoke. In every place where there are a certain number of huts, there is a kind of square fort built, without bastions, surrounded by a stockade, to which the old, the women, and the children retreat in times of war. The men go hunting, and the women tend a small field where they sow grain. The women look after all the agricultural work, which comes down to turning the earth over once with a grubbing-hoe. The soil produces peas, beans, cabbage, maize, melons, potatoes, and tobacco. The meadows grow good hay, the forests provide good timber, and are thick with wood-buffalo, bear, deer, panther, wolves, foxes, rabbits, and more. There are also an astonishing quantity of ducks, turkeys, partridges, pheasants, and all types of bird, so unafraid that children can catch them in the countryside.

"The Iroquois have a tanned complexion and the skin horribly blackened, or, as they like to say, pleasingly painted and decorated with shapes traced with cannon powder. They have shaved heads, with the exception of the poor; for among them, as among us (who are not Savages, after all), there are the poor and the rich, the noble and the commoner.[159] These latter classes are distinguished by a tuft of hair that they allow to grow on the top of their head and that they decorate with the feathers of birds, deerskin, or the tail of

---

159 This comment on the existence of rich and poor, and of social classes among the Iroquois, is in contrast to many accounts praising the natives of North America for their supposed egalitarian existence, such as we find in the literary fancies of Jean-Jacques Rousseau. The different roles of women and men in daily life (women work at home and in the fields, while men hunt and go to war), initiation rites for those coming of age as hunters and warriors, status differences in amounts and kinds of finery worn, and the widespread custom of holding a slave class among many Canadian Indian nations, suggests that the then prevalent belief among non-natives in an egalitarian moral and political ideal among the Indians of Canada, was more a product of fitting them into an abstract European ideal, than of close observation of actual Indian life. Class divisions were even more obvious among some West coast nations.

a rabbit. Their ears form the most arresting part of their finery. These people make their ears grow larger by stretching them. Then they split them — a very painful operation which, for forty days, causes those who submit to it to suffer agonies. Then, they weigh them down with heavy silver, copper, or lead rings. They also attach these to their nostrils. And nothing is more common than bracelets and necklaces made of shell, or metal, that constitute the ordinary finery of the most distinguished of the nation. A piece of material tied above the belt, a very short shirt, bits of cloth tied around the leg as if like a gaiter, a large coat, or, to be more exact, a rough blanket thrown over the shoulders, makes up their clothing. In winter they have stockings of rough cloth, and shoes of animal skin. In summer, most of them go almost naked. Some women wear skirts, let their hair grow to mid-thigh, and others, almost to the ground. They braid and decorate their hair with ribbons; others wrap it in a hair-bag, to imitate our young French women of Canada, whom they wouldn't be disconcerted either to resemble or to please. They let their eyebrows grow, too, but along with their hair, that is the only adornment of this type that they hold onto. They pluck out all their other bodily hair with extreme care. An Iroquois woman who has not done this will find neither a lover nor a husband. But they would strike you in general as quite well put together, with a pleasing figure.

The Iroquois Character, Marriage and Childbirth

"These people are gentle, civil, and affable with their friends; but cruel, villainous, and unforgiving of their enemies, whom they will pursue until they have exterminated them and their entire race.[160] In the past, the obligations of hospitality were sacred among them; they received strangers like the hosts of antiquity welcomed travelers. But thanks to the teachings and the example of the Europeans, they got civilized, so as to become hard, greedy, and cruel.[161]

---

160 Here again, the author balances the admirable with the execrable characteristics of the native to avoid the common stereotyping of the native either as a noble, or ignoble, Savage. This Indian with good and evil traits fits the Christian typology of all men as beings created with the moral capacity for good, but prone to evil when lacking the formation of an admirable "second nature" (Aristotle's phrase); in this case, without the character-formation brought about by revelation of true religion.

161 This remark gives voice to the growing Romantic notion of the mid-Eighteenth century, that "society" corrupts the goodness of natural man. Delaporte's ironic use of the term "civilized" here is to imply that the European "civilization" of his day was corrupt, and so to bring it to America was to corrupt the once naturally-good natives who used to uphold their sacred obligations, as did the noble ancients of Europe. Baron de Lahontan (1666–1715), in his widely translated and popular publication *New Voyages to North America* (1703) had so widely promoted the myth of the noble Savage through a central Indian character named Adario, that this popular anti-European literary-critical device is today commonly called "the Adario motif."

"Accustomed to the most rigorous conditions, they bear with unwavering constancy, the cold, the heat, hunger, thirst, and long treks; and in spite of these traits, they are the most intemperate people I know. The use of strong liquor carries them off in all sorts of excesses, and they blame the liquor itself for all the violence to which they surrender themselves.[162] Although they usually nourish themselves with game, sometimes they eat dogs, cats, and even grass-snakes. To roast their meats, they skewer it on a long stick stuck in the ground leaning toward the fire.

"The passion — rather, the fury — of gambling, is nowhere carried to a greater extreme than with the Iroquois. It is altogether typical to see them lose everything they own, piece by piece, including their own shirt, and the tatters of cloth that they use for a stocking or a belt. To this characteristic, which is closer to the civilized customs to be found in our cities, than to the natural selflessness of Savages, they also add a love of sex — another characteristic they share with all civilized nations.[163]

"Each man has his own wife, whom he takes, and sends back to her home when he wishes,[164] but they are in no way polygamous. For them, marriage is neither preceded nor followed by any contract or formality. The young

---

162 Liquor, or brandy, or firewater, as it became known, is a common symbol of the corruption and cheating of the pure Indian by the corrupt Whiteman, and there are many scenes in this book of Indian vulnerability to firewater, a loss of traditional stoic self-control, and, in Christian eyes at least, release of the devil within.

163 As mentioned, the eighteenth century was a period — perhaps this is true one way or another of all historical periods — of clashing worldviews. France, in particular, was in intellectual foment over conflicting views of political sovereignty, and linked to this, of the nature of mankind. Is man flawed and sinful, an unrepentant "Savage," as many felt the Iroquois likely were? A weak and fallen species, as the Christian heritage had been insisting for almost two millennia — and therefore in need of absolute Monarchy? Or, as the latest rational thinkers and social planners just then emerging, such as Rousseau, Condorcet and their colleagues, were to insist, is man basically a good and rational being, who has been corrupted by a society that ought to be overthrown, remade, and governed by popular sovereignty along rationalist lines? In this passage we can see hints of both views. The "Savage" is weak and susceptible to drunkenness, violence, gambling, and sex. And Delaporte makes sure to equate this condition with the modern "civilized customs" of European cities. But he writes that the Savage also has the trait of "selflessness," and speaks of him as innocent, and childlike, as man must have been in the Garden of Eden before the Fall.

164 This is of interest, as during the French Revolution (1789-1799), radical democrats and rationalists clamoured to end marriage as a sacred Christian sacrament, and replace it with a civil union that either party could dissolve at will, on the ground that if there is no meeting of the minds as required by a contract, then the marriage has already dissolved. It is possible — even very likely — that knowledge of native customs of marriage, and their "natural" union — or disunion — of man and wife, influenced the revolutionary program through romantic writing about native people such as may be found in Rousseau's widely influential work, and in popular travel narratives such as this book. At any rate, marriage in countries such as Canada is today more like that of the Iroquois union, as it is dissolvable by the will of either party without the necessity of consent from an observant spouse.

people of both sexes come to an understanding, and bind themselves, and it is, at most, a half-hour affair. Even though their marriages last only as long as they find them suitable to them, there are nevertheless marriages that last until death, especially if there are children of the marriage. At the very instant an Iroquois woman gives birth, the newborn is plunged into cold water, regardless of the weather, and this bath is repeated every day for two years. When the women have barely recovered from the birth — toward the end of the third day — they take their baby to the river themselves to wash it. I have seen them at the edge of a stream, bathing themselves, dunking the child, and returning to their home carrying the baby on one arm, and on the other, a bucket of water.

The Iroquois at War

"Ever since these people have traded with Europeans, their arms consist of a musket, a long knife, and a hatchet. To take up the hatchet, for them, means to declare war; to bury it, means to make peace. They handle the hatchet with so much skill, that even though it spins continuously after it is thrown, the sharp edge always hits the target. Before going to war, they have a grand feast, followed by a war dance. They take part in this with their bodies smeared with red vermillion dye, which makes them look frightening. They rouse themselves by chanting about their exploits and those of their ancestors, which fires up a military enthusiasm in all who are gathered there. The next day they set on a single-file march, one after the other, for a few miles, while remaining profoundly silent. After the procession is finished, they peel the bark from a large oak and make a carving on the trunk showing the expedition they are planning. The shape of a canoe signals the strength of their war party by the number of men it contains, and the animal they paint in the stern of the canoe designates the nation they intend to attack.

"There is nothing they won't do to stimulate the courage of the people, and nothing seems more fitting than the ceremony by which the return of a war party is accompanied. Before entering their village, two heralds advance sufficiently to make themselves heard, and utter a loud cry, the modulation of which announces either good or bad news. At the first cry, the people gather, and prepare a feast for the conquerors. They are led by a man who carries a bow at the end of a long pole, from which are hung the heads of the enemies they killed in battle. The parents, the women, and the children appear before the victorious heroes, and show them all the forms of respect. When the congratulations are finished, one of the warriors tells everyone what happened; all listen with the greatest attentiveness, and the feasting and the dancing begin.

"To toughen up the young ones — especially those who have not yet ever seen the enemy — the older ones insult them mightily. They throw hot embers on their heads; insult them outrageously; hit them; heap abuse on them; and push this teasing to the limit. And it is essential to bear all of this without the slightest reaction, for at the least sign of irritability, the young men would be judged unworthy of ever going to war.

Indian Tricksters

"Just as the hope of cheating death and healing their wounds helps a lot to bolster their courage, different kinds of medicine are prepared, and this is the job of the tricksters[165] of the nation, who act as their doctors. One of these impostors declares that he is going to communicate the powers of healing wounds, and restoring life and health to the dead, to the roots and plants he supplies. Then he starts to chant. His fellow tricksters respond to him; and it is supposed that during this concert, a medical power spreads through all their drugs. The head trickster puts this to the test. He begins by making his lips bleed. Then he applies his remedy to them, and the blood he sucked with such cleverness, ceases to flow, and … the spectators applaud with cries of joy! This same charlatan then takes hold of a dead animal, leaving the doubters as much time as they want to assure themselves the animal is effectively without life, and when he is satisfied that they are convinced, he blows powdered herbs into its face. Then, by means of a rod that he has inserted under the tail, he makes it wiggle. At bottom, this artifice does not fool anyone; but he amuses the crowd.

More of Indians at War, and the Adoption of Enemies

"These Indians never do battle except in skirmishes, by surprise attacks, and in small groups, which withdraw each night to their meeting place. They can detect the places where their enemies have passed so accurately by the bent of the grasses, that they just follow their trail. So as not to slow themselves down, they kill the women and children they overtake, cut off their heads without any pity, and take the men prisoners. If someone has lost a parent in war, and he chooses one of these captives to take their place, the captive is not only protected from the torments reserved for his fellow captives, but he actually enjoys all the rights of the other Savages; and the family adopts him. It would be infamy to send him back; it would be as if they had sold the blood of the deceased.

---

165 Most of the European and Jesuit observers of Indian "healers" considered them to be tricksters and charlatans. See: Pierre Charlevoix, *Histoire, et description générale de la Nouvelle France* (3: 426-7).

"In gaining all the rights of those whose places these prisoners take, gratitude or habit often causes them to take on the spirit of their new nation with such good faith, that they have no difficulty taking up arms against their own people. The Iroquois have only been able to sustain themselves thanks to this policy, for their perpetual wars with most other nations would have nearly destroyed them if they had not naturalized so many of their captives.

"The individual to whom the gift of the man he wants to adopt is being made, has one of his family go fetch him. And the council, in handing over the adoptive captive into his care, does so with these words: 'We give you what is necessary to heal the loss of such a person, and to purify the heart of his father, his mother, and his wife and children, even though you might rather make them drink a broth of this flesh, or that you would prefer to put the deceased back on his own bed, in the person of this slave, whom you may dispose of as you will.' A prisoner adopted in this manner is led to the cabin where he must live. All his shackles are removed, and then water is heated to wash all the parts of his body. His wounds are dressed, if he has any. Nothing is spared to help him forget the evils he has suffered; he is well fed, and properly dressed; in a word, the one whom he *resurrects* in his person would not have been treated any better: that is the expression they use. A few days afterward, a feast is held in which he is solemnly given the name of the dead one he has replaced, all of whose obligations he takes on, just as he assumes all his rights. If an adopted captive escapes, and falls into the hands of his conquerors a second time, he is considered as a deranged child, an ingrate who has taken sides against his own parents and his benefactors, and then the vengeance wreaked on him has no limit.

The Torture and Death of Enemies, and Invocation of Spirits

"Whenever a prisoner is condemned to death, they begin by invoking the ghost of a warrior who perished in combat, and whose death it is their intent to avenge. 'Come forth!' they say to the ghost of the dead one. 'We are going to assuage your soul; we will prepare a feast for you; drink in long draughts this blood we are going to spill for you; accept the sacrifice we make for you by way of the agony of this slave. We are going to take off his scalp; we will drink from his skull; we will apply red-hot hatchets to his bare skin; he will be burned alive, and put in the kettle. You will no longer have reason to complain, as you will be forever avenged.' A crier calls the prisoner from the cabin, and urges the young people to torment him mightily. Another speaks to the culprit and says to him: 'have courage, my brother, we are going to burn you.' The captive replies coldly, 'You do well; I thank you.' He is then led to the place of torture. The most common procedure is to tie him to a post in such a way that he can turn in every direction. Then he begins his death chant, recites his exploits, insults and defies his executioners, urges them not to spare him, and begs them only to remember that he is a Man. 'I am a worthy man,' he tells them, 'I am fearless. I fear neither death, nor torture; those who fear these things are cowards. Life is nothing for a man of courage. Oh, that anger and despair may choke my enemies; Oh, why cannot I devour them, and drink their blood!"[166] It seems that his objective is to rile up the anger of the judges of his fate against himself. In effect, a vanity such as this, in circumstances so ill-suited for it, costs him dearly, for his misplaced bravado stirs all who hear it to sheer outrage. And it won't be long before he suffers the terrible consequences. Soon, after untying him, he is made to run between two rows of men armed with stones and sticks, who strike him as if they want to kill him — but they are careful not to hit him so hard as to endanger his life. Next, a fingernail is torn off; then a finger, then an ear, and so on. One of them strips away some flesh; another pierces his lung. The women whip him pitiably. The only vengeance they don't allow themselves, and the only exception, at least insofar as they have not received permission for it (which is rarely granted), and which they don't even ask for; or, if they ask for it and get it, that they only exercise as late as they can, is mutilation. It is only after having inhumanely torn off all the parts of his body that they slay this pathetic final victim, who had been for so long the object of their pity and mercy. No doubt, it is to avoid an insult of this kind that the victim takes care to remind them that he is a man.

"Throughout these horrible executions, which have no other motive than ferocity and caprice, there is no uniform method to be observed. Often, all

---

166 The theme of satisfaction with the act of cannibalism — in this case, flesh-eating of enemies as an act of revenge and as a show of bravery intended to terrify (or impress) them, is recurrent in this book. There are many historical examples of the Whiteman's barbarism, of course, including starvation cannibalism, which would surely have shocked the Indians. But it was likely the ritual nature of Indian cannibalism and torture as a kind of military and religious blood-sport, that shocked Europeans. There is a detailed account of Indians delighting in the torture, slow murder, and cannibalism — drinking the warm blood and eating some of the almost raw flesh — of the French missionary Jean de Brebeuf (now the Patron Saint of Canada) in the *Jesuit Relations* (1678: 34:27-35, in Mealing, *Relations*, 67). There are also Jesuit accounts showing their tolerance of Indian famine-cannibalism such as they witnessed among the Huron after the destruction of their society by the Iroquois in 1649. But it is also true that many Indian nations abhorred cannibalism and associated it with a mythical evil monster known as the *Windigo*. A full study of this latter phenomenon by Professor Cecil Chabot may be found here: http://www.ruor.uottawa.ca/bitstream/10393/33452/1/Chabot_Cecil_2016_thesis.pdf. At any rate, eating all or part of an enemy, a slave, or a sacrificed victim usually had deep religious or ritual significance connected with revenge, intimidation of the enemy, or the incorporation of the powers, bravery, beauty, or other attributes of the one whose blood is drunk and flesh eaten. A parallel to the latter notion has long existed in Western society. For Protestants, the Christian religion includes a symbolic variation of this belief in assimilation-by-ingestion of attributes of the beloved Saviour, and for Catholics, an actual one via transubstantiation of the bread (the Host), consumed as the real body of Christ.

the inhabitants of the village, men, women, and children, fight over themselves to deliver the first blows. Sometimes they begin by burning the feet of the victim; and then the legs, and then successively, the entire body right up to the head. The more sharp and piercing the screams that the violence and the torment force out of the prisoner, the more the entire spectacle is amusing and enjoyable for the barbaric crowd assembled. The torture lasts for four or five hours, and sometimes even for a few days. Whenever the prisoner is not tied up, he is permitted to defend himself. Then his torments are increased; but he accepts this liberty, less in the hope of saving his life, than to avenge his death and die as a warrior."

A Story of Incredible Courage

The missionary told us that he himself had witnessed a singular and incredible example of the power and courage that these two passions are able to inspire. And I am only reporting all this on the good faith of this fine man, who guarantees he saw it all.

"An Iroquois chieftain preferred to brave the danger than to dishonour himself by fleeing. He fought for a long time as a man who preferred to die with his weapons in hand. But the Hurons he faced wanted him alive, and captured him. When they arrived in the village, he was condemned to be burned to death. As he was not tied up, he considered himself within his rights to do as much damage as possible to is enemies. He was made to mount a kind of theatre scaffold, where fire was applied to all parts of his body. He seemed not to be moved at all, and his executioners had a difficult time finding any sensitive places on his body, when one of them had the idea of cutting the skin around his head and violently tearing off his scalp. The pain caused him to fall over, but without his giving any sign this had happened to him. Everyone thought he was dead, and backed away. But a moment later, he revived from this fainting spell, and seeing no one around him any longer, he took a large firebrand in both hands, forced his executioners to back away, and dared them to approach him. His boldness surprised them. They hurled horrible screams at him; some armed themselves with hot firebrands, others with pieces of red-hot iron, and they set upon him all as one, But he met them with a vigour that made them retreat. The fire served him as protection on one side; and he used the ladders meant to help mount the scaffold, as another, and cordoned off by his own funeral pyre, he terrorized the entire village for a while. Then he made one mistake. In attempting to avoid a burning stake thrown at him, he fell back amongst his enemies, and grown furious, they made him pay dearly for the pain he ended up causing them. After having exhausted themselves in tormenting him, they threw him into the middle of a large pile of hot embers, and left him there, thinking he would soon be burnt up. But they were mistaken. They barely had time to think about it, when they saw him get down from the scaffold, armed with burning stakes, and run toward the village as if he wanted to burn it down. Everyone was frozen with fear, and no one had the boldness to face him and stop him. But, a few paces from the first cabins, a stick thrown from afar got tangled in his legs and made him fall down, and he was pounced upon before he had a chance to get up. First, his hands and feet were cut off, then he was rolled on red-hot coals. And finally, he was shoved under a burning tree-trunk. Then, the whole village formed a circle around him to share the pleasure of watching him burn to death. However, the dying man made a last effort to escape that started trouble once again. He began dragging himself on his elbows and knees with such vigour, and with such a frightening look that those closest to him had to step aside, less from fear, in truth, than from astonishment. But soon, a Huron came up behind him, and cut off his head.

The Peace Pipe, and Honour

"Though the Savages make war like barbarians, we can say that in their peace treaties and negotiations, they have as much skill as nobility. They send a deputy to the enemy with a pipe; he presents his proposals; if they are accepted, he ratifies these preliminaries by smoking with them, and from thence, all hostilities between both parties are halted. We French call this pipe a *Calumet*. It is considered something so sacred among these Indians, that any nation that violates the privileges associated with it can count on being at war with allies for about thirty years.

Indian Eloquence

"Eloquence is the only — or, at least, the principal way to elevate one's status among the Iroquois and to distinguish oneself in assemblies. Nothing delights them more than skill in speaking, or shocks them more than a bad speech, according to the difficulty to be had in remembering it. As soon as they have a reply to give, they repeat it from one end to the other with the greatest orderliness of which they are capable. They express themselves in very few words, and make great use of metaphors. Their orators speak with force, and accompany their speaking with energetic gestures. With a fierce countenance, their cape floating on their shoulders, their tone of voice, their confidence in the discourses they present, bare armed, to an audience around them in a semi-circle in the open air — all of this powerfully calls to mind the image of ancient Greek and Roman orators.[167] At each stage of the

---

167 Here we see a repeat of a theme likely present in the minds of most Europeans reading travel

discourse, whether they are ratifying an ancient treaty, or making a new one, a collar or shoulder-belt is presented, to preserve the memory of the event in question. These collars are about four inches in width, and about thirty inches long. They are made of many rows of little shells, threaded one after the other by means of a cord.

Some Examples of Eloquence in Treaty Negotiations

"To give you an idea of the way these people deal with their allies and neighbours, I will record a few fragments of their speeches, and the responses. Of the many examples of this nature, I am choosing one that shows both the eloquence of the Savages, and the method used by Europeans who imitate them, to make themselves understood. It's the harangue of one of our French officers to an Iroquois Chief:

"'The King, my Master, having learned that you have often violated the treaty of peace between us, has ordered me to come here with an escort, to summon you to follow me to my camp. The intention of the grand king is that we should smoke the Calumet of peace together. But only on the condition that you promise me to give full satisfaction to these subjects, and never to bother us with them in future. Your warriors have pillaged our merchants who travelled to the land of the Illinois Indians,[168] and the other nations that are subjects of my king. If you continue this vexatious behaviour, I have specific instructions to declare war on you. This shoulder-belt is given to confirm what I am putting forth.

---

literature in the Eighteenth century: how, as civilized people, do we Europeans compare with man in the state of nature, such as these Indians? In this passage, which comes just after truly horrifying and barbaric scenes of cruelty and torture, we are in effect asked to equate the latent nobility — the untutored goodness — of the these natural people, with orators like Pericles and Cicero, who were considered the most noble and civilized human beings known in all human history. This is an example of Delaporte being careful to balance the images of the noble vs. ignoble Savage for his curious European readers. He is balancing the Christian belief in the inherent sinfulness of all humankind (and the possibility of grace and salvation) against the Enlightenment belief that all people, when living free of oppression are guided by a natural light within (and therefore do not need religion). Jesuits such as Delaporte were despite themselves often promoters of this latter ideal, and were specifically so in their ongoing battle with their Jansenist theological foes, who believed that all human nature is fundamentally depraved, and the Indians mere beasts unfit for religion. In this passage, Delaporte is signifying that alongside the Noble Savage myth, there was a parallel myth of "the eloquent Savage" prominent in the eighteenth century (See: Mark Clatterbuck, *Demons, Saints, & Patriots: Catholic Visions of Native America Through* The Indian Sentinel (1902–1962), (Milwaukee: Marquette University Press, 2009), p.110-111, esp. note 22, on "The Noble Eloquent Savage". *The Indian Sentinel* was an American on-reserve newsletter publication prepared during this period by Catholic priests.

168 A map giving original locations of all American Indian tribes/nations, and much other information about them, can be found here: http://www.native-languages.org/illinois.htm

'Your warriors have led the English near the lakes that belong to the king, my Master, and taken them to the territories of nations that are his children, to destroy their trade, and to weaken their obedience to the great king. I would like very much to forget what has happened; but if the same ever happens again, I have express orders to declare war on you. This belt is given to confirm my word.

'In a time of peace, your warriors have made barbarous incursions into Illinois territory, and have taken many prisoners there. These people, who are the children of my king, should not be your slaves. If you refuse to grant them liberty, I have express orders to declare war on you. This belt is given to confirm what I have just said.'"

"One of the Chiefs began to speak, and made the following reply to the Frenchman.

'I honour you, and the warriors who are with you. As my words hasten to your ears — pay attention to them. You say you have only come to smoke the great Calumet with the Chiefs of the Five Nations. But I believe I understand the contrary. Your aim was to strike us on the head, if sickness had not weakened your army. Listen: our women would have taken up their clubs, and our children and old people would have brought their bows and their arrows in the middle of your camp if your soldiers had not disarmed them and kept them.

'We have not pillaged any French other than those who transported rifles, gunpowder, and bullets to our enemies, because those arms could have cost us our lives. In this, we have followed the example of the missionaries, who smash all the barrels of strong liquor that are brought into our homes so that our fighters do not get drunk and smash their heads open. We will not give up the arms we have taken, and our elders do not fear war. This belt confirms my words.

'We have led the English to your lakes to trade, just as the Illinois have led the French to negotiate on our lakes. We are born free; we are not dependent on you or on the English. We go where we please, take with us whom we please, and buy or sell whatever pleases us. If your allies are your slaves; treat them as such. This belt confirms my words.

'We have hit the Illinois over the head, because they have cut the trees of peace that served as the borders of our country. They have come to engage in a massive hunt of the beaver on our lands, and have left none of these animals alive; they have killed the males and the females — which is an unpardonable crime among us. We have done less than the French, who have invaded the lands of many Indian nations and chased them from their own country. This belt is given to confirm what I just said.

'Listen, Frenchman. Be careful that your soldiers do not choke the tree of peace, and do not prevent it from covering your country and ours with its branches. I assure you, in the name of the Five Nations, that our warriors will perform the dance of the calumet under its leaves, will sleep calmly on their beds, and will never dig up the hatchet unless and until their brothers, the French, attack the country where the Great Spirit settled their ancestors. This necklace confirms my words; and this other necklace confirms the power the Five Nations have given me.'

Aids to Memory, and Treaty Imagery

"It often happens in these kinds of treaty discussions, that the reply is not given on the spot, but rather, the next day. These Indians sometimes repeat, word for word, the speeches of the day before, and there is a device they use to assist their memory. The Chief who presides over the assembly keeps a packet of small sticks in his hand, and at the end of each key article of the speech, he gives one of them to a chief, another to another, and orders them to remember the article. After having then conferred with them, he is in a position to repeat all the articles and to reply to them. They observe this method faithfully in all their negotiations.

"The image these Savages form of the alliances they contract with us, is that of a chain that extends from a vase to a tree, and each time they renew these alliances, they call it *polishing the chain*. The part of the discussion in which they ratify their treaty is conceived in these terms: 'We promise inviolably to preserve the chain, and hope that the sun will always shine peacefully on all the heads linked in this chain.'

Manner of Trading, Complex Personality, and Decline of the Iroquois

"The Iroquois only trade with Europeans, to whom they offer furs, skins, and so on, by weight. But for any other merchandise, they have no idea of the numerical value relative to the value of exchangeable goods. They also often sell for the same price something worth one crown, and something that costs three or four. They don't understand any better the different qualities of merchandise, and they place the same value on a badly made knife, as on a better-tempered one. This happens because they have so often been cheated by Europeans; and also because they have made the decision to place a fixed and invariable value on each article.

"Even though superstitious, these Savages are neither intolerant, nor troublemakers. Each is free to think as he wishes, and there are among them almost as many different personalities, as persons. However, they acknowledge a supreme Being who created them, and who governs all things here below. If some misfortune befalls them, they do not surrender to their sorrows: *the Man on high wishes it to be so.* These few words console and bolster them. They have neither priests, nor temples, nor altars, nor sacrifices; they just render homage to the divinity, or to the beings superior to them, with public dancing.

The Gospel Not Very Effective

"The Gospel introduced by the Sulpician missionaries has not had much effect on them. There are, nevertheless, two Christian villages which in times of war are considered to be under the protection of Montreal. The first, called *Saut de Saint-Louis*,[169] is located on the south side, about three leagues beyond this town. Its inhabitants have always been one of the strongest defences for the colony against the idolatrous Iroquois and against the English from New York. The church, and the missionary hostel are two of the most beautiful buildings in the country. The second village is called *La Montagne*,[170] and the Sulpicians govern both of them.

The Manner of Living and Future of the Iroquois

"Such is the manner in which this Iroquois nation — or rather, this combination of five nations — is united by a league as ancient as it is inviolable, which has, due to its unanimity, stability, military prowess, and political savvy, made itself so formidable. For a long time they have been the most steady and most useful allies to the English. But having recently admitted into their league another people that is an enemy of Great Britain, this new confederation seems at the moment more attached to the interests of France. The Iroquois have subjected immense regions of the country to their domination; but their subjects have not increased proportionately. Because they make war excessively, and as real barbarians, they really only possess a vast desert inhabited by a few tribes spread throughout the country, whom they allow to live only because they are contemptuous of them. But also this nation, so powerful in the past, so celebrated for its conquests — and despite the precaution they have always taken to include a group of prisoners obtained during war as adoptees among their subjects — is today in decline. At the beginning of this century

---

[169] A map of the original village may be seen here: http://www2.ville.montreal.qc.ca/archives/democratie/democratie_fr/expo/montreal/hochelaga/piece13/index.shtm. *Saut* in French commonly refers to a cataract or *rapids*, and these were so named by Champlain, one of whose party, named Louis, drowned here.

[170] Charlevoix, in *Journal of a Voyage*, Vol. 1, Louise Kellog, trans., p. 218, writes that La Montaigne "was for a long time situated on the double-headed mountain that gave the island its name."

it made up more than ten thousand armed men, but would have difficulty now coming up with two or three thousand. The wars, sickness, epidemics, and the monstrous union of the vices brought to them by the civilized nations with the morals of the Savages, has reduced them to this small number. This nation nevertheless draws the attention of everyone surrounding, as much for their love of liberty, their passion for glory, their energy, and their merit, as for the universally accepted opinion of their superiority to all the other Indians of Canada. The little concern these chiefs have for riches has no parallel in our civilized governments. The Iroquois sent to Paris in 1666 were less charmed by the magnificence of the royal houses, than by the roast poultry, spread out in abundance in the stores of Huchette Street.[171]

Admirable Qualities of the Iroquois

"Honour and shame are the main motives for all their actions; the former is their principal satisfaction, the latter their greatest punishment. The maturity of their councils, their swiftness of execution, the good faith of their treaties and faithfulness in their observance, a courage when tested, a dauntless valour, an heroic steadiness under torture, a steadiness of soul that adversity or prosperity never alters — such are the good qualities of this barbaric people. They are light-minded, lazy, ungrateful, suspicious, traitorous, vindictive, and all the more dangerous because of their ability to hide resentment and perfidy. This is a people that carries out unbelievable cruelties against its enemies, and in the inventiveness of torture, surpasses the most awful inhumanities ever attempted by the worst tyrants of ancient history.

But this does not apply only to the Iroquois. There is so little difference in the customs, morals and the character of all these Savages of North America, that we can attribute to each of these particular nations what you have just been reading of one of them.

I remain, etc.

At Quebec, February 13, 1749.

---

171 The Rue de la Huchette is one of the oldest streets in Paris, running eastward along the Rive Gauche, just south of the Seine River from the Place Saint-Michel. It is today an animated Latin Quarter artery, with one of the highest concentrations of restaurants in the city.

Letter 102

CANADA – CONTINUED

Happy the country, Madam, such as the one you live in. You are already enjoying all the pleasures of spring, whereas here, even though as close to the sun as your southern provinces, we cannot stick our noses outside without first being covered with fur, like a bear. Before the end of autumn, the rivers are frozen; and the ground, so covered with snow, hides the beauties of nature from us for six months. You can't see any difference between the rivers and the fields, and as a result, there is no variety. The trees are loaded with hoarfrost, icicles hang from every branch, and it would be dangerous to stop under one of them. If the sky is serene, a wind blows from the west that cuts into your face. If it switches to a south or east wind, it warms up, but then snow falls so thick you can't see ten feet in front of you. If a thaw arrives, say goodbye to the fish, fowl, and game — I mean, all the meat, that was being preserved, thanks to the freezing weather. Those provisions are stocked at the end of October because of the difficulty of feeding livestock in winter, of keeping backyard fowl alive in the deep freeze, and of fishing through the ice.

There are many causes that contribute to making this season more rigorous than it is in France at the same latitude. There are simply no other countries where there are more forests, lakes, and mountains, and few where the land is such a mixture of rock and sand. This mixture of the humid and the dry produces the extremes and the length of the cold that we endure.

Life, War, Torture, and Ceremonies of the Hurons

But that has not stopped me from traveling among the Hurons, who think of missionaries as their fathers, the French as their brothers, and all foreigners as their friends.

They were actually at war with the Iroquois, for whom they harbour an implacable hatred, and against whom they have just won an important victory. I arrived at the very moment they entered their village in triumph.

The Hurons marched side by side, and between the files were their prisoners, crowned with flowers, faces and hair painted, their bodies almost naked, their arms tied above the elbows with a rope held by the victors. These unfortunate ones sang, without ceasing, their song of death, in a lugubrious and proud tone, and did not seem to be humiliated or to be suffering.

If they pass through a village allied with the victorious nation, the inhabitants come out to meet them, and get ready for some cruel entertainment at their expense. As soon as they meet, the prisoners are stopped, and while they sing their funeral hymn, the whole village dances around them; and it's about who can do them the most harm. It is not considered so bad that they defend themselves, and there is even laughter over this. But tied up as they are, and overwhelmed by numbers, defending themselves is useless. The victors, who have all the rights over the prisoners, back away as they enter the village, so that their allies can enjoy diverting themselves over this. For it's a kind of triumphal event, in which the people have all the fun, and the victorious warriors, all the honour. But as the latter only surrender their rights for a while, and as they have an interest in bringing back the prisoners in the least disfigured condition possible, there is a tradition that those who delight in mutilating them, offer a gift that compensates the persons to whom those prisoners belong. If these persons take this into account, they reach out to those they are eager to save, take them by the hand themselves, and by this means they spare these unfortunates the torments for which they were destined. From that moment, the pleasure consists in no more than watching them dance, and listening to them as they sing the songs of their country, or those they have learned from their conquerors along the route. They are led from one cabin to another, and they are paraded in this way for several days until their fate has been decided.

Our Hurons will stop not far from their own village, and the Chief will begin to alert the village of his return. A delegate advances to within earshot of the village, and shouts out different cries, which will give a general idea of the success and the principal events of the campaign. He signals first of all the number of men that have been lost, by the number of death cries. At that moment the young people of the village race forward to get more information, and soon the entire village has run to them. But just one man meets the delegate, learns from him the news that he brings, and then, turning each time toward those who accompanied him, he repeats the news for them with all its circumstances, in a high voice, to which they respond with acclamation. Following this, the delegate is led into a cabin where the elders will ask the same questions. When the public curiosity is satisfied, a crier invites the youth to march in front of the warriors, and the women bring refreshments to them.

The Savages have a certain mutual respect such that no matter how complete their victory, or what advantage they have enjoyed over the enemy, the first feeling they allow themselves is grief over those of their people they have lost. The whole village must participate in this, and there is no sharing of good news until all due regrets have been paid to the dead. It is only after having fulfilled this first duty that each one gives himself up to the joy that the return of the conquerors has inspired — a joy that is principally expressed in cruelty toward the vanquished.

Indian Cruelty

Our warriors will barely have taken a few steps before they stop and, seizing one of their prisoners, reproach him for all the violence he suffered upon the Hurons. Then, having announced to him that he must expect the same treatment, this miserable one begins to sing his funeral hymn. His torture, accompanied by all the horrors reported in my last letter, makes me tremble. What I was able to gather from these barbarians is that they would shorten the misery of their victim. One of them ended his life with a shot from a musket. The others slashed open his belly, threw away his entrails, and cut off his head, legs, and arms, which they scattered all over the place, keeping only his scalp, which they display with a lot of others taken on the battlefield.

Indian Cannibalism and Scalping

His heart was then cut into pieces, and the other captives were forced to eat it. Among them was a brother of the dead man, who was forced to put some in his mouth — but he as quickly threw up.

As soon as the conquerors came within sight of their cabins, they cut long sticks to which they attached the scalps they had taken, and carried them in triumph. The women rush to meet them in their canoes, jump in to swim towards them, take these symbols of victory from the hands of their husbands, and hang them around their necks.

The way in which Savages strip the scalps from their conquered, and sometimes still-living enemies, cannot be read without horror. They slice the skin that covers the skull, cutting above the brow and the ears to around behind the head, then tear it off as if they were stripping a calf, or a sheep. What is surprising is that the victim doesn't always die from this cruel operation. I once saw a woman who suffered this same ordeal, and lived, and it earned her the name, *skinhead* — and she carried herself pretty well. But these kinds of cases are rare.

The Savages prepare the scalp just as they would the skins of animals killed in the hunt. They stretch it in a circular shape, and paint it with a variety of colours. Sometimes, on the side opposite the hair, they draw a portrait, or a hieroglyphic painting of the person from whom they took it, and parade around in triumph with the scalp on a pole. Those who end up with these scalps take great care of them, use them as ornaments in public ceremonies, and then hang them at the door of their cabin, where the weather ages them — this is similar to the way our hunters decorate the entrance to their homes with the heads and feet of birds of prey or wild animals. There are nations in America, that skin the bodies of their dead enemies and make use of the skin of their hands for tobacco pouches.[172]

The Adoption Ritual

After the first transports of joy caused by the news of victory, the prisoners are split into groups. Those destined for adoption are taken under cover by their future parents, who have been alerted about this, and who are going to take them on indirect pathways to their cabins. Others, whose fate was not yet decided, were abandoned to the fury of the women, and I admired how these unfortunate souls were able to resist all the evils such ingenious cruelty suffered upon them. Two of these women, one of whom had lost her son in the war, and another, her husband, were like two furies who went to work on their victims with an unbelievable inhumanity. I could not even begin to communicate the limits of rage to which both were carried. All the laws of humanity and decency were forgotten.[173] Each blow delivered would make anyone think it was the mortal one, if they didn't know how on such occasions, the Savages are so ingenious at prolonging torture.

In the allotting of the captives, the women are always the first to be allotted. Then, the Chiefs must be satisfied with respect to any undertakings they assumed before their departure. If the number of prisoners exceeds

---

[172] Simon Harrison, *Dark Trophies: Hunting, and the Enemy Body in Modern War* (New York: Berghahn Books, 2012) contains some material on this gruesome topic, including descriptions of white settlers who claimed to own razor strops and purses made of the skins of dead Indians. The cured male scrotum was said to be in popular use as a tobacco pouch. This topic is beyond the scope of the present work, but suffice it to say that if some human beings could normalize such grotesque practices in specific historical circumstances, it is fair to say that given the exact same circumstances, any could do so. Delaporte was clearly aware of the dangerous conceit of assuming we are morally superior to our ancestors.

[173] This is likely a reference, by contrast, to widely-accepted European discussions at the time concerning topics such as "natural law", and "just war," that had grown out of the work of such as Aquinas, Grotius, and their followers. We sense throughout *The French Traveler*, a tension in the Christian conception of "the Savage"; between the conflicting images of the Savage as Angel, and the Savage as Devil. This naturally reflects the Christian theological, and hence linguistic paradigms of the day. See Clatterbuck, *Demons, Saints, & Patriots*, for a most interesting study of the Demon vs. Saint dualistic imagery of the Indian, a literary and moral trope employed until mid-twentieth century, and afterward.

those contending for them, the surplus is given to their allies, and if there are insufficient to go around, the difference is made up in scalps.

The Council of the nation regulates the distribution of captives and decides on their fate, at least if the mothers of families do not dispose of them otherwise, for they are always the ones who make the final decisions about life or death — even for those who have already been judged by the Council. After deliberation by the Elders, everyone is invited to gather in a place where the division will be made, without any resistance or fuss. Sometimes, instead of sending the surplus of prisoners off to neighbouring villages, they are given as gifts to various individuals who have no right to them at all, but who, because they enjoy a certain esteem in the village, have earned these attentions, and from that moment onward, they are in charge of the fate of their slave. The death of these captives is more or less assured if they end up assigned to a cabin where many warriors have been lost, or if there is any other person — even if only an infant at the breast — whose mourning has been recent. They run no less risk if their age, their body, or their character is unpleasing, if there is worry that not enough work can be gotten from them, or if they are bestowed upon a cabin of poor people who are in no condition to clothe or feed them.

The Duplicity of Execution

When a slave is destined to die, care is taken to conceal his fate from him, and right up until the time of his execution, he is treated with as much regard as would have been the case had he enjoyed the happiness of adoption. He is even given young girls to enjoy, and no clothing or food is spared, and as he must be sacrificed to the god of war, he is a victim who must be fattened up for the killing. When the moment approaches, if it is to a mother, or to a spouse that he was handed over, she suddenly becomes a mad woman, and changes from giving the most tender caresses, to indulging in the ultimate excesses of cruelty.

The Huron War With the Iroquois, and War Customs

This war of the Hurons against the Iroquois, the cruellest effects of which I saw with my own eyes, lasted for about eighteen months. The missionary whom I had the honor of accompanying in his apostolic work, had been a witness to the declaration of war, and told me his story in the following way. "I was then," he told me, "in a small fort that the French had just built. In the middle of the night I heard a horrible cry, that I learned was a war cry. Soon I saw a troop of Savages — friends of France — enter the fort, singing. Three or four of the bravest were in a dreadful group, followed by nearly all the Hurons who lived near the fort, and after having gone through all the cabins, they went to make themselves heard by the commander. I swear," added the missionary, "that this ceremony filled me with horror, for until then, I had not yet fully sensed that I was among the barbarians. Their cry always has something dark in it; but on this occasion, I found it frightening. It seemed to me that in their chanting they were summoning the God of War, whom they call *Areskoui*. Although at one and the same time he is the sovereign of the gods, the creator and the ruler of the world, the intelligence that governs all things and, in keeping with the expression of these people, the Great Spirit, he is especially invoked for military expeditions. His name alone is the war cry in the heat of battle. In the middle their marches his name is often repeated for encouragement, and to implore his help.

"Our Huron braves" — this is still the missionary speaking — "held the hatchet overhead, and he suspended the boiling-pot in the air. Of these two ways to declare war, the second is the most solemn. The origin of it is said to be the barbaric custom of eating their prisoners after having boiled them. It's another way of saying that they will fight with fury: that 'We will eat our enemies.' But the boiling pot is only lifted when it is a matter of a war between many nations. It's enough to raise only the hatchet for a simple quarrel, and each person has that right.

"The allies are drawn into taking part in a war by sending them the *Vase of Partnership*. It's a large shell inviting them to drink blood or, depending on their manner of speaking, to boil the flesh of the conquered. And it is seldom that these barbarians resist such an invitation. Often, even without having been asked, the slightest motive gains their agreement — especially the thirst for revenge, for they always have some old or new insult to punish.

"The desire to replace those who have died, to calm their souls, or the caprice of some individual, a dream, or any other pretext, will soon have a group of adventurers who were not even thinking about it the day before, running off to war. It is true that these little skirmishes, which are undertaken without the consent of the Council, generally amount to nothing much. But, in general, no one is upset to see the young men getting themselves worked up and talking about exploits of this kind in this warrior spirit, which by making them more formidable, makes the nation safer. This is not opposed without really good reasons, neither is any authority brought to bear on it, because each is considered the master of his own decisions. If there is concern that the number of these war parties will weaken the village too much, and that they will only be going off to insult some people who should be handled more carefully (or if there is need of them for some other secret project) then action is taken to stop the leaders of the expedition. Some are intimidated by false rumours; others are skillfully persuaded; the most obstinate are seduced with gifts into breaking up the party — which is never very difficult, for all it takes is a true or a false dream to destroy all the ambitions of the day before. But neither force nor ultimatums are brought to bear, so as not to compromise their inclination, or to snuff out the natural liberty of which the Savages are so proud.

"These small war-parties are usually made up of seven or eight warriors from the village, and so as not to compromise the nation with hostilities that could result in hostile consequences, they go off to make war with people the farthest away. Sometimes they will be away for two or three years doing this, and will cover two or three thousand leagues,[174] just to smash a head, take a scalp, or make a slave of a man they don't know — and they consider this heroism!

"I have been told of a certain Iroquois who, having sneaked up on a stockade without notice where he heard a war song being sung, saw two Savages on a kind of sentry-box. He climbed it secretively, delivered a blow with his club to the head of one of them, threw the other to the ground, took his time cutting his throat, took the scalps of both, and got out of there undetected. But these examples of brashness are quite rare. They usually strike in hunting or fishing areas, and sometimes lurking at the entry to the forest, like our thieves. After keeping themselves hidden in the brush for a few days, a few unfortunate passersby who are hardly thinking of defending themselves, offer them the advantage of surprise and of victory. Worried about being pursued, they flee, rather than fight a rearguard battle, smash the heads of the wounded, or of those who cannot follow them, and take with them only the prisoners they want, or that they can guard. They burn the others, and if they are pressed for time, they tie them to a tree, and set fire to the tree right beside them to ensure they suffer as long as possible. Abandoned in this way, these miserable victims die like madmen, either from a slow fire that consumes them, or from hunger that devours them if the fire has not burned hot enough for them to really feel it. A war that involves the whole nation does not end so innocently. The difficulties and the advantages are scrupulously weighed and balanced for a long time.

War Preparations and Methods of Attack

"As soon as these Hurons of ours have made up their minds to go to war, they begin to think about supplies of weapons and food, which doesn't take much time. Their superstitious ceremonies last a lot longer. The one named to lead them did not think about assembling his troops until after a fast of

---

174 This is likely a typographical error, and Delaporte intended to write: "two or three hundred leagues." A league is roughly four kilometers, or the distance a man can walk in one hour.

several days, during which he had his face, arms, legs, and chest daubed with black paint, and spoke with no one. His sole concern, night and day, was to invoke his guardian angel, and to carefully interpret his own dreams, which, as you can well imagine, always turn out the way he wants them. The time for prayer, fasting, and retreat having passed, the General assembles his troops, and with a belt in hand, he gives them more or less this speech: 'My brothers, my comrades, my children, my friends; the Great Spirit has approved of my feelings and has encouraged me. The blood of a certain one is not washed away; his body is not buried; and I wish to acquit myself of this duty.' He goes on to explain his motives for taking up arms, and he adds: 'And so, I am resolved to go into the country of the Five Nations, and take scalps, and prisoners. If I perish in this glorious mission, or if one of those who wishes to accompany me should lose his life, this necklace will be the reward for the one who undertakes to bury the dead — and we will not be left lying in the dust.' In finishing, he puts his belt on the ground, and the one who picks it up thereby declares himself to be his lieutenant, while thanking him for the outburst of zeal he has inspired to avenge his brothers and the honour of his fatherland.

"Immediately, water is heated to wash the face of the General and remove his war make-up. His hair is prepared with fat and paint. Other colours are painted on his face, and he is covered with his most beautiful robe. In this finery, he intones, in a mournful voice, his song of death. Then the warriors who offered to accompany him — for no one is constrained to do this — also sing their military hymn, one after the other. Each one has a particular song for himself or for his family, which no one else is permitted to use.

"After these preliminaries, the Chief goes to lay out his views before the council of the nation, which discusses them. The undertaking approved once again, the General holds a feast, where a dog is served as the one and only food. Before putting the animal in the boiling pot, it is offered to the God of wars, and this feast will be repeated for several days. But it was less a spirit of pity than a feeling of rage and fury which moved them to make this sacrifice, for their imagination got fired up by the sight of this meal, and they imagined themselves to be devouring the flesh of their enemies, and seemed to have no keener pleasure than to show the contempt they felt in comparing them to their dogs; for they give no other name to their slaves. The Warriors came to this gathering painted in a horrible and bizarre way intended to inspire terror.

"Not to be overlooked is that at each feast, the Chief, or first captain, made a speech, where he spoke of himself with sufficient modesty, but he never failed to say a eulogy for those who suffered the misfortune of dying in war, and for whom it was essential to avenge death with the death of their enemies. 'These were men,' he said, 'how could we forget them, and rest for so long on our beds? Oh youth, redouble your courage, trim your hair, polish your face, prepare your bows, fill your quivers, make our forests echo with your cries of war, make glad the dead with the news that they have been avenged.' Then, addressing himself to the God of war: 'I invoke you,' he adds, 'so that you will favour me in my undertaking; I also invoke the Spirits, good and evil — all those in the air and on the earth — so that they will protect me; me, and those of my war party, and that at the end of our successful campaign we will be able to return victorious to our cabins.'

"After the applause that this speech did not fail to excite, the Savages began their war dances. The Chief banged on one of the pots of his hut with his club, and they all responded in the same fashion: it was a public declaration of the resolution they had taken to follow him. A few of them, trying out their arms, pretended to strike some of those present, as if they had wished to say by this gesture that this was how they had killed or knocked out their enemies. It is only permitted to those who have already been designated by some praiseworthy action to do this kind of thing, and even then it is essential that they immediately make a gift to the one to whom this kind of insult is addressed.

"The General walks into the middle of the crowd, his club in his hand, and starts singing again. His soldiers respond to him in the same tone, and swear to conquer, or to die. But this commitment does not subject them to any dependency: it all comes down to promising a lot of unity and courage. Those who enrol give the Chief a piece of wood with their individual mark on it, and any who withdraw their word will be forever dishonoured. There was a time when those who did not fulfill their commitments were killed. But that custom is no longer observed, or at least not in a strict sense. However, there are still examples of severe treatment, and we have seen Chiefs, in cold blood, smash in the head of individuals who abandoned the flag under which they were enrolled.

"To get back to our Hurons, each made clear his expectations as to the number of prisoners he hoped to capture, for himself or his family, at his return from the campaign. Presents are given to the General, who gives his word that in the case of insufficient captives, he will give scalps to all those in the group meriting this favour. From that moment on, until the departure of the Warriors, the nights are spent in chanting, and the days working on preparations.

The War Expedition Underway

If the expedition is to be by water, canoes are either built, or repaired; and if it is winter, snowshoes are supplied for traveling on snow, and sleds for carrying the baggage, the sick, and the wounded. A single man, with the help of a long leather band around the chest, is sufficient to pull one of these conveyances. The women use them to carry their children, but they push the band in front of themselves. With only minor differences, the snowshoes our Savages use are quite similar to the different kinds of pads you[175] have been able to see among the Laplanders and Samoieds.[176] Their canoes are nothing more than huge trunks of oak, hollowed out, and thirty or forty feet long. In the past, they used fire to hollow out trees, but for a while now, they make very skillful and intelligent use of tools we have brought for them from Europe. These canoes can hold fifteen or twenty people, and these Hurons are so good at controlling them that we often see them traveling against the current, with incredible ease.

"The day for departure arrives, and the goodbyes of the Warriors are given with every evidence of a lively tenderness. Each of them wanted to have a pledge of their friendship, and to keep something that had been of use to them. Robes and blankets and such are exchanged; and such will be shed twenty or thirty times before leaving the village, in proportion to the degree of esteem a person holds among his own, or the number of friends he has in the village.

"All the soldiers presented themselves at the General's home, who has been armed ever since he took on his title. He comes out of his cabin chanting, and after a short but energetic harangue, everyone follows him in profound silence. At some distance from the dwellings, they fire a volley from their muskets in the air, and the Chief continues to chant until they are well outside the village. This same discipline is observed every day until they begin their march. The women go in front with the provisions, and as soon as their husbands catch up they give them their clothes, and are left almost naked, as they were then in the heat of summer.

"Ever since the French have provided them with firearms, the Hurons have abandoned the bow, the arrow, the spear, and have only kept the club. It's a small club of very hard wood, with one side of its head rounded, and the other sharpened. To identify themselves and to rally together, they have flags of a sort made of a certain tree bark, on which is drawn the mark of their

---

175 The "you" Delaporte adresses here, is the *Salonnière* woman in France to whom he is purportedly writing these letters.

176 Lapland is Finland's northernmost region, a sparsely populated area bordering Sweden, Norway, Russia and the Baltic Sea. It is known for its vast wilderness, and natural phenomena, including 24-hour summer daylight, and the Northern Lights. The Samoyedic peoples are a linguistic grouping, not an ethnic or cultural one. The name derives from the obsolete term *Samoyed* used in Russia for some indigenous peoples of Siberia. Delaporte wrote of the Laplanders in Volume VIII of *Le Voyageur François*.

nation, of their village, of their family, or of their general. They carry these standards at the end of a pole, and each one is in charge of carrying whichever one he deems appropriate. Each warrior also crafts a symbol for himself that represents his guardian spirit; for this people is persuaded that each of us has one of his own, just as we speak of our guardian angel.

Their Guardian Spirits

This spirit is called *Okki* among the Hurons, and *Manitou* in the Algonquin language. It is upon this spirit one relies in dangerous undertakings, or to gain some particular favour. But these people do not believe, as we do, that this beneficent spirit protects them from birth. That is a grace one must have earned, and for which one makes ready by way of certain preparations. They begin by blackening the head of the proselyte; then they are made to fast for several days, during which the future Spirit is supposed to appear to him in dreams, and his brain, overheated by fasting, does not fail to supply him with all sorts of them. It is always as some kind of symbol that Manitou makes himself known. Sometimes it's the foot of an animal; sometimes a weapon of war; a tree; a stone; a piece of wood; and so on.

"Under whatever shape that the Spirit shows itself, it is guarded with care. It is drawn on one's body, on weapons, on flags, and so on. It is believed that everything in nature has its own Okki or its Manitou. The number of them is unlimited, and the imagination causes them to be seen in all things natural — and especially in those things whose inner workings are not understood. Several ranks of them are also distinguished, and different qualities are attributed to them. To all things that are above the comprehension of these good people, a protective Genie of an eminent rank is attributed, and the common expression for this is to say: *it's a Spirit*. They also use this term for those who distinguish themselves by way of their knowledge, talents, or extraordinary acts: they are Spirits, which is to say, they are guided by a Manitou of a higher order. The priests, magicians, or tricksters — for here, these words signify the same thing — boast of the superiority of their Genie over that of other men. They have actually persuaded the Savages that they feel ecstatic transports in which their Angel protector reveals the future to them, and gives them knowledge of the most remote events. The women also have their Manitous; but they attach less significance to them than do the men, contrary to the custom of other countries, where the weaker sex is usually the most superstitious.

"The protection of these symbols is of the greatest concern to our Savages. They are put in a bag made of bullrush fronds, painted in various colours, and are held aloft at the front of the troop under the guard of the oldest and bravest of each family. A great distinction is attached to carrying this bag, which confers a right of survivorship on the leadership if the Chief and his lieutenant die in war. The Ark of the Hebrews[177] and the Oriflamme[178] of the French were less honoured by them than a bag of Manitous is honoured among our Hurons. The custom is to place them in a small stronghold surrounded with a stockade, and to invoke their spirit day and night. This religious act dissipates all fears, and the army marches and sleeps peacefully under the guard of these Spiritual protectors.

"Even though they are generally given names which equate them with the First Being, they are never confused with him. They are only subordinate Genies, in most of which the Savages recognize a bad character more likely to do evil than good.

Casualness and Skills On Route to War

"Our Warriors, when on route, will only march for a short while; and they develop predictions about everything they will encounter along the way, and have, like the Argonauts, their Orpheus and their Mopfus;[179] which is to say, they have their tricksters who, presaging good or bad consequences according to their principles, advance or slow the march as they see fit. As long as they do not yet believe themselves to be in hostile country, all precautions are dropped, and each hunts as he wishes, and only rarely are a group of them found together. But no matter how spread out, everyone gathers on time and in the place designated by the Chief. These people have

---

177 Jews do not normally venerate holy relics or man-made symbols. But in the history of the Jewish people, there was one exception to this rule. One man-made object — the Ark of the Covenant — was considered intrinsically holy. Constructed during the Israelites' wanderings in the desert and used until the destruction of the First Temple, the Ark was the most important symbol of the Jewish faith, and served as the only physical manifestation of God on earth.

178 The Oriflamme (from Latin *aurea flamma*, "golden flame") was the battle standard of the King of France in the Middle Ages. It was originally the sacred banner of the Abbey of St. Denis, a monastery near Paris. When the oriflamme was raised in battle by the French royalty during the Middle Ages, most notably during the Hundred Years War, no prisoners were to be taken until it was lowered. This tactic was employed to strike fear into the hearts of the enemy, especially the nobles, who could usually expect to be taken alive for ransom during such military encounters.

179 Orpheus was an ancient Greek hero endowed with superhuman musical skills. His singing and playing were so beautiful that animals and even trees and rocks moved about him in dance. Mopfus was the son of Apollo and Manto, and was a celebrated prophet during the Trojan War. In these passages, Delaporte is concerned to equate modern Indians with ancient heroes, as a way of emphasizing the universality of humankind over the ages, which was a core Enlightenment value in the rationalist Eighteenth century: all concepts must be clear, susceptible of rational analysis, and universal in application. But having himself published some of the thought of Jean-Jacques Rousseau, Delaporte was also intimately familiar with the rising Romantic ethos of his time: much truth is also natural, instinctive, and available to those who live naturally — as this scenario about Indians having an inner "compass" illustrates.

an admirable talent — something like an instinct — to orient themselves and find their way. In the thickest forests and most menacing weather, they go straight to where they want to go, and stay on course as surely as if they had a compass.

"Another talent even more admirable, which they possess to a high degree, knowing whether or not someone has passed through a certain place. On the shortest grass, on the hardest ground, even on rock, they discover certain signs, and they distinguish not only the vestiges of men as distinguished from women, but even the traces of different peoples. From the way in which they seem to be turned, by the shape of the feet and the way in which they are spread, from the very first glance they can tell, without being mistaken, from which nation, what sex, what age, and what size the persons are whose imprints they see, and how long ago they were made. If these person are known to them they don't hesitate to say, 'These are the footprints of a certain man, or woman'. If they perceive that this spot has been the place for a suspicious rendezvous, they will maliciously cut the grass to express what cannot be said with decency by mouth. This language is understood by everyone and it is rare that anyone mistakes it.

The Night Before Battle

"Once they arrive in enemy territory, a great feast is prepared, after which everyone sleeps. When they awaken, those who recall their dreams want to have them explained. If they cannot be figured out, it is permissible for those who had them, to return to their village, which, as you can see, is no small resource for cowards.

"After new information is gained, they set out marching again. The encampment, when they arrived at the place intended for sleeping, was soon set up. Some turned their canoes over on their sides for protection from the wind. Others laid a few branches of leaves on the shore, or spread them out on their beds. Some carried strips of birch bark with them, rolled up like paper, with which they soon formed into a kind of tent. The youngest of the troop, as there were no women, light the fire and look after getting the kettle boiling.

"At nightfall, they are careful to send runners to ensure they are still a good distance from enemies. As soon as they have been discovered from a long distance, by the smell of their fire, a council is held, and with the aim of surprising them during their sleep, it is resolved to attack them at first light. The whole night they lie on their stomachs, without moving. The advance is made in the same posture by crawling on their hands and feet, until they are within rifle distance. Then, they all rise up; the Chief gives the signal, and the whole troop replies with horrific cries. At the same time they fire the first volley, and without giving the Iroquois time to know what hit them, they sweep down upon them, clubs in hand. The fight was bloody, but the Hurons came out victorious. After the fight, the scalps of the dead — or the dying — were removed, and no thought was given to taking prisoners unless the enemy was caught trying to flee. Those fleeing were chased down, and a few were caught who surrendered with sufficient good grace. Others defended themselves by joining together for smaller individual fights. On these sorts of occasion, their smaller number allows them to fight hand to hand, so to speak, as did the heroes of the *Iliad* [180]and the *Aeneid*.[181] Often they know each other, talk, ask for news, harangue each other, and do not kill each other until after they have exchanged a few compliments, which makes the military dialogues of Homer and Virgil seem more believable.[182]

Treatment of Captives

"The captives whose wounds do not permit them to be transported, are burned on the battlefield, and this execution is carried out in the first heat of victory. In this way, they suffer far less than those who are reserved for a slower torture. Great care is taken to guard these latter. During the day they are tied up by the neck and by the hands to one of the thwarts of the canoe. The worst time for them is the night, when they are stretched out on their backs with no other bed than the bare ground, with four stakes driven into it for each prisoner. They are tied to these stretched out by the arms and legs in the shape of a cross, and a fifth is added with a collar with which the captive is secured by the neck. And finally, they are bound around the middle with a strap, the two ends of which are placed under the head of the one watching over them as he sleeps, so that he will be awakened immediately if the prisoner makes even one move to save himself. This cruel posture, held for a whole night, becomes even more cruel in mosquito season. It would be impossible to explain adequately the pestilential nature of these insects,

---

180 The *Iliad* is an epic poem by the ancient Greek poet Homer, which recounts some of the significant events of the final weeks of the Trojan War and the Greek siege of the city of Troy. Written in the mid-8th Century B.C., it is usually considered to be the earliest work in the whole Western literary tradition, and one of the best known and most loved stories of all time.

181 The *Aeneid* is an epic poem by Virgil, the pre-eminent poet of the Roman Empire. It tells the legendary story of the Trojan hero Aeneas who, after years of wandering after the fall of Troy, travelled to Italy to battle the Latins, eventually to become the Founder of the Roman nation.

182 This is a scene in which by linking the Canadian Savage to ancient heroes, Delaporte blends together the classical and romantic themes that run through his book. Rather than the poetic and historical European past authenticating the present, the behaviour of the Indians at war authenticates the historical and poetic past of European civilization, so to speak, and thereby suggests the reader is witnessing a universal and ageless human behaviour.

which flock by the millions and unceasingly sting to the quick, leaving a venom in each sting that causes inflammation and unbearable itchiness.

"After having ensured themselves concerning their prisoners, our Hurons learned from their runners that a sizeable group of Iroquois were entrenched and well fortified, in a camp they resolved to break into the next day. It is difficult to describe the sad spectacle presented by the attack and capture of a place by these barbarians. As the stockades are made only of wood, and the cabins of tree-bark, it is all well and good to try to repel the invaders with a hail of arrows. But the latter rain desolation with their flaming arrows, which turn the whole village to cinders. Then they move in without fear with their makeshift wooden shields, thanks to which they get right to the foot of the stockade. Thus did I see our Hurons break through the fortifications of their enemies and make themselves masters, despite the hail of arrows that rained on them from all sides. Just try to imagine the victors, slathered with black and red paint — such a scary sight, and so proud of their victory — running all over the place like maniacs, chanting of their triumph, and hurling insults upon the enemy with horrible shouting. Everything that fell into their hands was sacrificed to their fury; everything was put to fire and the sword in the first heat of their carnage. The Iroquois, for their part, knowing what awaited them from the ferocity of the victors, and preferring to die rather than expose themselves to horrific tortures, were extraordinarily valorous. Animated equally by vengeance and despair, they sought their own death in the death of their enemies, and never gave up until, overcome by their numbers, and by weariness, they found it impossible to offer any further resistance.

"As they were not able to keep a large group of prisoners, the Hurons separated them into two groups. One was sacrificed to their military fury; the other was kept alive, to be included among them. The elderly, whom age rendered useless, children, and the infirm who would be a burden on the trip home, as well as a few fit warriors who could still cause trouble, were the unlucky ones whom the victors burned in rage, under the guise of false prudence. They burnt many of them before leaving camp, and every night they sacrificed a few more."

A Touching Love Scene

The Missionary, interrupting his narrative at this place, drew my attention to a Savage who, at dusk, was hanging around a cabin into which quite a pretty young girl had just entered.

"I understand," said I, to the Jesuit. "This young man is waiting for nightfall, *to carry the candle.*"

"Do you know then," asked the Missionary, "what this expression means?"

"I read somewhere," I replied to him, "that this is the name the Canadians give to their nocturnal debaucheries."

In effect, if we are to believe certain travelers on this matter, courtship is never discussed with the girls of this country, especially in the daytime. To carry the Candle is the only way to tell them you love them, and to find out if you are loved in return. They will break out in insults against a man who makes any other declaration of love to them. But as the cabins are always open, even during the night, a young Savage waits to go in until the fire is covered and everyone is asleep. Then he shows up with a piece of lighted wood and approaches the girl, who is probably not asleep. If he is poorly received in this gesture, he leaves quietly. Sometimes, she will allow a suitor to sit at the foot of her bed, but only for conversation. However, if someone more to her liking shows up … she blows out the candle. This tells him she has a desire to treat him kindly.

I remain, etc.

At Quebec, this First of March, 1749.

Letter 103 [183]

CANADA ~ CONTINUED

I RETURN once again to my Missionary, who, without needing any coaxing, had the kindness to reply to all my questions on the morals, customs, and habits of the Hurons. On the occasion of the little adventure we just witnessed, he spoke to me about marriage.

Courtship, Marriage, and Divorce Among the Hurons

"The girls," he told me, "haven't much eagerness for this bond, because as you have just seen, they are permitted to try it out as often as they like, and the ceremony of marriage doesn't change their condition — except, to make it more disagreeable. As girls, there is nothing that can be said about this; they are masters of their own bodies according to the natural law of liberty; whereas the women, because they can leave their husbands whenever it pleases them, abhor adultery. But to this there are exceptions, because as free as Huron girls may be, there are certain rules of decorum to which they are subject. For example, they avoid lingering in public with men of whose gossip they ought to be leery. Modest in their bearing, unless they are completely loose, they strive to protect a certain reputation, for fear they may not otherwise get established. With respect to married women, those who engage in love-trysts, excel, as they do everywhere, in the arts so well known to French women, of arranging meetings and pleasing a happy lover. However, it must be admitted that contrary to the usual way this is done in France, the Huron women hold to higher standards of decorum after marriage, than they did as young girls.

"The slightest degree of kinship here, becomes an obstacle to marriage. But if the wife dies, the husband must marry the sister, or failing that, the woman

---

[183] This letter is numbered in Roman numerals as CI in Delaporte's text, or 101 in Arabic numerals, even though it follows CII, or 102, which is an obvious mistake; so I have re-numbered it as Letter 103.

presented to him by the parents of the deceased. The wife is in a similar situation with respect to her brothers-in-law, especially if she has not had children with her husband. A widower who refuses the sister, or the relative of his wife, will be faced with the full fury of her revenge. As for personal qualities? A man is expected to be brave, a good warrior, and a good hunter; a woman must be a tireless worker, docile, and enjoy a good reputation. But despite all these precautions, a good woman is as hard to find in America as in Europe.

"The marriage treaty is arranged between the parents, and even though the young people play no role in these details, nothing is finalized without their consent. They surrender themselves voluntarily to the decision of their families, and behave submissively only in this situation — the only one, perhaps, where they ought to be the least dependent.[184] The first steps are taken by the older women, and rarely by the parents of the girl: she must wait until she is sought out. If she is too slow to be asked, these same matrons are not above some underhanded intrigues to find her a partner who suits her well, but a great deal of care is brought to bear on the problem.

"When the marriage contract is completed, the parents of the young man send gifts that are less a witness of friendship, than signs of slavery, such as a collar,[185] a log for burning, and a cooking pot, to signify that the woman will carry the burdens, and will provide the firewood and the cooking. It is even the custom in some places that she will supply all the firewood necessary for the home during winter, in advance. The new husband also has his obligations and responsibilities. Besides hunting and fishing — two duties that are lifelong — he must build a bed for his wife, build her a cabin, and bring her all the small game he kills.

"As soon as these gifts are accepted, the contract is deemed fulfilled, and the marriage finalized. At nightfall, the boy shows up at the girl's house accompanied by his whole family. He is asked to sit down on a mat, and the new spouse bears him a plate of boiled food which she places at his side. Not only does she not speak to him, but out of modesty, keeps her back a little turned to him, and covered in a blanket. The husband eats what has been presented to him, and this is what the entire nuptial ceremony consists of. This boiled food is seen as a new obligation that the wife undertakes to provide the necessities and to prepare the food.

---

184 This opinion reflects the growing Romantic trend in European society to "marry for love," rather than according to the wishes of parents who were traditionally more concerned with the economic soundness of the marriage. In this case, the narrator has taken the Romantic side of the debate.

185 The French expression *collier de misère* signifies drudgery. But the passages here suggest that Indian women, while more sexually free and natural as young girls, are more honourable than French women once they make a vow to marry.

"The wedding is celebrated with singing, dancing, and feasting. The meal is eaten in the cabin of the husband, but the new wife pays for it and supplies the meats that must go into the boiling pot. While everyone is caught up in the celebration, the newly-married pair seems not to be taking any part in the joy of it all. The wife especially seems serious and even sad, from a fear that people may think she doesn't understand the price of her virginity if she surrenders herself to pleasure just as she is on the point of losing it. It is even said there are places where the bride may go a year without consummating her marriage. The mere suggestion that she might exercise her conjugal right before the year is up, would be an insult. For it would seem that her partnership may have been sought less because of esteem for her, than to satisfy a brute passion. This victory, if it qualifies as one following such a bizarre custom, is made all the more difficult because the newly-married couple sleeps in the same bed every night. It is true that the parents watch over them with the greatest attention, and take care to keep a constant fire burning as a guarantee that nothing happens that is forbidden. But a day came when one young husband, less continent than old Arbrissel,[186] wanted to follow the example of Europeans. The wife was so outraged over this, that even though in marrying him she likely got familiar with his inclinations, she could not be persuaded to get together with this indiscreet husband again, and so it was necessary to separate them. In places where this custom no longer survives, we still don't see a woman pregnant in her first year of marriage, without astonishment. She would lose a little of her reputation over this, and in some parts of the country, fingers would be wagged at her.

"In some other places, a husband is within his rights to cut off the nose of his adulterous or fugitive wife. But here, they can split up in harmony, and the separate parties are free to create new partnerships. These people can't conceive why there should be any difficulty over something like this.

"'My wife and I could not live on good terms,' one of them said, to a missionary who was trying to get them to understand the indecency of this separation.[187] 'My neighbour was in the same situation. So we exchanged

---

[186] Robert of Arbrissel (c. 1045 –1116) was an itinerant preacher, ascetic, and founder of the abbey of Fontevrault, in France. He was born at Arbrissel (near Retiers, Brittany); and died at Orsan.

[187] In this passage on marriage and divorce Delaporte compares and contrast the Enlightenment, anti-religious view of marriage and divorce rooted in a secular conception of Reason, with the predominantly Catholic view of marriage as an indissoluble religious sacrament. Civil marriage was introduced in revolutionary France in 1792 as an alternative and wholly secular form of union. Divorce was made possible by the initiation of one of the parties to the "contract" of marriage. At this point it was no longer a true contract as it could be ruptured by one party without the consent of the other. This was an expression of the growing emphasis on individual liberty and rights, as distinct from the religious and social rights held in common by society, and it signified a gradual change from a broader concern for the social and moral harm done to traditional institutions

wives, and we are all happy. What could more reasonable than to make each other happy, when it costs so little, and no one is harmed?'

Divorce Among the Hurons ... Continued

"So divorce is permitted among the Hurons, especially for very serious reasons, such as an acknowledged infidelity, the bad temper of the husband, their inability to get along, or their stubbornness toward family members by whom they let themselves be controlled. Their Jealousy and mutual fickleness may also provide them with lots of opportunity for break-up. If they have children, the husband always behaves as if he has the right to take the boys, but the mothers consider themselves the ones with the right to keep them — which they almost always do. As for the children, they do not seem to be bothered by the affront the father's abandoning of them has meant to their mother. A wife who suspects her husband of infidelity is capable of all sorts of outrage against her rival, and he doesn't dare defend himself. He would dishonour himself by the slightest show of resentment. At the return from a hunt, an upset or suspicious woman will march right up to the mistress, and without any resistance, take her entire share of the game killed. A Huron sees this and will not say a word. The wife is exercising her right, and he takes no further interest in the matter. If she considers herself still not satisfied, and torments her husband with her bad mood and her accusations, the husband hangs his head in silence, not daring to argue with his wife, much less to beat her; and finally, fed up with her fractious behaviour, he parts, and leaves her for good.

"If it is the wife in the wrong, the husband hides his jealousy as much as he can, and considers it a point of honour to appear unaffected by it. But he does not hesitate to repay, with interest, the infidelities suffered upon him, and in the end forces his wife to suffer, though with less punishment, the fact that he rejects her. Sometimes, an outraged husband takes his desire for vengeance much farther — as witnessed by what one of our missionaries told me, and which I relay to you in the same way.

Trickery and Murder

"A Savage who was unhappy with his wife, but concealing his resentment, took her with him on a hunt in the usual way. It was a good year, game was plentiful, and the husband was a good hunter. However, he feigned that he could not find any game, and gave as a reason that a spell must have been cast

---

by an individual's behaviour, to the more narrow moral justification we see here: an individual's behaviour is acceptable if "no one [i.e., no other individual] is harmed." French Jacobin moral reasoning has been put in the mouth of this Indian.

upon him. The season was ending, their stocks were dwindling, and the wife was suffering from hunger. The husband, having tired her out for a long time, pretended that he had a dream that ought to lift the spell that was exposing them to hardship. 'I must attack your cabin tonight,' he said, 'as if it were under assault by a war enemy, take you prisoner, and treat you as a slave.'

"The wife, who considered it possible to sidestep this dream, did not seem to oppose it, and encouraged him to carry it out. He did not fail in this. The next night, he laid siege to the home, took his wife prisoner, condemned her to the flames, stripped off her clothing, tied her up to a stake, and lit a blazing fire. The poor, unfortunate woman thought that the game should end there — but she was mistaken. The husband, suddenly turning serious, scolded her for her infidelities, and began to burn her slowly. The brother of this woman, worried that she was suffering from hunger, had set out to take her food, and he arrived at her home just when this cruel scene was unfolding, which he could see from afar. The cabin was open, his sister was screaming horribly, and the sight horrified him. So he crept closer without being seen, raised his rifle, fired a shot at his brother-in-law, and killed him. Then he ran up to his sister who was near death, untied her, and expressed his suspicions of her jealous husband to her, and the cause of his violence. But she was in such bad condition that she could not even express any desire to live. So her sympathetic brother thought it best to deliver her from her suffering and, moved by pity, stabbed her to death with her consent. After having rendered this last service to her, he went back to his village, where he recounted this dreadful affair.

"Sometimes, divorce here is only a simple abandonment, which doesn't entirely eliminate the hope of re-uniting. It's actually what happens quite often, either because their friends get involved trying try to patch things up, or because their original friendship, or their love of their children re-awakens, or because time passes and effaces the reason they were so upset.

Huron Women, Their Treatment, Their Pregnancies

"Among certain nations, the women have all the authority, in others, they play no role in government. The former are, in a way, the masters of the state, and form, so to speak, the most important group. But they must have reached a ripe age and have children capable of ensuring they will be respected. At any rate, they are esteemed for nothing else, and in the household, are nothing but the slaves of their husbands. In general, there is perhaps no other people in the world where this gender is more scorned. To treat a Savage like a woman is for them the bloodiest of outrages. However, as you have seen, the children belong only to the mother, and recognize no other authority than hers. The father is, for them, a stranger, who is not respected except as a master.

"The Huron women do not spoil themselves during pregnancy. They work as usual, and the closer they get to term, the more they give in to fatigue. They go to work the fields, carry their loads, and find that such efforts help with childbirth. When they go into labour — which rarely happens — the young people of the village are alerted. They gather in the fields near the cabin of the patient, and just when she is least expecting it, they sneak up to the door of the cabin and suddenly shriek in a loud voice. The surprise of this causes a shock that immediately starts her delivery.

"There is something surprising in the ease with which they customarily bring their children into the world. Most of the time they give birth without any pain or help. If they are surprised by this in coming back from the fields, they act as their own mid-wife, wash the baby in whatever water they come across, then go back to their cabin, and the same day go back to their ordinary routines. It seems as if they don't suffer at all, or have any pain afterward. It's not that they are not sometimes very uncomfortable, and even that some of them don't die in childbirth. But they conquer their pain with an admirable strength of mind, and refuse, so long as they are able, to show any sign of weakness. When they show a little too much sensitivity, the elders conclude they should not have any more children, because they will only bring into the world more weak ones like themselves. But again, these cases are really rare. Most of them give birth while working, or travelling. As soon as they feel close to their term, a small hut is set up outside the village, and they spend forty days there after they deliver the baby. When their term is over, the fire is extinguished in the cabin to which they must return, all the furnishings are shaken out, and when they arrive, a new fire is begun. These same formalities are more or less observed during their monthly periods, and while they nurse their babies. The nursing lasts no less than three years, and the husbands don't go near them during this time. We could perhaps applaud this custom if both of them observed their conjugal fidelity, but sometimes both parties slip up. It is claimed that the use of certain plants that have the power to block the consequences of their infidelity, is fairly common in this country.

Baby Care

"The mothers love their children passionately, and even though they don't demonstrate this by way of overt caresses, like European women do, their tenderness is no less real, no less robust, and no less constant. From the moment they prepare a cradle, their care of their children has no limit. However, even though they lose no affection for them after they are weaned, they leave them to themselves in the belief that nature should take its course. Their cradles, as attractive as they are convenient, consist of two thin boards of light wood, about two and a half feet long, decorated on the edges, narrowed at the bottom, and rounded at the foot to make it easier to rock. The baby is wrapped in furs, which serve as diapers, and two large straps hang out of the cradle, making it easy for the mothers to take the baby everywhere with them, and to suspend him from a tree branch while they are working. The infants are tucked away, warmly and softly, for in addition to the really soft furs, they put in a lot of down from the tufts of reeds, or from the powder of a certain bark that women use to clean their hair. They are also very clean there, thanks to a piece of leather that hangs out of the cradle, which allows them to satisfy their natural functions without dirtying the inside of the cradle — with the exception of the down, which is easy to replace with new down.

"The children are left free on their own as soon as they can crawl around on their hands and feet. They can go where they want, completely naked, in the water, in the woods, in the mud and in the snow. From this practice comes the vigour, toughness, and resistance to airborne illnesses, that the Europeans admire in them. In the summer, from daybreak, they can be seen running to the water, just like animals for whom water is natural. They spend a part of the day playing in the lakes and rivers.

Growing Up

"When they get a bit older, they follow their mothers and work for the family. They get used to hauling water, carrying small loads of wood, and little by little they are taught to help out more as they age. At a very early age a bow, and arrows are put into their hands, which they play with for a long time as a toy, but as their strength increases with age, this changes from an amusing pastime, to a necessary exercise, and emulation, the best teacher, causes them to develop a surprising ability in their use. It did not cost these people any more to develop their skill in the use of firearms.

"From their first years they are also made to wrestle together. If two antagonists get to fighting in a way that goes beyond play, the calmness of the spectators is admirable. They form a circle around the two fighters, and watch them as spectators, without taking sides with either, unless the game gets pushed too far, or the contestants become unequal. Then they enjoy ridiculing the loser. Their love of this is so great that they might often kill each other, if care were not taken to separate them. Those who succumb to their adversary consider it a vexation that gives them no peace of mind until they have a chance to get even.

"In general, mothers and fathers strive to instill certain principles of honour in their children that they will carry within them all their lives, but which they often apply badly. And this is about all the education they are given, even though it is indirect. Which is to say that their instruction is adapted from the fine examples of their ancestors. The young, stirred up by these ancient images, can barely wait for an opportunity to imitate whatever has excited their admiration. To correct their faults, exhortations and prayer are brought to bear, but never punishments or threats, persuaded as they are, that no man has the right to compel another. Moreover, they hope that as the years grace them with reason, they will follow its lights, and perfect themselves.[188] The greatest punishment is to throw some water in their face; and they are so sensitive to this, that some young women have been known to strangle themselves over a similar correction, warning their mother by telling her: *You will no longer have a daughter*. You would believe that such a poorly disciplined childhood would be followed by a turbulent and corrupted teen-age period of youth. But other than the fact that these people are naturally tranquil, and masters of themselves,[189] their temperament, especially among the northern nations, does not lead them into self-destruction.

The Use of Names

"Among the Hurons, the act that terminates infancy, is the bestowing of a name. The ceremony is held during a feast where only persons of the same sex as the infant about to be named attend. He sits on the knees of the father or the mother, who do not stop commending the child to the Spirits, especially to the one who is to be the child's tutelary Genie. New names are never created. Each family holds onto a certain number of names that come back again and again, and are allocated to it. These names change with age. An infant receives the name of a young man, who has just left his name behind to take on the name of a grown man, who is himself taking the name of an old man, and this latter, the name of an ancestor of the family. When a man dies, his name remains buried with him, and it is only many years later that anyone thinks of using it once again. It's less to perpetuate these names, that they are kept in the family, than to encourage the one who receives them to imitate the fine behaviour of those who carried them, to avenge them if they were killed or burned in war, and to comfort their parents. Just so,

---

188 In this passage, Delaporte echoes the progressive Enlightenment belief just then developing in eighteenth-century France, that if employed correctly, in a logical, and Cartesian way, "reason", considered as a technique for the discovery of truth, will lead to perfection of self, and therefore, in social terms, to the perfection of society as a whole. It is a bit odd to see this characterization of "the Savage" in such rationalist terms, as the tool of "reason" was at the time considered a specifically modern technique for the discovery of truth that had been hidden from all prior generations, and so it would not normally have been considered available to "barbarians" and pre-moderns.

189 This is again an allusion to the notion that natural human beings are "tranquil and masters of themselves" because they have not been corrupted by "civilization".

when a woman has lost her husband or her son, and finds herself no longer supported by anyone, she delays the least she can in passing the name of the one she is mourning to someone who can take his place.

"The custom is never to call a man by his proper name when speaking to him in a familiar way. This would be considered an impoliteness among the Hurons, just as it is when it is committed even very frequently among ourselves. He must be granted the dignity with which he is endowed in relation to the one speaking to him, according to his kinship relations or the affinity that exists between them. If there is no blood connection, he is treated no less well than a brother, an uncle, a cousin, and so on, according to the degree of friendship, esteem, and respect that they have for each other, while observing all the proprieties of age. The same civil manner is used with outsiders, who are given names derived from the father's bloodline, as if there were a real kinship — closer, or more remote — according to the degree of honour they want to bestow.

Naming As Bonding

"Now is the time to speak of another Huron custom, that is also found among the Iroquois. The children think of the sisters of their mother, as their mothers, and the brothers as their uncles. By the same reasoning, they give the name of fathers to the brothers of their father, and the name of aunts, to the sisters. So all the children on the side of the mother and the sisters, and of the father and his brothers, think of themselves as brothers and sisters. But when it comes to the children of the uncles and the aunts — which is to say, of the brothers of their mother and the sisters of their father, they consider themselves to be cousins, even though they share the same degree of kinship as those who call themselves brothers and sisters. In the third generation, things change entirely. The great-uncles, and great-aunts, once again become grandfathers and grandmothers of those whom they called nephews and nieces. This is perhaps similar to the custom established in other nations, where they say they have married their sister or their mother, when in reality it was really only the cousin or the aunt."

I have often been told of personal friendships developed between the young among the Hurons — and even among all the Savages of America, and as I have forgotten the precise details of these relationships, I have implored my missionary to refresh my memory on this matter, which is one of the most interesting aspects of the moral life of these people.

A Story of Unusual Friendships

"This custom," he told me, "which proffers only what is rather laudable, was especially well-established in the republics of Crete and Sparta. I know," he continues, "that we have slandered their legislators, as if they had legalized a monstrous vice which, regrettably, became only too common among the Greeks, and that the odious and disgraceful nature of it has forever rendered infamous the reputation of their republic. You can believe that if this abominable vice had been connected with pure friendships, Minos and Lycurgus would not have taken so much care to honour them, to the point of making them a subject of honour and glory. So their intention was to foster attachments that have innocent love as their foundation, a relationship from which even the inkling of a crime is excluded, a sense of reciprocity based on emulation. The Lover[190] took constant care to foster feelings of honour in the object of his affections, and he had a duty to set a good example for him, to prevent or correct any faults he might commit, and the law held him responsible for the conduct of the Beloved, who was like his disciple. If the latter happened to fail, the former received the punishment as if he were the only one responsible. Misfortune fell upon the Lover who, rather than shaping his student through virtue, set an example of vice. If it so happened that he developed criminals feelings[191] for his student, he could only save himself from an infamous death by shamefully fleeing the country. It is in this manner that many heroes in ancient times became united with their companions of work and adventure, such as Hercules and Iolas,[192] Theseus and Pirithous,[193] Achilles and Patrocles,[194] Aeneas and Achate,[195] Orestes and Pylade.[196] The Lovers and the Beloved sent offerings to the tomb of Iolas, and tightened the bonds of their compact by the vows they made in his name.

---

190 The terms Lover/Beloved here refer strictly to male friendship, by many philosophers considered the purest form of love, because not adulterated or compromised by sexual feelings of any kind. Some ancient philosophers referred to this non-sexual form of affection as "love without wings."

191 The reference is to homosexual feelings.

192 Heracles (not "Hercules", as Delaporte writes) was a son of Iphicles, and Iolaus (sometimes spelled Iolas, as above) was a nephew of Heracles. He often acted as Heracles' charioteer and companion. The shrine to him in Thebes was a place where males worshiped and made vows of friendship, mutual help and protection, etc.

193 In disjointed episodes that have survived, Pirithous had heard rumors about Theseus' courage and strength in battle, but he wanted proof. He rustled Theseus' herd of cattle from Marathon, and Theseus set out to pursue him. Pirithous took up arms and the pair met, then became so impressed by each other they took an oath of friendship.

194 The relationship between Achilles and Patroclus is a key element of the myths associated with the Trojan War. Its exact nature has been a subject of dispute in both the classical period and modern times. In the *Iliad*, the two heroes have a deep and meaningful friendship.

195 Achates was the faithful companion of Aeneas, in Virgil's *Aeneid*.

196 Orestes had been sent to Phocis during his mother Clytemnestra's affair with Aegisthus. There, he was raised with Pylades, and so considered him to be like a brother.

"This is what we seem to have again today," continued the missionary, "in these friendship unions among the Savages. The bonds in them are just as firmly tightened as those of blood and nature, and cannot be dissolved unless one of them, in becoming indignant over some cowardly behaviour that brings dishonour upon his friend, forces him to break their compact. These friendships are gained with presents given to the one sought as a friend, and are sustained by gestures of mutual kindness. They become companions in the hunt, in war, and in the lottery of life. They live without any distinctions between them in their own, or in their friend's cabin, and the most flattering compliment that can be given is to call him, "friend". This bond, which ages along with them, is so strong, that we sometimes witness in it the same heroism as occurred between Pylade and Orestes. We learn in these old stories that among many war prisoners, there were often found two so bonded in friendship, that when one of them was condemned to death by fire, and the other saved for adoption, the latter was so distressed that his comrade did not receive the same pardon as himself, that he rejected his own pardon, and with complaints, prayers, and threats, begged that he should receive the same torture as his friend.

"One feels that two men so united in their common interest, owe each other a mutual assistance, even at the risk of their own lives. And according to what they believe, even death will only separate them for a while. They are certain that after death they will be re-united, never to be separated again, and are convinced they will need each other once again in another world. A Christian Savage, who did not actually live as much of a Christian, when threatened with hell by a missionary, asked him if his dead friend was in this place of torture? 'I have reason to hope,' replied the Jesuit, 'that God has taken mercy upon him.'

"'Well then I don't want to go there, either,' continued the Huron, and this feeling got him changing his life around. It was all the same to him, whether he ended up in hell or heaven, as long as he was with his friend."

Indian Appearance, Clothing, Tatooing, and More

I have been with the Canadians long enough to give you some sense of their appearance, their dress, and their character. Many people believe that Savages are men covered with hair, living in the forest without a society, and having nothing human about them but their shape, albeit imperfect. However, with the exception of the hair on their heads and their eyebrows — and many of them even pluck these out — these people have no trace of hair on their bodies, and if it so happens that some of it grows on them, they tear it out by the roots.[197] They are born white, like us, but their skin, exposed as much as it is to the elements, takes on a dark red colour. This unpleasant and dirty colour is made worse by the way they paint the body and the face, whether to be recognized from afar as an enemy or ally, or to make themselves more attractive in love, or more fearsome in war. To this veneer, they add rubbings of fat to protect themselves from the unbearable bites of gnats. You can add to these coatings the smoke that is used to further fight off these insects, or that these people breathe in their cabins, where they warm themselves, and smoke their meat in winter. Is anything more required to give them such a hideous coloration in our eyes — even if it is without doubt more handsome, or at least bearable, to their less delicate eyes?

In general, their bodies have a beautifully-proportioned shape, but more suited to bear the rigours of running, than the exertions of work, and they have less vigour, than agility. In their ordinary features they have a ferocious look that they get from the habit of hunting, and the perils of war. They are tall, and of greater height than our people, and there are no one-eyed men, hunchbacks, or blind, or lame people. They have a healthy constitution, and live a long time if they know how to look after themselves, because the only sicknesses they know are the ones that sometimes come from their overly-violent exertions, or from a surfeit of food after excessive privation. At any rate, you have seen that from infancy they have their bare feet in water, on the ice, or in the snow, and that alcoholic spirits — the disastrous gift made to them

---

197 Many explorers and travel writers have commented on the almost hairless bodies of Indians. From about 1750 to 1900 there was a ferocious dispute over the New World. Georges-Louis Leclerc, the Comte de Buffon (1707–1788) a widely-influential naturalist, argued that the animals and humans indigenous to the New World were "degenerate." American animals were obviously smaller in size than their Eurasian counterparts: there were no elephants, giraffes, camels, hippos, or lions, in America. But Buffon was unaware of the ancient extinction — some say the extermination — caused, some argue, by Paleo-Indian over-hunting of many giant North American species such as the Mastodon, giant beavers, etc., over 10,000 years ago, the bones of which have been found by paleontologists since his time. On the evidence of their near-hairlessness and a meagre population, Buffon was also convinced the Indians of the Americas were weaker and more effeminate than Europeans. The work of his contemporary, Cornelius de Pauw (1734–1799), who thoroughly denigrated the New World as a degenerate place with inferior plants and animals, as well as effeminate and undeveloped savages (hence their low population) was influential as a counterpoint to the romantic characterizations of Rousseau. At the time, while he was the American Ambassador to France, Thomas Jefferson was so angered by Buffon's claims, that he urged an American compatriot to hunt, kill, and ship to France the antlers and hide of an American giant moose. When Buffon saw the giant carcass, he retracted his argument — at least in the case of the moose. Pierre Charlevoix, Delaporte's richest source for this volume, argued that Indians may be hairless either because both sexes smoke tobacco too much, or because of the purity of their blood, which in turn is due to the naturalness and purity of their food. He also remarked that Europeans "appeared hideous" to the Indians because of their long beards, and that "the flesh of the French and the English seemed of a disagreeable taste to them, because of its saltiness" (Charlevoix, *Journal of a Voyage*, Vol. 2, Louise Kellog, trans., p.85).

by Europeans, which they love with a passion, and which they only drink to get drunk — has almost ruined them. As for the rest, they have vision, smell, and hearing and all the other senses, of a fineness and subtlety that alerts them to all dangers, and to all their needs. Despite the snow that dazzles them and the smoke that overwhelms them, their vision never weakens. The smell of perfumes makes them uncomfortable, and they only find agreeable the smells of the things they eat or drink.

These people have looked after their decency and their needs with clothing; such as: a truss, a jacket, breeches, shoes, and a robe. The truss is about a foot wide, and three feet long, is worn between the legs, and is folded over a small cord of gut from which it falls down in the front and the back. It is the only piece of clothing they are never without, so as not to offend modesty. This simple piece of clothing is often the only thing the men wear when it is hot. In winter, they cover themselves more or less according to the weather. The women, instead of a truss, have a piece of cloth or animal skin that serves as a skirt, which surrounds them from the waist to mid-thigh.

The jacket is a shirt without arms, made of two pieces of deerskin, thin, light, stripped of all hair, and cut at the back like a fringe. For men, it hangs to the waist, and for women, to the knee. It is the one piece of clothing that seems least essential to them, and many of them take it off as they please. In winter or when traveling, they have added sleeves that are not attached to the jacket — they are tied together by a cord that runs behind their shoulders.

The breeches are a kind of stocking that the men wear to mid-thigh, and the women a bit lower. The men attach them to their hips with the belt that holds the truss. The women hold them up, like us, with garters. These stockings, which have no feet, fit into shoes with no heel, or into a kind of slipper made of smoked deerskin.

The robe is more like a blanket, also made of cured animal skin, made like the rest of the clothing, and fringed with notches. The Savages wear it in a casual way, adjusting it only with their hands, and only fastening it tightly on their travels. When they are loaded down with baggage, they tie it to the middle of their body so they don't have to bother with it. In bad weather, they carry it on their head, which is normally uncovered, for they don't wear hats or bonnets. Those who live with Europeans, while maintaining their old way of dressing themselves, only change the materials used for clothing. They have shorts of cloth instead of animal skin, a truss and breeches made of cloth, and in place of their fur robes, they wear a woollen blanket. The richest of them wear scarlet ones that they buy in the colony. They are especially keen to have shirts, which they cover with jackets only when they are dirty, and they stay dressed this way until the shirt rots and falls off, because they can't be bothered to wash them.

If you want to know how they prepare the skins they use as clothing, listen to the Missionary:

"The preparation of these skins is neither long, nor difficult. After having soaked them in water for a while, they are scraped, and become soft from handling. To soften them further, they are rubbed with the brain of some animal — and soon they become white and soft. They are not oiled, but rather are exposed to smoke, which produces more or less the same result. All these skins are put to good use, and in the art of preparing them there is no risk of burning them as with us.[198] The Indians paint them and trace shapes on them that enhances their beauty and makes them more enjoyable. Before applying colour to them, all the lines that are to be coloured are cut into the leather. This paint is a kind of cinnabar,[199] gotten from red earth that is found on the shores of rivers and lakes. They also use the sap and cinders of certain plants."

It is not just on the skins of animals that these people have skill in drawing shapes. They are also in the habit of decorating live flesh — of creating a bit of clothing that costs them a lot, in truth, but which lasts all their life. This work is the same as what they do on leather. They first of all colour the design on their stretched out skin; then they trace over all the lines by pricking the lines with needles — either sharp bones, or fish bones — on open skin, into which pulverized colours are rubbed that settle so deeply into the skin that they never fade. This is a magnificence that is only permitted for those who have distinguished themselves among their compatriots. One has to be singled out by bold acts, to have killed many men in war, or many animals in the hunt. This tattooing is not at all painful when it is performed, but the skin swells up soon after, and scabs over, with inflammation. Often this is followed by a fever that can last several days, and in a heat wave, there is a danger of dying.

Some, like the Picts[200] in the past, pricked themselves in this way all over their bodies, others, only in certain parts. Most of them are content to paint

---

198 This is a reference to the fact that leather tanneries in Europe used — and still use — various acid-bath treatments to soften and tan raw animal hides. If left too long in their acid bath, the hides can dissolve altogether.

199 Cinnabar is the historic source for the brilliant red or scarlet pigment termed vermilion, and associated red mercury pigments that has been used for its color since antiquity in the Near East, including as a rouge-type cosmetic, in the New World, and in the Olmec culture, and in China, since as early as the Song dynasty, where it was used in coloring lacquerware.

200 Known as 'Picti' by the Romans, meaning 'Painted Ones' in Latin, these northern tribes constituted the largest kingdom in Dark Age Scotland. They repelled the conquests of both Romans and Angles, creating a true north-south divide on the British Isles, only to disappear from history by the end of the first millennium — swallowed whole by the history of another group, the Gaels. In his *Commentary* on the Gallic War (*Commentarii de Bello Gallico*, 58–49 B.C.), Julius Caesar describes the frightening appearance of shaved

themselves with various bird figures, snakes, or other animals, in no particular order, without any symmetry and according to their caprices. These are not mere ornamentation. They consider them to have other advantages, such as to make them less vulnerable to airborne illnesses and to protect them from toothaches — especially if these prickings are made in the parts of the face near the jaws. These permanent colours on their bodies do not prevent them from enjoying other, temporary makeup colours that they renew whenever they want to get dressed up. The warriors also paint themselves whenever they go to battle, to intimidate their enemies. Perhaps also, to hide their fear, for they are not always free of it. The young warriors do it to disguise their youthfulness, for which they will be teased by the older warriors; others, to give themselves an air of beauty; and then, the colours are much brighter and more varied. They also paint the prisoners they have condemned to be burned; and they paint their fathers, and their dead friends, to hide the pallor of death that disfigures them.

The other ornamentation that the men add to their finery, are such as the down of birds, sprinkled instead of powder on spiked or plaited hair that they have greased with oil; feathers of all colours; puffs of hair from various animals, bizarrely arranged; pendants hanging from their ears, and others from their nostrils, a large shell on their neck or on the stomach; the feet or heads of birds; deer-horns, and more. Each one of them dresses up according to his own taste as soon as he is of an age for these amusements. But as soon as this age is passed, they take pride in entirely different distractions, to show that they are thinking of more serious things.

The women take great pride in their coiffure, and will consider themselves dishonoured if they are obliged to cut it. Their hair, and in general the hair of all the Savages, is quite beautiful, and of a very deep black. They oil it, powder it, comb it, braid it, and let it hang like a canadette,[201] wrapped in a snake or eel skin. When it comes to the face, they are happy to trace a few lines on their skin with vermillion. Their nicest looking attire is their robes, painted with different designs, and ornamented with shells.

The oil with which these people grease their hair and their bodies renders them as smelly as it does dirty. But it is absolutely essential to protect them from vermin. Because they are not refined in anything like luxuries, they have not been able to offset terrible odours with the essence of perfumes,

---

and blue-painted warriors who appeared on the cliff-tops as he attempted to land his ships on beaches of England, hurling their spears down upon his men.

201 A canadette was a popular Eighteenth-century male hair style that consisted in two side braids worn in front of the ears, while the rest of the hair was gathered in two more braids behind the ears. Those were tied on the nape to form a tail. This hair arrangement, often reinforced with small wooden rods at the center of the braids, protected the cheeks and back of the neck in close combat.

which we have long since substituted for the rudeness of ointments. From all this you will conclude that the Hurons, instead of adding to their natural beauty, only work at spoiling it. However, when they are dressed up in their own fashion, the strange assemblage of all these bizarre embellishments does not give them a totally bad look.

Their Character

With respect to their character, they don't differ much from the Iroquois, and have good and bad qualities. Like them, they are volatile, fickle, dull, ignorant, ferocious, suspicious, traitorous, and two-faced.

"However," the Missionary told me, "as contemptible as they may seem to you, these are mortals who esteem themselves most the more they scorn others. Revenge is a passion that time has not quelled in their souls; it passes from generation to generation until the offended race decides to appease its hatred. Friendship, compassion, gratitude, and affection are with them less the effect of a good nature than of reflection, or prejudice. The care they take of widows, orphans, and the infirm, and the hospitality they show to strangers, follows from the widespread opinion among them, that everything should be common to all men. The inequality of conditions that we consider so essential to the preservation of society, is in their eyes, the height of madness.[202] They are equally scandalized that any one man should have more worldly goods than a thousand others; and believe that this original injustice generates a second one that is far more serious. What strikes them as humiliatingly low, a senseless debasement, is that men who are equal by nature would degrade themselves by their dependency on the will and caprices of a single man. The

---

202 Before the onset of egalitarian democracy in the Western world, especially as introduced into European life by the French Revolution of 1789, the commonly held opinion was that the different social classes, from the laborer, the merchant, the cleric, the soldier, to the magistrate, the duke, and the King, formed a vertically-integrated and natural social, moral, and economic system of interdependent rights and obligations distinctive to each level that each person recognized according to their position in this structure. *Noblesse oblige*, for example — the belief that the nobility had obligations to those less fortunate, and that the preservation of their privileges could only be justly defended if these obligations were fulfilled — served to sustain the "natural inequalities" inherent in the system. The rising democratic notion — so radically introduced by certain Jacobin revolutionaries such as the Abbé Sieyès, thirty years after the publication of Delaporte's book — that because all men are equal in their substance, private property and class privilege must be banished and all things held in common (the root belief of "communism") — was considered heretical and possibly treasonous, especially by aristocrats and highly-cultured thinkers. Native communism is introduced here to reflect this tension, and to echo this strand of belief in the natural equality of all men — a belief unlikely to have been shared by Delaporte, but that without romantic sentimentalism, he is nevertheless committed to explaining accurately, in keeping with the pledge in his "Notice to Readers", that "as his main aim is to interest and to instruct; anything that does not produce these two results will not be deemed worthy of remark."

respect we have for titles, dignitaries, and especially for hereditary nobility, they consider to be an insult and an outrage for all humanity.[203]

"The fathers and mothers have an affectionate tenderness for their children that is purely animal. The latter, on their part, have no such feeling for their parents, and sometimes treat them with indignity. I will cite just one example of this.

Filial Disrespect

"A Huron who had served for a long time among our troops fighting against his own nation, bumped into his own father in a fight, and was about to run him through, when he suddenly recognized him. He stopped himself just in time, and said to his father: 'I received life from you once; so I give life to you today. But don't let me find you under my power again, for I no longer owe you anything.' This alienated son was named *la Plaque*,[204] and the French had made him a lieutenant to ensure he would continue fighting with them, because he was a brave and fine warrior. But he couldn't stay with them very long, and returned to his nation, having adopted only our vices, without having corrected any of his own. He had a wild love of women, and his reputation gave him a great lustre in their eyes. He also led many wives into infidelity, making their husbands unhappy. This disorderly behaviour went so far that the Council deliberated whether or not they should rid themselves of him, once and for all. But it was decided to let him live, on the ground that because he was just as bold in love as in war, he would populate the country with brave men and soldiers.

Their Compensating Virtues

"If the Savages err due to their qualities of heart, is this not more than compensated for by those of the mind? Most of them have upright judgement, are quick thinking, have a lively imagination, and an admirable memory. They reflect justly on their own affairs, and much better than our people do. They reach their objectives by a safe path; but to train them in the arts, of which they have no notion, they would require a lot more work if they did not have the good sense to scorn things that are not essential for them. They laugh at

---

203 This may be the overt social philosophy of these Indian groups, but we have seen plenty of ranking in this book, as between children and parents, chiefs and warriors, elders and their inferiors, insiders and outsiders, friends/enemies, free and slave, and so on.

204 La Plaque was the nephew of the Iroquois chief of the *Sault-Recollet* Mission, near Montreal. In 1690, he warned the colonial authorities of an imminent attack on Montreal by the English. In 1691 he went to France to meet the King. In January of 1693, he led an Indian War Party against Fort Orange (built in 1624), the first permanent Dutch settlement in New Netherland — today, Albany, New York.

our contrivances, our manners, and our customs, which, the more removed they are from what is natural, the more they encourage vanity in us. They are not comfortable either, in applying themselves to purely intellectual matters. But they are not careless when it comes to things that interest them, and as much as they are phlegmatic and circumspect prior to deciding to do something, they are full of ardour and vivacity when they actually do it. They engage in quick, and often witty repartee, as witnessed by the Huron who was asked: 'What is Brandy made of?'

To which he replied: 'It's an extract of languages and hearts; because when I drink it, I speak wonderfully, and I fear nothing.'

Their Nobility of Soul

"These people have a nobility and an equanimity of soul that is rarely found in civilized nations. For example, a prisoner left in uncertainty as to his sentence, or even certain that he is about to die soon, doesn't lose more than a quarter hour of sleep over it. Whether it be the intoxication of enthusiasm that gets rid of, or suspends, their feeling of distress, or whether it is habit or education that produces these prodigies of heroism, the victim dies without fire or the sword tearing a single sigh from his breast. It's a combat between the victim and his executioners; it's a horrific contest between steadfastness in the face of suffering, and the fierceness of torment. A Huron that the Illinois Indians burned with the latest barbarities, having spied a Frenchman among the spectators, begged him to join in with his enemies, 'so that I have the consolation,' said he, 'to die by the hand of a real man, for, among so many, I see only you who merits this name.'

Character and Climate

"Such imperviousness to pain — does it come from their style of life, or from the climate?[205] Blood which is colder, thicker bodily fluids, a temperament that the humidity of the air and the soil renders more phlegmatic, can without doubt dull one's nervous reactions. Men continuously exposed to the harshness of the seasons, to the weariness of the hunt, the perils of war, incur from this a toughness of moral fibre and a habit of suffering that changes into a kind of impassiveness. From the most tender age, the Savages seem to want to get used to this. One sees young boys and little girls joining

---

205 This segment is likely influenced by the French philosopher Montesquieu (Charles-Louis de Secondat, baron de La Brède et de Montesquieu (1689–1755), who proposed in his famous book, *The Spirit of Laws* the controversial theory that geography and climate can influence the nature of men and societies. He believed that people living in warmer countries present a fiery, but vicious personality, whereas northern tribes are braver, but cold and rigid.

themselves, one to the other by the arm, and placing red-hot coals between them to see who will be the first to agitate them.

"What surprises with the men, whose exterior speaks of so much barbarity, are the mutual considerations they observe between themselves; the marks of esteem they lavish upon each other on the basis of what each demands of himself. One is no less charmed by the natural gravity, without pomp, that regulates their manners, their actions, and even their amusements. Thoughtful and reserved, they weigh what they say, they listen attentively, and there is nothing more rare than to see one of those quarrels arise of the kind that are so frequent among people in even the most civilized of nations. Convinced that no man owes anything to another, they conclude that no wrong should be done to anyone either, if one has received no offence from them. Unfortunately, this maxim only extends to their nation,[206] and does not prevent them from attacking an entire people against whom they have no grounds for complaint."[207]

Today this remains the character of the Hurons, notwithstanding any changes in their customs that contact with Europeans may have caused. They have resisted the bad examples of our compatriots for a long time, and only allow themselves to be conquered by our alcoholic spirits. Unable to corrupt them, we poison them.

I remain, etc.

From Quebec, March 18, 1749.

---

206 Delaporte's use of the French word *nation* in this context, which I have translated as "nation" in English here, as elsewhere in this book, is clearly used to name a people, or clan, or tribe of the same blood or ethnic origin. There were also territorial hunting, fishing and travel rights implied by this word as used in the Indian context. But the later sense of the word "nation" as used to describe a legal, surveyed, and bounded political and militarily-defended territory with internationally-recognized borders, containing "citizens" of a sworn allegiance to the nation regardless of their ethnicity, was a concept that began with the French Revolution in 1789, the foundational philosophy of which rested on a new conception of millions of citizens sharing in and democratically expressing a unitary *General Will*. This novel conception of a "people" united by a common Will, rather than by blood or ethnicity, found its most complete (if confusing and rather mystical) formulation in Jean-Jacques Rousseau's *Social Contract* (1762), a copy of which Rousseau reputedly kept by his side as he slept.

207 This remark reminds us of the controversy in the Christian religion, then and now, with respect to the command to "love thine enemy," and "turn the other cheek," and the like. The disputed question is whether Jesus meant only that your tribal enemy ought to be loved because solidarity with one's own in war (or under occupation, as in his case by the Romans), is essential, or also that alien enemies, including even those determined to kill you ought to be loved.

Letter 104

CANADA ~ CONTINUED

MADAM, I will not leave the topics of the Hurons and the Missionary until I have satisfied your curiosity on all the matters of interest.

Animal Symbols

These people, like most of the other Savages of America, have taken the name of an animal, the shape of which can be considered as the symbol and Arms of the nation. It is the seal that is applied to all the treaties with them, unless there are special reasons that call for the substitution of another. The porcupine is the animal that designates the Hurons. They have three principle families among them that they believe are as old as the country they inhabit. They all come from the same stock,[208] but there is one that is accepted as the first among them and that enjoys a kind of pre-eminence over the other two. Each branch has its own separate Chief, and in matters that concern their government these Chiefs get together to deliberate everything.

In addition to the animal that represents the whole nation, each of the three families has another of which it takes the name. The first is the Bear tribe, the second the Wolf, and the third, the Turtle. The Iroquois have the same animals as the Hurons, of which they are believed to be a colony, with this difference — the family of the Turtle is divided into two branches called the Big and the Little Turtle. The Chief of each tribe takes the name of its symbolic animal, and takes no other in public affairs. It's the same for the Chief of the whole nation. But in addition to this name, which is only for ceremony, there is a second one that is regarded as the title of a dignitary, such as: *the most noble,* or *the most ancient,* and so on, and even a third

---

208 All American Indians, whom it is believed came to North America more than ten thousand years ago across the Bering Sea land bridge, when oceans of the world were hundreds of feet lower, and eventually spread to South America, were of the same stock, and shared the same gene pool then and now as their Siberian forbears express today.

that they consider personal and that signifies them alone. These names are not always taken on according to the age of the one in this position, but according to the character with which he is imbued, to which they want to accord respect by means of a title that signifies the maturity, wisdom, and all those other qualities expected in fathers, pastors, and protectors of the people. They consider names so celebrated that no one dares to use a name for themselves after the death of someone who has made it honourable.

Power, Succession, and the Role of Women

Among the Huron, where the dignity of the Chief is hereditary, succession continues in the female line. It is not the son of the dead Chief who succeeds him, it is the son of his sister, or, failing this, his closest relative in the female line. If a branch of the family dies out, the noblest matron of the tribe becomes the one with the power to choose the successor. She does not always observe a birthright, and usually she will name the man who seems to her the most capable of filling it with distinction, to the vacant spot. Then this choice is proclaimed throughout all the villages of the nation, and among its allies, a choice met with rejoicing. Moreover, these Chiefs may not always be highly respected. If they are obeyed anyway, it is because they understand the limits they must set to their power. They propose more often than they command; so their power has nothing absolute about it; the obedience rendered them is entirely free. This liberty serves to constrain them, and subtly convinces them not to command anything that may be followed by a refusal. It contributes equally to persuading their inferiors to carry out the orders given them, with good grace. Even though these Chiefs carry no mark upon them that distinguishes them from others, no one fails to grant them certain prerogatives. The councils are called to assembly by their orders, and are held in their cabins. The business of the assembly is then carried out in their name. They have a large role to play in feast-making and in the general distribution of goods. They are often given preferences; and finally, because they have onerous duties of their position to fulfill, they also enjoy the many privileges with which they are compensated.

From a fear they may try to usurp too much authority and make their power absolute, each family has the right to name a Councillor and an Assistant, and the Chief has no right to interfere with that decision. It is the women who choose them, and who sometimes take this role themselves. They hold their meetings apart, and give the result of their deliberations to officials who communicate these to the Elders in a special Assembly. If the matter is in the public interest, they all gather for a General Assembly. This is a kind of Senate, composed of the Chief and his Assistants, and is of the highest rank.[209] The Assembly of the Elders — which is to say, of all those who have achieved an age of maturity — is held afterward. The last Assembly, which is of the Warriors, consists of all the men fit to bear arms. They often have the Chief of the nation as their head, or the Chief of the village, but in any case, one who has distinguished himself by acts of valour, without which he serves only as a regular warrior.

The Role of the Warriors

There are no military grades among the Savages. Each submits only to the General, and can also quit fighting whenever he wishes. And this Commandant has no real authority, for he can neither reward nor punish. Nevertheless, it rarely happens that he is disobeyed. As the qualities expected of him are high spirits, selflessness, and bravery, the one who displays them all can count on a perfect obedience, always freely and voluntarily given. The Warriors also have a separate council for all things that fall within their competence, but their actual proceedings are always subordinate, and subject to the judgement of the Elders.

To help you form some idea of these sorts of councils, try to imagine a slovenly group of men and women, dirty, seated on the ground, or squatting like monkeys, their knees up by their ears, pipe in the mouth, discussing in cold blood the destruction of an entire people, and the ruin of their enemies. Each one giving an opinion takes up the views of those who have spoken first, then gives his feeling about it. They don't give up discussing a thing until it has been looked at in all its aspects. They never get heated, even when they have differences of opinion, and would not know what it means to interrupt the one who is talking. The Chiefs with the highest standing defer so much to the authority of the senate that they only lay out the subject to be deliberated, after which they finish by saying: "Think upon this, Oh

---

209 Much of the appeal of the imagined Noble Savage for a pre-revolutionary eighteenth-century French public, was the belief that Indian societies were maximally free and egalitarian, and were therefore examples to be followed by highly stratified European societies. But here, as in several other places, Delaporte describes a few Indian social, moral, and religious rankings. Jenness, in *Indians of Canada*, describes many cases of Indian social classes as well as rigid military, medical, gender, and wealth distinctions (such as the painted tents of the Assiniboine tribes, and the material wealth of some of high rank made so visible in the potlatch ceremonies of the West Coast Kwakiutl Indians of Canada). We also read of the ranking distinctions held by the leaders of various secret societies and dancing societies, and of graded military classes made available to men only, and only by purchase, among the Blackfoot. Among some West Coast Tsimshian and Gitskan tribes, there were multiple levels of clans and "houses", and rigid ranks of "slaves, commoners, nobles, and, above the nobles, a class of ruling or 'royal' families who strictly prohibited marriage outside their own order" (p.337). Jenness states that of the two or three thousand strong Bella Coola Indian population of British Columbia in 1793, "30 per cent perhaps were slaves" (p.339).

you Elders, and give us orders." The women are given the appearances of command, but the men exercise it in reality.[210] Only seldom is something important communicated to the women, though everything is done in their name, and the Chiefs are, so to speak, only their lieutenants.

The Orator of the Tribe, and its Deliberations

Each tribe has its own Orator, who alone has the right to speak in the general assemblies. He must know the interests of the nation perfectly, and also understand how to make a case for them. His job consists strictly in laying out everything that has been urged in each of the councils, in announcing the result of all deliberations, and to speak with authority in the name of all the people. These discourses are not long harangues; the elocution is lively and concise, as among the Spartans.[211]

You are surprised that people who possess nothing, who have neither ambitions to exploit, nor any desire to conquer, could have anything to discuss? But as it happens, they negotiate unceasingly: there are alliances to renew or to enter into, services to be offered, reciprocal civilities, invitations to war, or compliments on the death of a Chief — all things that are handled with great care, and with a gravity appropriate to the highest objectives. A single topic, no matter how insignificant, will be deliberated for a long time, and nothing is decided until after all the voices of those wanting to take part have been heard.

Continuous distrust toward their neighbours commits them to taking advantage of every favourable situation, either to cause problems without seeming to do so, or by winning their loyalty by making themselves necessary. In this respect, their caution has infinite flexibility, always moving, always in play. While they handle their allies by way of frequent visits and civil duties, they busy themselves within their own group by watching everything that happens, and they deliberate over the slightest events.

Within their own villages, serious issues are so few in number that they can be drawn to a conclusion without difficulty in a short time. Sometimes they don't even rouse the attention of the Chiefs. Those who arbitrate are usually friends held in common, or parents.

---

210 Here again, we see a conflict between the earlier general comments about equality of rank among the Indians, and the many remarks, such as this one, about the different ranks and privileges accorded to women, men, chiefs, warriors, friends and enemies, slaves and owners, adolescents and adults, married and unmarried, trickster and commoner, and so on.

211 The contrast intended here is between the tough, war-like, and disciplined autocratic Spartans, and the effete, indecisive, democratic Athenians at the time of the 27-year war between Sparta and Athens (431–404 B.C.)

Their Way of Dealing With Criminals

The greatest fault of their government is that they have no conception of criminal justice. It is true that because self-interest — the principle cause of social disorders — is not known among these people, crimes are rare among them. If one man kills another, it is assumed that he did not go to this extreme without some reason, and there is even some sympathy that he fell into the sad necessity of resorting to such violence.

If he was drunk, as they sometimes feign to be to satisfy their desire for revenge or their hatred, they content themselves with sympathy for the dead man, while blaming the excess of wine for the wrongdoing of the guilty one. Anyway, it is up to the parents of the dead man to punish the murderer, because they are the ones most involved. They have the right to condemn him to death. But we don't see this very often. And if they do that, it is without any formal justice. Often this sort of event is used to get rid of a bad citizen.

A murderer of great concern to an entire village would be caught up in much more angry consequences, and often a crime of this kind enrages all the people. But the counsel of the Elders takes every care to reconcile the parties, and it is ordinarily the public that takes action on the part of the offended family. But if this family does not forgive, and the guilty one falls into its hands, the body of the dead victim is hung up on poles under the roof of a cabin, and the killer is placed immediately below the cadaver for several days, so that everything that flows out of the body falls upon him — not only on him, but also on his food. The most common custom these days is to buy back the life of the killer by means of gifts, to which everyone contributes. They are hung on a pole over the head of the dead man, and the Chief distributes them. "So you see," he says, pointing to the gifts, "with what means I remove the hatchet from the wound, and make it fall into the hand of the one who would avenge this death. You see how I clean up the blood that is still flowing." Then, as if it had been the whole country that had received the mortal blow that struck the dead man, he adds: "In this way, we restore our country, in this way, we re-unite divided hearts, and smooth out the way ahead so we can travel safely, from one place to another, with no fear of ambush. "So you see, finally," he continues, now addressing himself to the parents: "You see how to calm those who bear the main burden of this death, to give a medicine to the mother of the deceased to heal her of the sickness that the loss of her son has caused, to spread a bed for her on which she can lie sweetly during the time of her grieving."

When the presents are accepted, the parents consider themselves fully satisfied. But if the accused is wise, he wastes no time in making himself scarce — especially if the family of the dead man is powerful. He uses the excuse that he is going to war to get a prisoner to replace the dead man, and he doesn't come back until time has diminished the feelings of loss of which he is the author. If the captive he brings back is adopted by satisfied parents, the captive assumes all the rights of the one whose place he takes.

A man who thinks that the murder he is going to commit ought to concern the whole nation, as judged by the number of gifts they are obliged to furnish, should — if he is capable of figuring this out — take great pains to plan a violent act that will affect as many as possible. This kind of reparation is the consequence of an admirable politics, more effective, perhaps, at restraining a killer than the sight of the gallows or the wheel.[212]

The Criminal as a Slave

If the parents are not appeased by the gifts, the guilty one is delivered to them as their slave. Often, if they are satisfied by the submission offered to them, they rid themselves of the rights they hold over him, so they will not have an object of hatred continuously before their eyes. But there are occasions when the crime is so atrocious that the council, using its supreme authority, takes on the duty of ordering the correct punishment itself. But once again, there is no formal procedure of justice observed.

Executing a Criminal, and Keeping the Law

When the death of the murderer is decided upon, he may be stabbed to death wherever he is found. But most often, he is lured outside the village under some pretext or other, and his head is smashed in a few steps from the stockade.

If someone has made himself despicable by an act no one wants to make public, such as to become known as an habitual thief, or for having kept up suspicious connections outside the group, he is accused of casting spells and causing evils. You have seen that this crime is hardly ever forgiven. Soon, witnesses are found, who are willing to testify against the man they are trying to undo; he alone, it is said, is the cause of all the problems of the village: he has killed the mother of one; the brother of another; we have seen fire come out of his mouth; he has been digging up graves; or prowling around the cabins at night; and so on. No more is required for him to deserve death, and the first to show up … is his executioner. The parents of the guilty one do not dare to oppose this, and sometimes blame themselves for not having taken

---

[212] The breaking wheel, also known as the Catherine wheel, or simply "the wheel", was a torture device used for capital punishment from antiquity into early modern times for public executions by breaking the criminal's bones and/or bludgeoning him to death. As a form of execution, it was used from classical times into the 18th century; as a form of *post mortem* punishment of the criminal, the wheel was still in use in 19th-century Germany.

the law into their own hands in the first place. Most often, they are asked if they abandon the one whom the village has condemned. This is a courtesy offered to them, and at the same time a political move to get them out of the equation, in case they had the slightest desire to show any resentment. They also take care to appear to want to protect the criminal, and it is in this way that these people, without any written laws, do not allow themselves to dispense justice harshly, and preserve a mutual respect for each other, through an apprehension which demands that every individual must keep watch over his own conduct. So don't be surprised that people who seem to know so little of subordination, and who live so independently, and who give the impression of being governed only by chance and caprice, nevertheless enjoy nearly all the advantages that well-regulated power can provide to a civilized nation.[213] They hold arbitrary power in horror, and rarely depart from certain principles grounded in good sense that for them, take the place of law and, in some fashion, take the place of legitimate authority. Constraint of any kind incenses them. However, as you[214] have seen, they do have crimes punishable by death. They even sometimes make criminals submit to questioning, to force them to admit their complicity. A man who commits a disgraceful cowardice, is judged unworthy to live. As for robbers, it is not only permitted to take back what they stole, but more — to take away everything found in their cabin, to leave them naked, them, their women, and their children, without them being allowed to resist in the slightest.

With the exception of these unusual cases, a Huron lives in perfect independence, and no distinction of birth, nor any prerogative prejudices the rights of the individual; there is no pre-eminence that arises from merit, nor any that inspires a false pride that would make another feel inferior. In a man, what is esteemed, is man himself.[215]

---

213 This section presents the Indian to European readers of the eighteenth century as the real, living, cultural and political symbol of a natural, free, and self-governed human being. In a French society fed up with class oppressions and arbitrary monarchical power, this was far more than casual insight from a popular travel writer. It was incendiary imagery laid before a populace on the verge of revolution. Among the first lines of Rousseau's *Social Contract*, were: "Man is born free, and is everywhere in chains." The Indian had his own chains, of course — the powerfully social and moral binding powers of his own society — but these seemed insignificant to European observers faced with absolute monarchy and a rigid post-feudal class system.

214 Here, as elsewhere, Delaporte is addressing as "you" the woman of high society to whom he wants the reader to believe he is writing these "letters". The objective of this narrative device is to personalize the events being described, by means of the familiar letter form, as contrasted with a third-person essay form. This gives the reader a sense of eavesdropping on a private conversation.

215 In this passage we see a typical eighteenth-century Enlightenment focus on the universal qualities of "Man" as a species, stripped of all cultural and moral distinctions. This was typical of political and moral philosophers of the day such as Voltaire and Rousseau, and it became institutionalized in such as the *Declaration of the Rights of Man and of the Citizen* of (August, 1789), the

The Huron Religion

You ask if these people have a religion? It is a question I have posed to our Missionary myself.[216] "We cannot say," he replied, "that they lack it absolutely. But it is difficult to define what they have. They certainly recognize a supreme Being, the master and creator of the universe. But when we press them a little on such matters, we get only bizarre imaginings, and fables, poorly conceived, and even more poorly digested. They don't go back to the first creation. First, they have six men appear in the world without knowing who placed them there. There was not yet an earth. They wandered at the whim of the winds; didn't know of women, and felt as a consequence that their race would come to an end. One of them rises up into heaven, like another Prometheus, not to steal the sacred fire, but to find a partner. The birds took him up there by making a cart with their wings. As soon as he arrived there, he rested at the foot of a tree. A woman came to draw water from a nearby well. He began conversation with her, as did the serpent with Eve, gave gifts to her, which she accepted, and they began a union together that made her a mother. The master of heaven cast her from the heights of his empire, like Adam from his terrestrial paradise; and she was received, like another Latone[217] in an island that the fish had formed on the back of a turtle. This island grew, and imperceptibly took the form of our globe. This woman gave birth to two children, one of which became the murderer of the other, as Cain did of Abel.[218] After this event, there are no more questions about these men, or their posterity.

---

founding constitutional document of the French Revolution, which in spirit at least, was written not just for French people, but for all people. It differed substantially from the American *Declaration of Independence* of 1776 (which inspired the former document), which was specifically composed for Americans seeking independence from England, and not for all mankind, and was a demand for the restoration of the traditional English rights of which they had been deprived, not for new, revolutionary rights. In this sense, the "American Revolution" was not a revolution at all — it was a war of secession, or independence.

216 Here again, we see the double-utility of Delaporte's narrative device: a question is posed to him by a fictional "reader" of his letters, and he immediately tells us he has asked his fictional "missionary" the same question. This works rather well. We feel that we are party to events Delaporte is relating as they actually happened to him, rather than events transposed from other eyewitness or historical accounts, whether first, or second hand.

217 Classical Greek myths record little about Leto (French: *Latone*) other than her pregnancy and her search for a place where she could give birth to Apollo and Artemis. Finally, she finds an island that is not attached to the ocean floor so it is not considered land, and she can give birth. This is her one active mythic role: once Apollo and Artemis are grown, Leto withdraws, to remain a dim and benevolent matronly figure upon Mount Olympus, her part already played.

218 Cain and Abel were the two sons of Adam and Eve. Cain committed the first murder by killing Abel. Interpretations of Genesis 4 by ancient and modern commentators have typically

"The Savages, as I have said, believe there is a God, and they prove his existence by the creation of the universe. From which they conclude that Man was not made by chance — that he is the work of an origin that is superior in wisdom and knowledge. The Great Spirit contains all, is manifest in all, and gives motion to all things. And finally, all that we see, and all that we know, is this God, who exists eternally, and without limitation: they adore him in all things visible, and whenever they see something beautiful, curious, or surprising, they cry out — *'Oh, Great Spirit! We see you everywhere.'*

"In addition to this first Being, they recognize subordinate divinities, which have bodies like our own, but without any of the inconveniences to which we are subject. They are all subordinate to the Great Genius; they are invoked; they speak with them; they believe they hear what is said to them; that as a consequence they act and make things good or bad according to the various concerns that animate them. So this is all that can be elicited from these barbarians. It is still only the elderly who are initiated into these mysteries.

"These Spirits are honoured by different kinds of offerings and sacrifices. They throw tobacco, birds with their throats slit, the skins of animals, necklaces of shells, entire animals, and especially dogs, ears of corn, fruit, and more, into the lakes and rivers for the God of the waters, and into the fire for the sun God. You can run across these same offerings beside difficult trails, on rocks, or beside white-water rapids, left there to appease the gods who preside over these dangerous places. Sometimes, live dogs are hung from a tree by their back feet to die in fits of rage. The Savages accompany these gifts with prayers, and even with special pleading whereby they beg the sun to light their path, to guide them well, to grant them victory, to make fallow fields fertile, to grant them good fishing, happy hunting, and so on.

"The Hurons honour these same Gods with vows — if we can so describe their promises to give the Chief of their village a portion of the first animal they kill in the hunt, and not to eat any food before having fulfilled this promise. If the fulfillment of this vow becomes impossible, because the Chief is too far away, they burn whatever they had destined for him as a kind of burnt offering.

"Also to be considered as acts of religion are not only their songs of war and of death, which are like their prayers, but also, the custom whereby they make sure not to use knives during certain meals; not to break the bones of the animals they eat at these meals; to have no leftovers of the feast they make at the return from a hunt; and if they cannot finish everything, to get

---

assumed that the motives were jealousy and anger. The story of Cain and Abel is found in the Christian Bible, Jewish Torah, and Muslim Quran.

help from their neighbours; to draw foreshadowing from everything that happens, and to think of them as signs from heaven.

"Some have believed that in the past there existed a kind of religious people among the Hurons, who had no contact with other men; hermits who devoted themselves to chastity. I cannot tell you what their functions may have been. All I have been able to learn from a few Savages is that these virgins never came out of their cabins, wherein they busied themselves with small projects; that the people respected them and left them in peace. A small boy, chosen by the Elders took them whatever they needed to live on; care was taken only to send in another boy before his age might have rendered his services suspect. So this is all I have been able to learn of this sort of vestal virgin, and of these supposed hermits, of whom, I can assure you, I found no trace here.

Their Notion of the Soul

"Our Hurons accept the immortality of the soul, without believing it to be spiritual. They believe it to be like a shadow or image of the body, and believe that after it separates from the body, it preserves all the same characteristics it had during life. They also bury with the dead, everything customary to them in life that could satisfy their needs. They are even convinced that the soul lingers a long time near the body after their separation, and then passes into another country where it is transformed into a turtle-dove. This is a place where the souls of prisoners of war who were burned, are tormented. They go there as late as possible. That's why, after the death of these unfortunates, in the fear that their shades may linger around the cabins to avenge the torments they were made to suffer, they go about everywhere making a great noise beating sticks together, howling with frightening shrieks, to get these shades to leave.

"The happiness these people believe exists in paradise is less a reward for virtue, than for having been a great hunter and warrior. These two qualities, together with a great success in all their ventures, and the glory of having slain a great number of enemies; this is what gives them the right to that happiness which consists in an abundance of all things: good fishing, and a hunt that is always successful, an eternal spring, women, and rest — that's all they ask of their gods, both in this world, and the next. Their minds are never elevated to more sublime ideas or more spiritual pleasures.[219]

---

219 This criticism of Indian spirituality is made in the context of a kind of Christian Platonism, which holds that there is a so-called "Great Chain of Being" from the very lowest, most mundane things in all existence, upward, in increasingly rarefied and ever more spiritual (and so, less material) forms of existence, ending finally, in union with the pure essence of God. Man is held to occupy a very high place in such a chain, above all merely material and insensate substances such

The Role of Dreams

"Dreams form an essential aspect of their religion. They consider these as the ordinary means by which the gods manifest their will, and they make it their duty to defer to them. They are convinced that their souls benefit during their sleep by taking leave of them to wander about. When they awaken, they believe the soul has really seen what was made manifest to it during sleep. When they have had an angry dream, and upon awakening differ with the outcome of it, they believe their life is in danger. A Savage, having dreamed a finger was taken off in the night, cuts if off the next day himself; another, who dreamt that he was a prisoner, burns a few parts of his body. In this way, they believe they escape the prediction of a fateful dream, for their superstition in this respect is really unbelievable.

"It is not only the one who has had a dream who must satisfy the obligations he imagines to have been imposed upon him: it would be a crime to refuse him the things his dreams have made him long for. A Savage, having seen in a dream a Frenchman who had a blanket nicer than his own, asked him for it. The Frenchman gave it to him out of good manners, counting on getting something similar back. A few days later, he went to find his man, and seeing him dressed in a beautiful fur, feigned that he had dreamed of this, and the Savage gave it to him without any coaxing. These alternating dreams went on for a little while. But the Savage, tiring of it first, because he always lost the most in these clever exchanges, went to find the Frenchman, and promised him that he would never again dream of anything that could belong to either of them. But here's an even better story. A Huron, who dreamed that the greatest happiness of his life was connected to possession of a woman married to one of the most important men of the village, went and asked him for her. The husband and the wife were living in a perfect union, and a separation would surely pain them. However, they didn't dare refuse this demand, and they split up. The abandoned husband took up with another woman, to avoid all suspicion that he was still thinking of his first wife.

"If what is desired is not within the powers of a single man to procure, the whole nation gets busy and tries to obtain it, whatever be the price, and they look after it with great care when they have finished the job of finding it. If it is an animal, the fear that it may die on the way home can cause dreadful worries. This business gets very serious when a Savage makes it known that he has dreamed of smashing someone's head in. It is believed that he will actually have to smash the fellow's head in. But this goes just as unhappily

---

as rocks and plants, and all lower animals, but below the angels and, of course, below God, union with whom, first in contemplation, and then in death, is considered the purest spiritual objective.

for the murderer, if it so happens that another has in his own turn dreamed that he ought to avenge the deceased. On these occasions, they take sides, with gifts, and appease their Genie; but there is not always the time for this.

"One day, a Savage came into a cabin and said, 'I have dreamed I killed a Frenchman.' At that moment, the master of the dwelling threw him a French-style piece of clothing, which this angry man then began to pierce with a thousand cuts. Then the one in the cabin became angry in turn, and said he was going to avenge the offence and burn down the whole village. He began with his own cabin, and went on to do the same to all the others. A dog was dragged before him, in the hope he would take out his anger on the animal; but it didn't work, so they threw another dog before him, which he cut to pieces; and suddenly, his fury was calmed. A Chief had dreamed he saw human hearts, and this dream caused the greatest upset for the entire village. It became necessary to use other dreams to counteract the effect of this one. Examples are cited where similar dreams have been carried out in reality. A Huron, shocked that against his will and his opinion that the life of a prisoner be spared, dreamed that he had to eat the flesh of this slave. Efforts were made, in vain, to avoid the influence of this barbaric dream. Little men were made of dough, and cooked in the embers for him to eat; but he spurned them. Everything was done to make him change his mind. But he would not give in. So in the end, they had to smash in the prisoner's head.

The Feast of Dreams

"What is called the Feast of Dreams, or of Desires — which ought rather to be called craziness — is a kind of baccanalia that lasts for fifteen days. It is proclaimed by the Elders, with the same gravity as if it were an affair of state, even though there is no manner of extravagance in which they do not indulge. The feast is barely announced, when you can see men, women, and children nearly naked, even in winter, or disguised in a thousand ridiculous ways. These latter are dressed like satyrs, covered with leaves, and led by women dressed as shrews, their faces blackened, their hair wild, a wolf-skin covering their bodies, and a stake in their hand. These women wear masks made of bark, and a bag with holes cut in it for the eyes and the mouth. In this get-up, they run around in a frenzy from cabin to cabin, without knowing either where they are going, or what they want. You would think them drunkards, or mad people, or that some trance has made them not themselves. Things are smashed, and overturned, and no one dares to oppose this. Whoever does not want to be caught up in the confusion, or even to be exposed to it, has to leave. This, in effect, is what the wisest ones do, because a lot of people profit from this crazy-time to satisfy their hatreds, or to take a private revenge. On some, full buckets of water are thrown, and as this freezes, those who suffer this become numb with cold. Others are covered with hot ashes, or with garbage. Some take flaming sticks and throw them at the first person they see. Others leap with fury on all who show up, and if they feel like it, they beat them black and blue. Everyone shouts aloud that they have had a dream, and asks everyone what the object of their dream is; and it is up to the one who guesses correctly, to pay up, and to satisfy the desire of the masked one — which is done with pleasure, for they are flattered to have resolved the question. Soon they are loaded with gifts, which are handed over after the feast. Then a grand feast is prepared, and everyone focuses on repairing the unfortunate damage done by the masquerade which, on most occasions, is not insignificant.

"The Tricksters play a central role in the Feast of Dreams. These charlatans mount all sorts of farces, and above all brag about their special ability to interpret dreams. They say they only have a relationship with beneficial Genies; that they can reveal the cause and the nature of the most mysterious illnesses, and that they possess the secret for healing them; that they can discern what ought to be done in the most complicated situations to make the most difficult negotiations work out, and that they can render the gods favourable to hunters and to men of war. The imposters with the most bravado are the most respected, and with a few deceptions, they easily win over these ignorant and superstitious people. It is mostly when they act as qualified physicians that they generate the most confidence. Among people more enlightened and civilized than those of Canada, we can also find charlatans who impose themselves with their shamelessness, for whenever it is a question of regaining one's health, such confidence is easy to stimulate in any country.

"It is true that among these barbarians we can witness scenarios quite capable of deceiving the masses. When they emerge from their sweatings, which are the usual preparation for their illusions, they don't differ much from the ancient Pythian priestesses.[220] A sudden ecstasy relieves them of their senses, and we see them become very agitated, speak in a different tone of voice,[221] and make movements like the convulsionists seen in France. Many Missionaries are convinced that the devil is working through these

---

220 The Pythia was the priestess at Apollo's oracle in Delphi. The name comes from Python, the creature with the body of a snake that was slain by Apollo. The Pythia operated as a vehicle for making Apollo's will known to those on earth. Once again, Delaporte is equating ancient European life with modern Indian life represented here as the timeless universality of mankind.

221 Likely a reference to possession by spirits, such as found in the New Testament phenomenon, still witnessed today among certain religious groups such as Pentecostals and Charismatics, as Glossolalia, or "speaking in tongues."

imposters, and tell incredible stories about their supposed spells — which only attests to the extent of their credulity.[222]

Their Art of Medicine

"The main pastime of these Tricksters — or at least the one that earns them the most profit — is medicine. They practice this art through principles based on a knowledge of medicinal plants, on experience, and mostly, as in every other nation, on the conjectures and imbecility of the people. But they have figured out a way for them never to be held responsible for the outcomes of their treatments. As soon as they see a sick person veering toward death, they don't miss the opportunity to make a prescription, the fulfilling of which is so difficult that they always have their excuses ready, aimed at blaming the patient for what has not been precisely followed. Sometimes they order their patients to feign madness; sometimes they make them perform grotesque dances. Those near-dead are at the mercy of these operators, who blow on them, suck on them, and put pressure, with frenetic violence, on the parts of their bodies where they suffer the most pain. They are executioners rather than doctors, and you would say that it is less the healing than the death of their sick patients that they have in mind. But what makes you realize the force of imagination — or the caprice of chance — is that these supposed doctors heal people just as often as ours do. What is certain, is that they have secrets and remedies that are not those of Europe.

The Sweating Cure

The main one, and the most ordinary, used for all sorts of illnesses, is the sweating they work up in their sweat lodges. They use this just as much for the sick as for the healthy. They have a little round cabin, about six or seven feet high, where seven or eight persons can arrange themselves. It is covered with blankets and furs to block the outside air. In the middle of the hut, stones that have been on the fire for a long time are laid out, and above them a pot full of water is suspended. Those who want to sweat enter the cabin naked, whereupon they begin to sing and get very agitated. Water from the pot is spilled onto the hot rocks, and a steam and heat immediately fill the cabin. In no time their bodies begin to drip all over with sweat, and in this condition they then go and throw themselves into a river, or spray themselves with cold water. Often they use this remedy just to relax, or to calm their soul, and to get more in the mood to talk about serious matters. If a

---

222 Is Delaporte, a Jesuit, equating Christian belief in the Devil to the credulity of Indian Tricksters, or simply saying that the beliefs of Indian Tricksters are so banal they do not rank as works of the Devil?

stranger comes into a cabin? They make a fire for him, they rub his feet with oil, and lead him into their sweat lodge, where the host keeps him company. They have a different way of stimulating a sweat for certain illnesses: they place the sick person on a small platform, under which they boil the wood of a thorn bush and fir branches. The steam which arises causes abundant sweating, and the smell of it, they say, is very healthy for you.

European Diseases Unknown Here

"These people never suffered the sicknesses to which we are subjected in Europe, until they came among us. They have gotten smallpox from us — of which they had no idea, and which has ravaged them terribly.[223] Gout, kidney stones, and apoplexy have not as yet penetrated into this happy land among those natural to the country. If we have not as yet gotten venereal disease from them — because this began in America — we must nevertheless admit that Europeans have done their utmost to keep it alive.[224] We build cabins in the forest for those attacked by this; we pluck them from amidst the people, as the Jews used to do with lepers.

---

223 North American Indians, who are believed to have come to North America more than ten thousand years ago across the Bering Sea land bridge, and eventually spread to South America, were all of the same genetic stock (as Delaporte mentioned earlier), and shared in the same restricted gene pool. They suffered from various local diseases such as tuberculosis, and endemic and venereal syphilis. But because they had no experience in childhood with virulent European diseases such as measles, mumps, scarlet fever, smallpox, typhoid fever, pneumonia, or influenza (and more), they lacked all immunity to them, and therefore died in unbelievable numbers. These European diseases arrived in North and South America and took root in "virgin soil," sprouting a virtual holocaust of disease among native people. In the two centuries after contact, almost 90% of Northeastern coastal Indians were decimated. Yale University virologist Francis Black has worked on specialized molecules called "Human Leukocyte Antigens" (HLAs), which do the important work of ridding most people of what HLAs recognize as cell-garbage, such as viruses. Overall, he writes, "Indians have fewer HLA types" than other populations. Most of us have thirty-five main classes of HLAs, "whereas Indian groups have no more than seventeen." As a result, Black argues, "people of the New World are unusually susceptible to diseases of the Old." The one group that Black found was just as susceptible to these diseases then, as now, is their closest genetic relative: Indigenous Siberians. See Charles C. Mann, *1491: New Revelations of the Americas Before Columbus* (New York: Random House, 2005), for more on this mournful topic.

224 Delaporte seems unaware that the first recorded epidemic of syphilis in Europe occurred in 1495, after Columbus returned from the New World. There is some contradictory evidence that this disease existed prior to this time in Europe — critics believe many cases thought to be leprosy were actually syphilis — but consensus is growing that it came from the New World via Columbus (and this is called "the Columbus theory"). Increasing evidence for the theory has been gathered from paleoanthropology. Syphilis leaves distinct lesions on human bones, and many studies show these markings on ancient North American Indian skulls and bones, but few studies show markings on European bones prior to the return of the Columbus crew. An interesting discussion of some of the evidence, pro and con, is here: http://www.scienceclarified.com/dispute/Vol-2/Historic-Dispute-Did-syphilis-originate-in-the-New-World-from-which-it-was-brought-to-Europe-by-Christopher-Columbus-and-his-crew.html

"A sickness is never taken seriously until one's appetite is completely gone. Even the most violent fevers do not stop them from feeding a sick person if they demand it. But once they reject food of all kinds, more attention is paid to them. However, nothing they want is refused, because their appetites are considered commanded by the Genie who watches over and preserves them. Also, when the Tricksters are called in, it is less for their skills than because it is supposed that they know the Spirits better, the reason for the pain, and the remedies that ought to be used. It is rare that a sickness is considered to be the result of something purely natural. Most of them get it into their heads that is caused by some evil spell, and so the whole effort of the Trickster is to reveal the spell. He starts by making himself sweat, and when he has tired himself out by yelling and beating himself, and invoking the help of the Genie, the first extraordinary thing that enters his mind, is considered the cause of the sickness. It is imagined that the presence of the Spirit is revealed in a violent wind that may arise suddenly, or by a howling sound that can be heard beneath the earth. And so, full of his supposed divinity, he pronounces on the health of the patient in a very positive tone, and is sometimes fairly accurate.

"The professional Tricksters don't normally have this wild character until after they have become that way due to excessive fasting. During all that time, they just cry out, howl, sing, and smoke. The set-up takes place in a kind of bacchanalia, with ceremonies so extravagant, accompanied with so much fury, that you would think the devil had taken possession of their person.[225] It's the time for initiation; it's the moment they receive the spirit, and take on the sacred character of the priest and the healer.

I remain, etc.

From Quebec, March 28, 1749.

---

225 As pointed out by Pierre Berthiaume, in *L'Aventure Américaine*, especially in the section "L'univers satanique," (satanic universe), pp. 250 ff, the Savage condition invited much speculation from Missionaries as to possessions by the Devil and the conceptual allegorization of everything in the New World in terms of a cosmic struggle between good and evil.

Letter 105

CANADA ~ CONTINUED

Funerals and Burial Customs

I HAVE already spoken about the sicknesses and healers of the Hurons, and so I will begin this letter speaking about their burials and funerals. When a sick person is without any hope, there are parts of this country where they are abandoned. In others, their death is hurried along so as to prevent them languishing too long. Old age itself is a burden from which these people seek to free themselves. Wandering people are especially subject to this inhumanity. As they are almost always moving from one place to another, and are reduced very often to extreme famine, the inconvenience of old people whom they must carry and feed becomes much more of a problem. These unfortunate elders are often the first to say to those who carry them: "My children. I am causing you a lot of trouble. I am no longer good for anything. Break my head." They are not always listened to, but sometimes it happens that a young man, exhausted by fatigue and hunger, replies coldly: "You are correct, my Grandfather," and in a single motion, takes off his backpack, grabs his hatchet, and smashes the old man's head, who, no doubt, was not so pleased to be taken at his word.

With respect to those who die of sickness, they come to terms with this with a certain resolve. Also, they don't have to worry about not being able to tell the dying person about the dangers of his condition, for fear of frightening him. He is told quite naturally, that his hour has come, and that he should not hold any hope of living much longer. They even try to console him with signs of the affection they feel for him, by showing him the precious robes and ornaments he will wear in the grave. Often he is the first to condemn himself to death.

No sooner has the death sentence been announced, than he gathers his strength to harangue all those gathered around him. If he is the head of a family he gives advice to the children; and, so that he can say goodbye to the entire village, he orders a meal whereby all the foodstuffs of the cabin are to be consumed. Then, he receives the gifts that will accompany him to the grave. They cut the throats of all the dogs they can catch, as they are convinced that the souls of these animals will make an announcement in the next world that the dying one is ready to arrive. The dog meat is put into the cooking pot to add to the food for the feast. After the feast, the tears begin; but they are interrupted to wish the sick one a good journey. He is then left in quiet. But to make sure he does not grimace upon dying, his eyes and mouth are closed until he enters the point of death.

After he has drawn his last breath, everything reverberates with moaning, and this scenario continues for as long a time as the family is able to keep it up at its own expense, for during this entire time they are still seated around the dining table. Then, the first cares are devoted to the corpse in preparation for burial. Those who must busy themselves with this sad ministration, are informed of this at the moment of death. They wash the body, cover it with their oils, and the dead person, dressed in his best finery, with his face painted, and having beside him all that was useful to him, is lifted on a platform and set out for all to see at the door of the cabin in the same posture as he will have in the grave.

Once the body is all dressed and in place, the tears and the sobbing, which have been withheld for some time, begin in an orderly and rhythmic way. One woman in tears gives the signal; and then other women follow her lead, keeping to the same rhythm, but adding-in different words, suitable for each person, according to the different blood relations, or closeness they have with the deceased. This music goes on for a few minutes, after which one of the Elders commands a silence — and everything stops immediately. You will notice, Madam, that it is only the women who express their sadness with tears. The men consider tears and sobbing to be beneath their dignity, and keep their sorrow within their hearts. They keep their heads bowed and covered by their robes, without saying a word, and with no outbursts of emotion.

After these first lamentations, a man leaves the cabin to go tell the Chief of the tribe about the loss they have just suffered. The Chief sends him off to spread the word throughout the village, and also sends delegates to the neighbouring villages where the deceased had relationships. If it was a person of high station, everyone in the nation who ought to come and pay last respects, is alerted. When everyone is gathered, the main griever begins a discourse wherein she tells what has happened throughout the whole course of the sickness, from the first symptoms until the moment of death. Tears begin again, for the third time, and are once again interrupted by one of the Chiefs, who begins to speak a eulogy for the deceased. He does not leave out any of the qualities that made him commendable in his life, nor any of the reasons that ought to moderate the grief of those present, and most of all, of those most interested in him.

The assembled crowd breaks up with a great show of sadness, and then, individual families are invited to come to grieve in turn, and each is assigned a day and an hour for this ceremony. The main griever repeats her discourse for all newcomers; then the moaning and sobbing begin all over again. And always, a new eulogist is found. And as long as the dead is on show, he is always watched over, cried over, praised. Then he is carried, without a lot of ceremony to the burial place, accompanied by everyone, walking in silence. When he is laid in the ground, he is covered with great care so that the earth will not touch him. Erected over the grave is a pillar to which small figures are attached that represent the finest acts of his life. Each day, food is brought there, and what the wild animals take away, they feign to believe (or perhaps they really do believe?) are things the soul of the dead person has enjoyed.

The body of a man who dies during a hunt is placed on a scaffold, and remains there until the hunting party is ready to leave, when they take him back home with them. Those who die in war are burned on the spot, and their ashes taken back for their family. There are cemeteries of a sort situated at some distance from the village. Some bury their dead in the forest; others keep them in a box after drying the body in the sun. When it comes to a drowned person, or those who die due to some accident, the ceremony is more peculiar. Convinced that such tragedies only happen due to the anger of the Spirits, they believe heaven is wrathful and that the entire country is threatened by some great desolation. So they forget nothing when it comes to appeasing this wrath. They search for the missing body with great care, and are of the opinion that if they don't find it, the unhappy souls of these unfortunates will never enjoy any rest. Meanwhile, the whole time is spent in singing, dancing, and feasting. These celebrations just become greater if the body is found, and it becomes a full meeting of all the villages, as an event that interests the whole nation. Then the body is carried to the cemetery, where it is first laid out on a mat. On one side is the grave, on the other, a large fire. Many young people go up to the cadaver, and cut off pieces of flesh from places that have been outlined by an Elder, and throw them in the fire. During this procedure, young women, revolving without cease around those who are working, exhort them to fulfill this ministry, and pop small shellfish into their mouths to encourage them to do their duty, just as sugar-coated candies are given to children. The body stripped of flesh is then buried, and everyone gives a present to the sorrowing family. If one of these customs is omitted, every misfortune in the days following would be considered a punishment sent by the angry gods. If the death was of an important man, a kind of jousting match is celebrated in his honor. A Chief throws three sticks, each about a foot long onto the grave. A man, a woman, and a young girl each take one of them, and those of their own age and sex try to wrestle them from their hands: victory goes to the those who get them.

Their Mourning Laws

The mourning laws are very severe among the Hurons. Upon the death of a father or a mother, they cut their hair, they blacken their faces, and their heads are held high and covered with a cloth; they don't look at anyone, don't visit anyone, don't eat any warm food, and don't warm themselves, even in the depths of winter. After this first period of mourning, a second, more moderate period is begun, which lessens by degrees.

Just as funeral rites are not the same for every kind of person, the laws of mourning are not the same for everyone, either.[226] The ones who adhere to them most strictly are the husband and wife. But the husband never cries over the loss of his wife, because tears are not suitable for men. But the women bewail the loss of their husbands for a whole year, call out for him unceasingly, and fill the village with their cries at sunrise and sunset, and whenever they go out to work, or return from it. If the spouses have lived well together, they observe the mourning rituals strictly; but the parents, pleased with this exactitude, may moderate it with certain exceptions which they announce by way of feasting and gifts. In the contrary case, they are released from whatever duties they may owe each other, and are given liberty to provide for themselves elsewhere. Notwithstanding all this, they expose themselves to endless outrage if they remarry prior to the time prescribed for ordinary mourning. The mourning of mothers has the same term for children. The highest compliment made to friends, and even to strangers received in one's cabin, is to mourn for the parents they have lost.

Like us, the Hurons have an All Souls Day,[227] which they call the *Festival of Souls*. Of all the activities that interest Savages, this is the most solemn. It is so important to them that they prepare for it from one celebration to another to build up the ceremonial excitement. When the time gets closer, they begin by designating a spot for the gathering, and the king of the celebration is chosen. His duty is to be master of ceremonies and to invite guests from neighbouring villages. On the appointed day, everyone gathers, and they walk side by side in procession to the cemetery. Once there, everyone gets busy uncovering the dead bodies. Then, they stay for a while and reflect in silence on this gloomy and horrible spectacle. Try to imagine the opening

---

226 Here, we have another bit of evidence for status differences among Indians, even after death.

227 All Souls Day is a solemn celebration of the Catholic Church commemorating all who have died and are in Purgatory.

of these graves, where death takes pleasure in presenting itself in a thousand different ways according to the degree of bodily corruption. Soon, cries of lamentation are heard; and this scene, which I have witnessed with the Missionary, causes a trembling of soul I cannot adequately express to you.

Gathering Up the Bones of the Dead

After the first transports of sadness, the bones are collected; any flesh is stripped from them, they are washed, then wrapped in beaver pelts. Everything that has rotted is thrown into the fire; all that can be carried is placed on stretchers; others carry it on their shoulders; then everyone returns with it to the village where each one places the sad remains of their dead parents in their cabin. Throughout this death march, the women continue their wailing; the men show the same signs of mourning as on the day of the death. The return to the village is followed by feasting, dancing, games, and fights, for which there are set prizes. At intervals, there are piercing cries made that are called the cries of souls. Gifts are given to strangers, among whom are sometimes some who have come from quite far away, and gifts are received from them. They take advantage of these occasions to speak of common interests.

On the third day, they go in procession into a large room, all decorated for the occasion. Suspended from the walls are the bones dug up at the cemetery. In certain places they are paraded from one village to another, and everywhere they are greeted with lively displays of sadness and tenderness. People come out of their villages to meet them, and the order of things is so well established that each one has a shelter for his group, and for his dead, without the slightest confusion. These funeral marches are accompanied by the sound of musical instruments and the most beautiful voices, and every step is marked by a cadence. At the end, the remains of the dead are carried to the burial place, where they must now be buried forever. They are unwrapped again, before the eyes of the parents, who want the satisfaction of contemplating upon them once again, to handle them, and to adorn them, before saying their last goodbye. The grief is renewed over this sad sight, and soon the whole village rings out with new cries and howling.

A large hole is prepared in the middle of a space where they have gathered, surrounded by a gallery. Above this, poles that are stuck in the ground arise, with crossbars intended to hold the bones that must be exposed to public view. As they arrive, they are placed on the ground along with gifts, and these are spread out over the whole space, like pottery at a fair. It's not unusual to see about twelve hundred packages — as many gifts as bones of the dead. The hole is covered over with pelts, and the gifts are placed aside. New furs are placed over the bodies, then covered with the bark of trees, on which wood, stones, and earth are thrown. Each family is in a row on the scaffolding around the hole, and they go down to get a few handfuls of the grave-sand, which they preserve with great care. Finally, all of them leave. But for a few days, the women come to spread sagamité[228] over the grave. That's the name they give here to a kind of gruel that is the main meal for Savages.

Mother's Milk on the Grave, and Feeding the Dead

These people conduct themselves with respect to their dead parents with a generosity and affection that cannot be too much admired. Mothers have been seen to keep the bodies of their children for years on end, without being able to leave them, and others draw milk from their own breasts to sprinkle over their children's graves. If a fire takes hold of a village where there are dead bodies, these are the first thing they try to protect from the fire. They strip themselves of their precious things in order to dress up the dead, and sometimes their coffins are dug up to change their grave-clothing, and they will deprive themselves of food, even in the most pressing conditions, rather than leave the dead without food. In a word, they place themselves under less hardship for the living, than for the dead.

During the mourning period, it is not permitted to call the dead person by any of the names they used when alive — this would be a lack of respect for their memory. Even those who have a similar name are obliged to drop the name and take another, until these regrets have passed. Not only can they not pronounce the name of the dead person — they cannot even say in a crude way that he is dead. They must use circumlocutions, for example: *the captain who left us*, or *whom we mourn*, and so on.

The Dance of the Calumet Pipe

To freshen up this discussion of funerary matters, I am going to tell you about the most important dances of the Savages, the most celebrated of which is the dance of the Calumet. You know that this calumet is a pipe that has a very long stem, and the bowl very large. The Savages consider this a gift from heaven, and use it for their most important ceremonies, but more often in peace than in war. To smoke the same pipe is to contract a sacred engagement, and these good people believe the Great Spirit will punish any infraction. If the enemy presents a pipe in the middle of a battle, it is permitted to refuse it; but if it is accepted everyone must immediately drop

---

228 Sagamité is a Native American stew made from hominy, or Indian corn mixed with fat. Additional ingredients may include vegetables, wild rice, brown sugar, beans, smoked fish or animal brains.

their arms. There are pipes for all kinds of treaties. In matters of trade, the exchanges have no sooner been made, than a pipe is brought out to cement the deal. It is like the basis and the guarantee of a mutual good faith. These people, taught by their experience that smoking gets rid of melancholy, and frees the mind, have introduced it to their Councils, where they more or less have a pipe in their mouth at all times. Also, after having taken all their resolutions in the wisest way, they believe there is no better symbol with which to seal them, nor a better measure to assure their execution, than the very instrument that has played such a role in their deliberations. In the end, they cannot imagine a more natural sign to mark a clear agreement than to smoke from the same pipe — especially if the smoke they draw from it is offered to the sun, or to some divinity who puts the seal of religion on it. The size and the ornamentations of the calumet — which are the feathers of birds of different colours — are proportional to the distinction of the persons involved, and the importance of the topics.

The calumet dance is properly speaking, a military feast in which the warriors, with painted faces and heads decked out in feathers are the only actors. Sometimes they honour an invited nation with this dance, sometimes it serves to honour a person already there. The Hurons have often used this dance for the arrival of a French Governor in a Canadian fort. In winter, a spacious cabin is built where the whole crowd is gathered. In summer, it is held in an open field surrounded by greenery. A large mat is spread out to place the Okki or the Manitou of the one who leads the dance. To the side is the calumet, in honour of the one for whom the dance is given. It occupies the most visible spot, and the warriors form a circle around it. Each person, on arrival, comes to salute the Manitou, and breathes in a large puff of smoke drawn from the calumet. Then they spread out, to one side or the other, in small groups, the women separate from the men, all seated on the ground, dressed in their finest outfits, giving loud shouts periodically, to applaud the dancers.

The one who is supposed to begin goes up, with respect, and takes the calumet; holding it in both hands, turns it in every way, always in rhythm. Sometimes he shows it to the crowd; sometimes he presents it to the sun; sometimes he bends it to the ground; at others he puts it near his own mouth, and then near the mouths of others present. At each pause, a warrior comes and strikes a post set in the ground a short distance away with his war-hatchet. Upon this signal, a profound silence descends, and this man begins to tell stories about some of his acts of prowess. He gets applause, takes his seat, and the dance continues. Another invites the dancer to fight to the sound of a drum. So he approaches and accepts the duel, with no other defence than the calumet. The first makes a few punches, and the other wards them off; the first flees, and the second chases him; and the victor is always the one who manages to hold onto this instrument of the feast. Then he presents it to another, who wins the same advantage; this one then passes it to a third, until all have danced in their turn. Then, the one presiding over the assembly makes a gift of the calumet to the invited nation, to mark the eternal alliance they wish to establish between their two people.

The Discovery Dance

The dances of the Savages almost always portray the image of war, and are carried out, weapons in hand. They are so varied, so quick, and so terrifying, that a European seeing them for the very first time, cannot avoid shuddering. He feels that at any moment the earth is going to be covered in blood and scattered limbs, and of all the dancers and spectators, not a single man will remain alive. The dance they call *The Discovery*, is an imitation of what happens during a military campaign. A man always shows up alone, and at first he advances slowly through the crowd. He stays immobile for a while, and then he makes a pantomime of the departure of the warriors, their march, and their encampment. He goes off to explore; he advances; he pauses, as if to catch his breath; and then, suddenly, he breaks into a fury, and seems angry at everything he sees. Calming himself from this excess, he chooses someone from the crowd, as if to make them a prisoner of war. He pretends to smash in the head of another. He takes aim at third; and then he breaks into a run with all his power. Then he stops, and regains his senses; retreats, at first hastily, then more slowly. Then he explains with various shouts and cries the different situations he found himself in during the last war campaign; and to wrap it up, he tells them about his exalted exploits. Each of them has the right to boast about their victories so they can be the first to march into danger; to tell about what they have done; to demonstrate what they are going to do; and it is almost always this way that these Indians end their dances. For vanity produces in them a pleasure so sweet and agreeable that they are always ready to start over.

Those who give these feasts use a drum to call everyone from the village, and they gather around his cabin. The warriors dance there, each in their turn, so they can have a chance to begin their lofty public speeches. The Savages find that it befits them to show themselves off as a seasoned hero who shows his battle-scars. Applause is only reserved for true merit; but if anyone esteems himself more than is his worth, the others are permitted to punish him with a few snubs. They blacken their faces, and tell themselves this is to prevent any paleness when they first see danger; but despite this cover-up, here, as in France, the most cowardly are not those who brag about themselves the least. The one who has snubbed a braggart in this way, takes his place, and if he succumbs to the same fault, another replaces him. No one is exempt from this little humiliation, and no one is allowed to get angry over it.

The Savages are natural mockers, and especially like satirical dances. One man takes another by the hand, and leads him to the middle of the crowd. The one being led obeys without resistance, and the dancer stops periodically to rain all sorts of biting comments upon him, which he listen to without saying anything. With each witty word, each sharply satirical verse, there is uproarious laughter from the crowd, to which he reacts by hiding his face in his blanket. The one who is running the show, after having ridiculed his victim in every way, tops off this ignominy by pouring ashes or flour on his head. The Indians love this sort of farce; but the passive one gets even in his turn, at the expense of the one who dragged him in front of everyone. This diversion is so agreeable to them that the young folk, whenever they gather together, form two files, and begin to speak their truths to each other, until one of the two adversaries raises the white flag and admits he is beaten. All these mockeries are spoken in cadences, to the measured beat of the sound of instruments, and it is incredible that this teasing never breaks down in anger or violence. The one who comes to dance, first asks someone, then gives them a gift to entice them to respond favourably, and this generosity makes their reciprocal humiliations more bearable.

There are also dances among the Hurons that are organized by the Tricksters for the healing of the sick, which are of the nature of fortune-telling; and there are others that are purely for amusement, and have no other purpose. These various kinds of dance are for men and for women, but they dance separately, and the men dance with their weapons. Even though they do not hold hands to dance, they never break out of the circle, nor ever break their rhythm — which is all the more difficult, because the music of the Savages has only two or three sounds which repeat continuously. These dances are always announced by a public crier, and everyone shows up decked out in all their finery. The orchestra is in the middle of all the dancing area, and as the musicians accompany their voices with their instruments, the spectators beat large cooking pots with sticks. Those who dance make various movements with their hands and feet, each according to their whim, and even though these motions are each different — and in general quite bizarre — no one, despite this, loses the beat. Those who know best how to move their bodies in the most creative way, are said to be the best dancers. Very soon, they are covered in sweat, and are as if in a trance: you would think you were watching a gang of frenzied people, and what tires them even more is that with their voices and their actions they mimic the noise of the kettle-drums and the sound of the other instruments. Each dance segment is followed by a cry — *ouww!* — from all at once, and very loud, which is a cry of approval to indicate that the refrain has really succeeded. There is something barbaric about this music, which is repellent at first, for no clear idea of what it is can be formed. But one gets used to it little by little, and eventually listens with pleasure. The Savages love this kind of all-out festivity with a passion, and they can carry on this way for days and nights at a time, and their shouts of pleasure make the whole village rumble.

Many Reasons for Feasting

Their dances are always preceded and followed by a huge meal, because feasts are designated for every solemnity and holiday. They distinguish different kinds of them according to the reason for which they are given. They have them for the birth of a child; for those who become adolescents; for their entry into the ranks of the Warriors; for the first animal they kill on the hunt; for each change of name; for the initiation of a trickster; for the promotion of a captain; for the healing of the sick, the seeding and gathering of fruits; to decide the right time for fishing; to settle on a war expedition; to solemnly put a slave to death; to consult their divinities; evoke the spirits; mourn the dead; and so on. There are feasts for marriages; funeral feasts; feasts of souls; dance feasts; feasts for eating everything; feasts for giving gifts; and so on. There are feasts where everyone in the village takes part, and others where only a certain number of persons are invited.

The feast for eating everything is, as I believe I have already mentioned to you, a kind of sacrificial event where it is not permitted to leave anything remaining of the victim. A profound silence is observed, and nothing is to be taken back home of what is served. Everything must be consumed on the spot. It is true that each participant is allowed to have a parasite with him — which is to say, a second person who is allowed to make up for his failure to finish everything. If he cannot find one, even with the lure of gifts, and he cannot finish what is offered to him, he is punished there and then. He is driven into a spot in the corner of the cabin, where he is as if in prison, and sometimes he is left there for a whole day. After the meats are devoured, they bring out the large pieces of bear fat, and the broth in which the flesh was cooked. But if, despite the greatest efforts they cannot finish everything, they throw what is left over on the fire, just as the Jews did for the Pascal Lamb.[229]

The singing feasts are the most magnificent and the most solemn. Sometimes they have as many as thirty deer in their pots; and while they are cooking, they figure out the number of people who ought to be invited. The

---

229 The Paschal Lamb, in Judaism, is the lamb sacrificed at the first Passover, on the eve of the Exodus from Egypt, which is the most momentous event in Jewish history.

calculation is made with the help of kernels of corn, which are sent to the various cabins. They are thrown down onto the mat, with these words: "you are invited," and the number of guests coming corresponds to the number of kernels.

Nevertheless, a town crier goes through the village to alert people that the kettles are boiling in a certain house, and to set the hour they must show up there. Each one arrives at the hour prescribed, carrying his own bowl for the portion of meat he will be given. While the crowd gathers, the chief of the feast sings all by himself to entertain the company. His songs go over the heroic feats of the nation, and end when everyone has taken their place. He almost always has an assistant who takes over when he gets tired.

An Orator opens the proceeding, asks if all the invited guests are present, names the one hosting the feast and the motive for it, and gets into a description of what is in the pot. As he mentions each item of food, the invitees respond with an excited *Oh!, Oh!* as a sign of their appreciation. Then he reveals the topics of which all the guests need to have some understanding; for, as these feasts are held on every occasion important to the village, they are, properly speaking, occasions for public hearings.

As soon as he has stopped speaking, some begin to sing, and others to eat, and some eat and sing at the same time. The host of the feast doesn't touch anything, for he is busy serving others, or serving himself, and he names aloud the pieces he serves to each person. The best pieces are given by preference to the people he wishes to honour. If the meal is to last all day, parts of the pot are left for evening; the rest is edible for dinner; in between, there is singing and dancing.

This is how comradeship is kept alive among these people who, living in common, so to speak, enliven the happiness of the meal with their gaiety, tie more tightly their bonds of friendship, and make their society sweeter and more enjoyable. The only fault I find in all this is that the women never take part.[230] A few show up out of curiosity, and linger at the far side of the cabin. The children, the young ones who have not as yet been enlisted in the band of Warriors, climb up on the scaffolds, or up on the roof of the cabin itself, to see what is going on, by peeking down through the chimney-hole, while others make holes through the bark wall covering the cabin, and no one dares to find fault with this.

The Savages have other feasts where, instead of songs, gifts are given to the guests. They are given robes, hatchets, necklaces, pots, and so on. The

---

230 This is another of the many examples of gender-division among the Huron, just as saving the best pieces for those who are to be honoured, is an example of status division among them.

Chiefs distinguish themselves by this sort of generosity, which can leave them bereft of all they own.

I have spoken elsewhere about their wedding feasts, and those that are held for funeral ceremonies. They add different sorts of games to these, mostly games of chance for which these Indians have a decided passion.

Their Gambling Games

The game of which they are most fond is *The Plate Game*. They sometimes lose sleep over this — and may even lose their reason. They risk all they possess; their clothing; their furniture; their cabin, and even their liberty. It is only played between two people, each of whom takes six or eight knuckle-bones with unequal faces, of which the two most important ones are painted, one white, the other black. They are thrown up in the air while banging the ground or the table with a plate in which they were all mixed up. For lack of a plate, they are thrown by hand, and if, upon landing the same colour is showing, the one playing gets five points. A game goes to forty points, and the earnings go to the first one to reach this number. He then continues to play, and the loser surrenders his place to another.

These games are played in the presence of the entire village, which takes a very strong interest in them. Even though there are only two who hold the plate, we could nevertheless say that everyone plays together. First, they place bets both on the colour and the face of the knuckle-bones they think will show, and their adversary stakes his claim on the opposite. At each throw, all start shouting, and you would think the players had lost their minds — and the spectators are no quieter. Everyone is jumping all over the place, talking to the knuckle-bones, aiming expletives at the Genies of their adversaries, while the whole village echoes with their frightening shouts. They all speak vivaciously, with surprising volubility, and sometimes they just cut off their own words. Then, they turn their anger against themselves, and strike themselves with terrible blows, and begin such violent motions that, even though half-naked, they are soon covered in sweat. If their luck does not turn for the better, the losers can put off the game until the next day, which will only cost them a meal for the participants. At the break of day, the game begins again, and no effort has been spared to ensure that the Genies are onside. The happiness of the moment always hides from them the misfortune that may follow, which may be, alternatively, imbecile children, and dreadful men.

The large parties go for five or six days, and often through the night. Sometimes they are held because a sick person has asked for them, or by the order of a doctor. Then the parents assemble to try the game, and hope to choose a lucky hand. Their Manitou is consulted; they fast; they remain chaste so that they will have a happy dream, and the one they think is favoured by his Genie is placed beside the player.

Another game they play is called *Straws*. These are little straws about the thickness of wheat stalks, about two inches long. A certain number are collected, which are usually about two hundred and one. After having shuffled them well, the Spirits are called upon with a thousand contortions of the body, and a pointed bone is used to separate them into small piles of ten. Each player takes his lucky pile, and the bundle that has eleven straws gets a certain number of points.

In the game called the *Game of Down Feathers*, a few posts are placed in the middle of a cabin, crowned with piles of down of different colours. Young people of both sexes dance around them together. The boys who see in the clothing of their mistresses, the colour that would be most to their liking, pluck that colour from each of the posts, place it on their heads, dance around the girls, and make signs to them of precisely where, despite the vigilance of their mothers, they may later be found.

The *Game of Lacrosse* has a certain resemblance to tennis. You have to move a ball by striking it with a racquet-pouch in a wide-open space, and get it to a goal without it ever falling to the ground, or touching it with your hand. If either of these happens, you lose. These people are so good at catching the ball with their racquets, that a game can last several days.

I would also consider hunting and fishing to be among the diversions of Savages, if the work involved did not turn them into such a burdensome undertaking. The whole nation does this as if they are going to war; each family, each cabin, as if for its upkeep — except for old folks who are prevented by their decrepitude. Everyone goes off into the countryside, the men to hunt game, the women to carry them and dry them. It is advantageous for such a people that winter is the best season of the year. Bear, deer, stags, moose, and the beaver, cannot flee much even at top speed through four or five feet of snow. As the hunters are impeded neither by brush or gullies, or by marshes or rivers, and as everything is soon traversed by the shortest straight route, the hunt is rarely disappointing.

The Bear Hunt

I have already spoken about the hunt for the beaver and the caribou, so now I am going to tell you about the bear hunt. It is of the highest rank of hunts for the people of Canada, and among the nations that have not embraced Christianity, it is still accompanied by, preceded by, and followed by superstitious practices. It is always a war Chief who sets the time for the hunt and who takes charge of alerting the hunters. He commands a fast of eight days during which the most strict abstinence is observed. The extreme weakness this produces in them does not stop them from singing from morning to night. Some of them even cut their flesh in various parts of their body so they can learn from the Genie where the bears will be in the greatest number. They do not ask for the strength to bring them down, but just for the happiness of finding them. It is dreams that produce the hunters' resolve, and they always predict a good hunt when they believe they have seen a lot of bears in the same area in a dream. They also voice their hopes to the manes of the animals they have killed in prior hunts, and as this thought alone fills their minds, it is natural that during sleep they dream often of the thing that is the constant focus of their desires.

After the fasting and the choice of hunting ground, they prepare a huge feast for all who want to go on the hunt. But no one shows up who has not bathed first, which consists of throwing themselves into a river, no matter what the weather, as long as it is not covered in ice. Here, as for all the other ceremonial meals, the one who does the honours doesn't touch anything, and while the others are eating only busies himself with boasting about the success of his previous hunts. As soon as the meal is over they leave in full war dress, cheered on by the whole village. This expedition is undertaken in winter, and the bears are then hidden in the hollows of trees; or, if they find trees fallen down, they make a den of their roots and plug the entrance with branches. If these means of protecting themselves fail them, they dig a large hole in the ground, and are careful after they crawl in, to close the opening. They are so well confined within their cave, that you have to be very close to them to find them. Once they have chosen such a retreat, they don't leave it for the whole winter; so first of all it becomes a question of knowing the places where they tend to hide. Once the hunters are confident, they form a circle around the cave proportional in size to their number, and then, advancing as the circle tightens, they find them tucked away in their holes, and kill them easily. The bears in this country are not dangerous unless they are really hungry, or wounded. They rarely attack, and they even flee at the sight of a man, and the sight of a dog is enough to frighten them off.

As soon as a bear is killed, the hunter puts the stem of his pipe between the bear's teeth, and blowing from the other end of it, fills the bear's mouth and throat with smoke. He is begging the spirit of the animal not to be angry over his death. "Do not have evil thoughts about us," he tells him, "because we have killed you. You can see that we, our women, and our children are suffering from hunger. But they love you, and want to put you into their bodies — is it not an honour to be eaten by the women and children of Warriors?"

As the Spirit of the bear makes no response, the Savage, to see if his prayer has been fulfilled, cuts the cord of flesh under the tongue of the bear, and keeps it with him until the hunt is over. Upon their return to the village, a large bonfire is lit, and they all throw these cords on the fire with great ceremony. If they sparkle and curl up, which normally happens, they believe the Spirits are appeased. If not, they believe the Spirits are unhappy, and they worry that next year the hunt will be unsuccessful if they do not take care to appease them with invocations and gifts.

The welcome given to these hunters and the praise heaped on them when the game is plentiful is just as if they had returned victorious from a long war. The whole village echoes with songs of joy, and the refrain is always that to kill a bear you have to be a real man. This applause is always followed by one of those feasts where everything is eaten, and for a first course, they present the biggest bear of the hunt. He is served as a whole bear, and they believe the Spirits will be irritated if they leave even a single scrap. Everything is eaten, even the skin, and the intestines. Even the soup left from cooking the bear, or rather, the melted fat, the bones, the nerves — all must be consumed: even to the extent that most of the guests are made ill from over-eating, and even some eat themselves to death. Although the main objective of this hunt is the bearskin, you can see that the meat is also in great demand. The Savages eat it when on their expeditions, and still bring back enough to treat their friends and feed their families.

Here, the hunt is a pursuit just as noble as war, and marriage with a good hunter, due to his usefulness, is held in even higher regard than with a soldier. To gain one's reputation in this endeavour, you have to have killed at least a dozen wild animals in a single day. Many dogs trained for this are taken along with you on this exercise. They all seem of the same breed, with straight ears, and a long muzzle, like the wolves. There is boasting about their attachment to their masters, who nevertheless feed them poorly, and never pet them.

The Hunt for Moose

There is another type of hunt that keeps these Savages no less busy: the hunt for moose, the meat of which is very tasty, and the hides strong, sweet-smelling, and soft. It could be mistaken for a chamois; and buff leather cloth is made of it, all the more valued when most light. This animal is the size of a horse, with a large rump, a tiny tail, high thighs, with the legs and feet of a deer. Long hair covers his neck and withers. This hair is never any trouble to him, and it never loses a kind of elasticity that straightens it out spontaneously. Mattresses and horse-saddles are stuffed with it. The head of the moose is more than two feet long, and his way of sticking it forward makes him look inelegant. His muzzle is large and rounded from the top, with nostrils so large you could stick half your arm in them, with an antler rack much larger than that of a deer and almost as long; and it's flat like the antlers of a buck deer, and grows anew every year. You would think this animal is the same as the elk, of which I spoke in my letter to you about Norway. But the moose is a little larger. He loves cold weather, and grazes on grass in summer, and in winter gnaws on bark.

When the snow is deep, the moose gather together under the trees to shelter themselves from bad weather, and they stay there as long as they have food. So it's easy to follow them, especially when the sun begins to melt the snow. The cold of the night then forms this wet snow into a crust, which they break through with their feet, plunge their legs deep into it, and cut them while trying to pull out. In this situation they are taken without much trouble. But in other seasons, you can only approach them with great difficulty, and the slightest wound enrages them. This animal will turn suddenly on a hunter and trample him underfoot. The only way to escape this fate is to throw him your clothing, on which he will take out his anger, while you get behind a tree and figure out how to finish him off.

These northern nations of Canada engage in this hunt without risking anything. They divide themselves into two groups; one of which goes off in canoes that keep a certain distance from each other and form into a semi-circle, the two ends of which touch the shore. The other group, which stayed ashore, sweeps across a large area that corresponds to the semi-circle. Then the dogs are let loose to chase after the moose who are trapped in that area, forcing them ever forward, so that eventually they have to jump into the river, whence they are fired upon from all the canoes, and it is rare that even one gets away. Another very common method is to capture them with rope snares. A large section of the forest is enclosed with an enclosure of posts interwoven with branches of trees, in which only a narrow opening is left where nets are stretched out. The animals pass through there and get tangled, either by the neck, or by the horns. They try hard to shake them off, and sometimes they either break, or carry off the ropes; sometimes they even strangle themselves, whereupon the hunters can easily kill them.

How the Wolverine Kills a Moose

The moose has other enemies besides man, which make no less cruel a war against them. The most terrible of all is the wolverine, a kind of cat with an extremely long tail. As soon as he has a prey in his sights, he jumps on him, attaches himself to his neck, around which he wraps his tail, and cuts his jugular vein. The moose has only one way to save his life: to throw himself into the water. Then his enemy, who is afraid of water, immediately lets go of his grip. But if the water is too far away, he dies before getting there. We are told that the Wolverine is accompanied by foxes that he sends to reconnoitre. The moment they have found a moose, two of them set up alongside him, with a third positioned behind, and all three manoeuvre so skillfully in harassing this beast, that they force him to go where they have left the wolverine, with which they then arrange to share the prey.

I remain, etc.

At Quebec, April 3, 1749.

Letter 106

CANADA ~ CONTINUED

More on Life, and War Among the Hurons

I AM not yet ready to finish my discussion of the Hurons: what they do inside and out constitute matters I don't want to forget. During war, the party for whom the war has become fateful, takes advantage of every opening to begin peace talks. If the feelings on both sides are still too bitter, they rely on mediation by some neutral nation; and then, when everything is set up right, they send in their ambassadors. These are welcomed, and treated with the friendship owed to all those who come to speak of peace or an alliance. It is never for a scheme of conquest or for an intent to dominate, that these wandering nations negotiate, for they don't have any notion of their own domain.[231] Even those who settle in permanent habitations, don't ever dispute the right of others to settle themselves on their land, provided they do not decide to bother them. So all their politics boils down to aligning themselves with others against an enemy too numerous or powerful to beat, so as to suspend all murderous hostilities. For wars among the Savages, when they are entered into nation to nation, are almost never-ending; and so you cannot count on an enduring peace whenever one of two peoples can create jealousy or unrest among the other.

Once it becomes a question of entering negotiations, the first concern is not to appear to be the one who takes the first step, or at the least, to convince the enemy that neither fear nor necessity have any part in the negotiations.

---

231 This comment is intended to underline the fact that the Indians did not have a notion of absolute property rights in land. So war to acquire or defend the land itself was never in question. Indians had a sense of migratory hunting and fishing rights over the territory they happened to be in, or were moving into, or back to, and they had a concept of ownership of objects such as a hatchet, a canoe, a blanket, family plantings, and so on. But they did not have a legal concept of absolute land ownership in fee simple, as we say. They had no tradition of animal husbandry, either, perhaps because in conditions of plenty, where animals to hunt could usually, if not always be found, this was unnecessary. It may be that historically, rights of land ownership arise, and are essential in conditions of scarce food resources, where a tradition of permanent agriculture and animal husbandry already exists, but not otherwise.

A negotiator does not diminish his pride, even in the most regrettable condition of the affairs of his nation. Sometimes, he is even artful enough to prove to the conquerors that it is in their interest to end the hostilities. To fill this role, the Council chooses the one in whom it recognizes the most talent and capacity; and after having received their instructions, which have been deeply considered by the Assembly of Elders, they set out on their trip with gifts, and a certain number of young people with whom they form this conciliatory procession.

Before their arrival, the chief ambassador ensures that his visit is preceded and announced by someone from his group, so that they are ready to receive him. He stops about half a league from the village, and sends an emissary ahead once again, to warn of his arrival. Councils are held in the village, and a deputy is sent to him to respond in kind. The oldest of the deputies sits down beside the ambassadors, lights his pipe, congratulates them on their arrival, thanks them for having undertaken such a difficult trip, and so on. Then he retires with his entire group, and the ambassadors make their entry without any fuss. They find their cabin prepared, and a pot on the fire. The feast is paid for by the public treasury, and no one except the newcomers touches it. During their whole stay, their costs are picked up by the public. First, they take a few days of rest, then ask to be admitted to the Council, present their necklaces, and make their proposals, which are deliberated upon with much maturity. If they are such as likely to be accepted, the foreigners are sent home with a favourable response and with gifts.

Disaster If the Meeting Fails

But they are out of luck if the feeling the war ought to be continued prevails in the Council. All respect for their character and the rights of men, is lost; and sometimes their heads are smashed in on the same mat where they were holding forth. But most often, so as not to violate hospitality, they are honourably dismissed, and then the hosts go and assassinate them on their way home, a few leagues from the village.

It is no longer the custom to burn ambassadors, or to treat them as slaves. However, the Missionary has told me that the Iroquois have taken their barbarism to that extent with respect to certain Frenchmen that a governor of Canada sent to them as his deputy. If I understand this same Jesuit, the Iroquois are practiced in the game of the most refined politics. They look after their enemy lodgers, and make certain that by means of a kind of caution that causes them to distrust self-interested opinion, they no longer accept anything from such secret agents unless they are accompanied by some gift.

Barter Trade Among Them

Other than treaties of peace and alliance, these Indians now consider trade as one of their most essential occupations. For them, this is pure bartering, which they do nation to nation, where they exchange furs, mats, tobacco, canoes, for robes, brandy, household tools, and for all things that are essential for living. The feasts and the dances they hold when they go to trade with other people, are an agreeable part of these diversions. They begin with presents for the Chiefs, or for the most important of the nation, and receive the equivalent in return, and this politeness is considered by both sides as a kind of reciprocal right that arises when trading goods. Then, they trade from individual to individual, or from cabin to cabin, and the desire to have something is only what sets the price placed on it.

When they pass through the lands of a nation where they must not stop, they have to pay for this right, which is never refused. A single man will stop thirty canoes, by saying: "I am blocking the river, because the body of a certain captain was not buried", or on some other pretext. We don't know what resistance would lead to in a similar case; but for the giving of a gift, the matter is settled; and this is something they ask for with a respect unknown in France from barbarians more Savage than these ... whom we call *employees* and *shop stewards*."

Their Notion of Money

Even though trade among them is only by barter, certain representative signs equivalent to our notion of money are recognizable.[232] The same holds for their speech, writing, and contracts: this is what we call *Cowry*, which is not baked earth, as in Europe; they are little sea-shells, distinguished by the differences in shape and the variety of colours. They are fluted, elongated, a little pointed, without appendages, and fairly thick. The inside of these shells is of such a beautiful sheen, and colors so brilliant, that no art could match it. These are the most precious belongings of the people of Canada — their jewelry, their precious stones, their gold, and their silver. There are two main types. One is white, is the most common and is used for most of the things with which men and women dress themselves. The other is of a deep violet colour, is more sought after than the first kind, and the more dark it is, the more valuable. They are mounted in two ways, as branches, or as necklaces. The latter are like large belts, where the shells, laid out in rows, are tied off by small bands of leather laid out in very neat rows. The public treasury consists

---

[232] In this example, Delaporte hints that the sophistication of a possible coin and paper money economy is latent in their barter trading habits.

mostly of this kind of wealth. The Savages, who do not have any kind of writing, attach different significations to them, each of which expresses a particular matter, or a circumstance that the necklace must represent as long as it lasts. To avoid any confusion among the many of them, care is taken to vary them, and to make them in such a way that they are recognizable at first glance. By this means, everything is demarcated, and nothing forgotten.

The length of these necklaces, their size, and colour, are proportional to the importance of the matters, and the dignity of the persons, and the rank held by a nation. It is an inviolable and sacred measure that sanctions speeches, promises, and treaties. No matter what task we agree to, what oath we have sworn, if all that is not cemented by the gift of a necklace, which is sent by both parties, the whole matter is dropped as if it had never been brought up. The chiefs of the villages are the keepers of these splendours of the nation. They understand what they signify, and interpret their meanings; it is these things that by way of custom transmit the history of the country to the young.

When these people lack cowry, they make up for it with other gifts. Commonly, these are such as the pelts of stags and deer, for which the Europeans who trade with them give them haberdashery of little value in exchange. The public treasury, which is kept in the Chiefs' cabins, is kept alternatively by one, then the other, for no determinate term; and it stays in one spot for as long as jealousy permits. Other than the branches and necklaces of shells, they also bring pelts, corn, flour, smoked meats, and generally, everything that can be used for the common expenditures of the village. It is only things of consequence, that are traded with necklaces. For the less important things, they use the shell-branches, hides, blankets, and the like. When it comes to inviting a nation to join in a war, a flag stained with blood is attached to the necklace.

Trading by Canoe

Trade among the Canadians takes place by waterways, thanks to the great number of lakes and rivers sprinkled across the land. Their boats are of different kinds and are made of different materials. I have seen boats made from animal skins that hold one person, from twelve to sixteen feet long. They are flat, and resemble a weaver's shuttle. The top is covered with skin, like the bottom, and there is only an opening in the middle into which a man fits to halfway up his body so he can sit on his bottom. He closes it like a purse, and tightens it around him like a belt, such that, as he is himself covered with animal skins, he seems to be of a piece with his boat, and not a single drop of water can get in. He steers it with a double-ended paddle which has a blade at both ends, and strokes on both sides with such speed that he seems to glide as if on ice. A spear that is attached to a cord allows him to spear fish, which he eats raw; and as he has no fear that the water will overcome him, he sets out on the longest voyages without fear as long as he has reason to hope that he will not lack for food.

The other boats are of the usual form, of different sizes, and can hold from ten to fifty people. In calm water, they are propelled with oars; but when the wind is right, sails made of skins are attached to the mast. I spoke earlier of canoes — the ones made of bark, which are the masterpieces of the art of the Savages. Nothing is better made, nor more admirable than these fragile devices with which, nevertheless, immense loads can be carried; and they can go anywhere with extreme rapidity. The bottom is made from one or two pieces of bark, to which others are sewn with roots that are glued from within, such that many pieces seem to be only one. The pieces on the bottom are only as thick as two pieces, but they are covered over by a wicker-work of cedar wood that strengthens the whole body of the boat.

It is in such craft that the Hurons cross inlets of the sea, navigate perilous rivers, and tour around lakes four or five hundred leagues in length. I have made several such trips with them, without ever encountering any danger. There was only one time, when crossing the St. Lawrence River that I found myself suddenly surrounded by a pile of ice of huge size. The canoe got smashed around, and the Indians who were leading me through began to cry out: "We are dead! It's over! We are going to perish!" However, with a huge effort, they jumped onto one of these floating pieces of ice. I could do nothing better than follow their lead, and after having pulled the canoe up, we carried it to the far end of the ice-floe. Once there, we got back in the boat, and went for another ice-floe, and jumping in this way from one to another, we eventually got to the bank of the river, soaked, and chilled to the bone.

There is one thing about these little boats that is very unsettling: you have to be extremely careful getting into them, and take care not to overturn them. It's even worse if they touch the rocks or the sand, for then there will be rips where the water will enter and spoil the goods on board. There are very few days where one is not obliged to patch a few holes with pine-gum. As soon as you get onshore, the canoe must be unloaded, and sheltered on the river bank, for fear that the wind cause it to be damaged. Two men can carry it on their shoulders with great ease, while the others carry the baggage, and in this way the difficult passages are avoided, such as cascades, waterfalls and cataracts, for their extreme height in the rivers of North America makes them impassible. It is even advisable to begin this portaging from afar, and get off the river well above the falls, so that you don't court an inevitable disaster. However, in the rapids that are less high, we just let ourselves go with the current. The whole skill consists in knowing how to shoot the rapids; of choosing the right narrow passage between the lines of rock, and avoiding the random rocks that are found in the current, for all it takes is to hit one rock for the canoe to break in two, and you are shipwrecked. You cannot conceive of the compromises that are made in such dangerous narrows when at the mercy of a single bit of bark; however, our Savages are so capable in this kind of navigation that many of them prefer to shoot the rapids than to bypass them on foot.

The Missionary's Aggravations Traveling With Indians

"For us Europeans," the Missionary told me, "this sort of vehicle has other inconveniences. Among them — the fear that its extreme fragility engenders from the start; the annoying body position you have to keep; the inactive state you are in (and that it is impossible to avoid); the slowness of the pace, which the slightest rain or a headwind can make even slower; the lack of socializing one finds with these people, who don't know anything, and who never speak at all when they are busy; who contaminate you with their bad smell, and cover you with dirt and vermin; the rough manners that have to be suffered; the rebuffs one has to suffer from a drunk man, or whom an unexpected accident puts in a bad mood; the greed that is so easily aroused in the hearts of these barbarians at the sight of something that excites them," this, he continues, "is what one often feels when travelling in such a vehicle with these Savages."

The Wilderness as a New Eden

"I admit," he adds, "that there are places and times where this kind of boat trip is less troublesome. I recall with pleasure a trip I went on last year on Lake Erie. I became very close with that charming country, with its serene sky, and water crystalline, as from a fountain. Everywhere I found sound and agreeable encampments, where I could indulge with very little effort in a hunt, breathe pure air at my leisure, and rejoice in the beautiful views of the countryside. I imagined the ancient patriarchs who, with no fixed habitation, lived under tents, were masters of the country through which they traveled, and benefited from the things produced without the bother of having to cultivate them.[233] How many oaks reminded me of the Oak of Mamre![234]

---

233 Here, through his imagined "Missionary," Delaporte introduces the notion of a perfect Holy Land, imagined as it was when peopled by the scriptural Fathers, a place of natural perfection, and overpowering natural forces that engender deep and mysterious emotions.

234 The *Oak of Mamre*, two kilometres (1.2 miles) southwest of Mamre near Hebron, Palestinian Territories, is also called *The Oak of Abraham*. It is an ancient tree which, by tradition, is said to

How many fountains made me recall the Fountain of Jacob!²³⁵ Each day, there was a new situation of my choosing: a naturally clean and roomy cabin, set up and furnished in a minute, sprinkled with ever-fresh flowers, on a lovely, evergreen carpet; in all aspects — simple and natural beauties that no art could alter or imitate.

"If these pleasures suffer a few interruptions, whether from bad weather, or from some unforeseen accident, that only lends them a more vivacious aspect when they return. This unlimited space offers a visually pleasing scene of sombre, thick, and deep forests, where their height alone attests to their ancient age. Rivers without number have come here from a great distance to irrigate this immense country, and everything in this intact region of the New World bears the stamp of the grand and the sublime.²³⁶ Nature here displays an wealth of fecundity, a magnificence, and a majesty that commands veneration. It is here that a painter, or a poet, would feel the exaltations of their imagination as it is fired up, filled with ideas that become ineradicable in the memories of men. The whole countryside exhaled and breathed in the air of a long life. And the temperature, which the circumstances of climate render so delightful, gives up none of its healthfulness due to the singular rigours of the excessive cold.

The French Government Meets With Indians

"I made this trip with two French officers that the Commander of Montreal sent among the Hurons to communicate orders to them, just received from the Governor-General of Canada. The morning after our arrival they assembled the Chiefs from three villages, who listened to them quietly, and without interruption. And when they finished, the Savages withdrew to deliberate; for their custom is never to respond on the spot whenever it is a matter of great importance. Two days later, they re-assembled in much greater numbers, and to give you an idea of this Council, try to imagine about thirty Savages, almost naked, their hair dishevelled in all sorts of ways, each one looking more ridiculous than the next, some of them wearing a rimmed hat, all of them with a pipe in their mouths, and with the demeanour of people

---

mark the place where Abraham entertained the three angels, or pitched his tent. It is estimated that this oak is approximately 5,000 years old.

235 Jacob's Well, also known as *Jacob's fountain*, is a deep well hewn of solid rock that has been associated in religious tradition with Jacob for roughly two millennia. It is situated a short distance from the archaeological site of Tell Balata, which is thought to be the site of biblical Shechem.

236 Delaporte is soaring now: the *Grand* and the *Sublime* were the most common adjectives (and as used here, nouns) denoting the rising Romantic sensibility in Europe. In this passage we see the rawness and potential hostility of nature transformed verbally, so to speak, into a highly emotionally-charged, Edenic vision.

who have nothing on their minds.[237] It's a big deal if they say even one word in a quarter hour.

"It had to do with two matters that lay heavy on the heart of the Governor. The first was to gain approval of the three villages that they no longer be sold brandy, for the French Marine Counsel[238] had absolutely forbidden using brandy for trading. The second, was to persuade them to unite against other Indians that were committing all sorts of robbery and violence in the country. The Huron orator began to speak. His air, the sound of his voice, and his movements, even though they included no gestures at all, had something noble and important about them. He didn't bother with an introduction, and went straight to the point. He spoke for a long time, and calmly, pausing at each topic to allow the interpreter to explain in our language, what he had just said in his own. The conclusion of all this was that the French were in control of never selling brandy to the Hurons; that they had done very well by not ever having sold it to them, and that they could not imagine anything more forceful than what is said against the disorders caused by this drink. But he added that they were so accustomed to it, they could no longer do without it, from which it was easy for us to figure out that if the French couldn't provide it, the English knew how to do so. As for the second topic, he declared that nothing could be resolved except by a general Council, which, undoubtedly, would arise from the necessity of this war."

Their Knowledge of Astronomy and Time

These people have some sort of understanding of astronomy, which helps them keep track of time, go in the right direction, and to determine the right season for fishing and hunting. They designate the seasons and the months by means of seeds, the different heights of the grains, and their harvests. They don't know anything about the allocation of the weeks, nor the regulation of

---

237 Clatterbuck, *Demons, Saints, and Patriots*, writes of the persistent and contradictory dualism expressed in "a pair of imaginary opposites: the dirty, repulsive, painted Indian on the one hand, and the strong, vital, and beautiful Native body on the other." We see many examples, as here, of this combination of disgust and admiration in *Le Voyageur François*. At the time, the America's were envisaged as sites where a corrupted European Christianity could be salvaged and restored to its original purity through conversion of the Indians, duplicating the passionate work of conversion achieved by the first Christian Friars that we read of in the *Book of Acts*. It was surely the appeal of this visionary motive of human perfection that supplied the all-or-nothing characterization of the Angel Indian when it worked, and the Devil Indian when it didn't. There was much speculation in the early period of North American exploration that the Indians of the New World were actually descendants of the Lost Tribes of Israel.

238 The "Conseil de la Marine" was a French institution under the pre-revolutionary *Ancien Régime*. It was created by an ordinance of November 3, 1715, and for a time governed French relations with her colonies. It ended operations in 1723, when Louis XV reached maturity.

daytime by hours. They have only four fixed points: sunrise, noon, sunset, and midnight. But in place of clocks, they can mark very exactly by pointing a finger, exactly where the sun ought to be in the sky. They don't make fire by striking stones together, but by rubbing two pieces of wood together. As soon as this wood makes a spark, they put it in powdered cedar bark, and blow softly on it until it starts to burn.

If they are so little interested in procuring the conveniences of life in the place where they live, what would you think of their encampments? The Missionary who went with them on a winter hunt, gave us the following description.

A Winter Hunt

"The place they choose is rough and wild. You have to walk a long time to get there, and carry on your back everything you might need for the next five or six months. If they have not taken the precaution to supply themselves with tree-bark, they will find nothing with which to shelter themselves from rain or snow along the route. Upon arriving at the hunting ground, everyone gets to work, and as much was expected of me as of the others. They didn't give me a separate cabin; I stayed in the first one willing to have me.

"These shelters, somewhat in the shape of our ice-boxes, are round, and terminate in a cone, with nothing holding them up except a few poles stuck in the snow, attached at the ends, and covered with poorly joined bark, such that the wind comes in everywhere, and it takes about a quarter of an hour to build them. Pine branches take the place of a mat, and serve as table and as beds. The snow that builds up around the hut forms a kind of parapet, in the shelter of which one sleeps rather tranquilly, when there is not too much smoke; for ordinarily, it fills the top of the hut so much it is impossible to stand up. Accustomed as they are from childhood to be lying down or seated, our Indians are not inconvenienced by this, but for me, this position was a cruel torture. Most of the time, you can't see anything even two feet in front of you, and eyesight suffers from constant weeping. There are times when, in order to breathe, you have to stay lying on your stomach with your mouth right on the ground, because you can't even think about going outside: the cold there will bitterly slash your face.

The Indians' Dogs

"The persecution of their dogs is really unbearable. These people have a lot of them that follow them everywhere, and are very attached to them. They are not affectionate, because they are never petted, but they are tough and good hunters. No one bothers much with feeding them — they live on what they can catch. They are also very thin, and have so little hair, that to protect themselves when they can't get close to the fire, they sleep on the first beds they come across; often, one is awakened during the night, almost suffocated by these bothersome animals. You want to chase them away; but they return as quickly. Their pestering begins at daylight, for they don't see any food appearing in which they can hope to share. Try to imagine a poor missionary, lying by the fire, beating back the smoke that barely allows him to say his breviary, but exposed to the insults of a multitude of dogs who run back and forth in front of him after a bone they have seen. If he wants to eat, they have put their noses in his plate before he has barely raised a hand, and while he is busy defending his morsel of food from the ones attacking him from the front, another comes from behind and takes half of it, or causes it to fall into the ashes.

"Hunger is another problem, much greater than what I have been speaking of. We counted on a hunt that was not successful. Our provisions ran out; and even though these people know well how to abstain, they often find themselves reduced to such a scarcity of food, that they succumb. How many times have I not seen my own self reduced to the necessity of eating the skins of eels and of moose with which I have patched up my clothing? How many times have I not had to nourish myself on tender branches and the bark of trees? My health, fortunately, has not suffered from this; but the same hardship has hurt a lot of others more.

The Mosquitoes and Gnats

"In summer, the mosquitoes, and a prodigious quantity of other gnats mount to a persecution even more troublesome than the smoke in winter; we are even obliged to use the one to rid us of the other — to bring the smoke to our rescue to fend off insect bites. It's the only remedy we can use; the only one that stops them from setting your body on fire with stings. Add to this the frequent forced marches, always very tough, that one must make in following these barbarians, sometimes through water up to your waist; or in mud up to your knees; in the forest we get tangled in brambles and thorns; in the open countryside nothing protects us from the sun which is just as burning in summer as the wind is sharp in winter.

"But if we are made to suffer at the beginning of the hunt, it is more than compensated when we succeed.

A Successful Buffalo Hunt — How They Do It

"We took back as many hides of wood buffalo as our sleds could carry. These animals, much larger than the buffalo of Europe,[239] have low horns, short

---

[239] As mentioned in note 197 of this book, Buffon made a notorious case for degeneracy based on the small size, meagre population, and hairless bodies of Indians, and the absence of large animals

and black, and two tufts of hair — one on their muzzles and the other on their heads, which falls over their eyes and gives them a frightening appearance. On their backs they have a bump that begins around their hindquarters and rises up over their shoulders. They are covered with a really long hair, verging on red, and the rest of the body is a highly-valued black wool. They have a large chest, a narrow rump, a short tail, and a huge head on a narrow neck. The very sight of a man starts them running, and just one dog can startle the whole herd into flight. Their sense of smell is so good that to get close to them with a gun you have to approach from downwind. A buffalo that is wounded becomes enraged, and will immediately charge the hunters. Its meat is very tasty, but so tough that eating it is a job. The meat of the female is the most tender, and so unless in great hunger, it is the only part the Savages eat.[240] "As for the hide? There is no better; and although very tough, it is also becomes very supple, and as soft as chamois. Very light shields are made of this hide that musket-balls can pierce only with great difficulty.

"Our Indians begin this hunt by forming four lines of men into a square shape, and they set fire to the grasses before them that are very dry and tall.[241] As the flames advance, they advance, while tightening their ranks.

---

in the Americas (though Delaporte remarks here that North American buffalo were much larger than European buffalo). Something of which no one at the time could have been aware was that the modern fossil record proves there were once single-humped camels, giant tapirs, three-hundred pound beaver, large sabre-toothed cats, mastodons, mammoths, and other very large species living in North America. But in a mere 1,000 years, they suddenly vanished from North America, and this disappearance happened to coincide with the arrival of the first Paleo-Indians ten or eleven thousand years ago. The geochronologist Paul Martin has argued that Paleo-Indians were very hungry, and were, he said (in a phrase that stuck), "super-predators." Many have objected, because this fact, if it is one, flies in the face of the standard notion of Indians as children of nature and its careful stewards. Martin insisted that "the destruction of fauna" by Indians, "was far greater before Columbus than at any time since." His detractors insist as adamantly that the disappearance was more likely due to climate change. See Chapter One, "The Pleistocene Extinction," in Shephard Krech III, *The Ecological Indian* (New York: W.W. Norton, 1990) for a discussion of this phenomenon, and his extensive notes.

240 The standard narrative concerning the extinction of the buffalo in North America lays the blame primarily on the Whiteman, and portrays the Indian as an ecologically conservation-minded hunter. Krech, in *The Ecological Indian*, provides some balance in his "Buffalo" chapter where, in addition to the unconscionable slaughters of buffalo by white hunters, we read of Indian buffalo butchery, wasteful killing, the taking of only choice parts of the kill such as tongues and humps, leaving the rest to rot; or of taking only the choice meat of females and fetuses rather than of the males killed, because their meat is more tender, and of "communal hunting" — slaughters managed by driving large herds over "jumps", into pounds, or bogs, or across frozen rivers to drown them in large numbers in excess of need, just to kill them more easily. The buffalo hunt in the Western part of Canada became a colossal slaughter on all sides. Jenness, in *Indians of Canada*, writes: "The tribes that jostled together on this amazing hunting-ground combined the buffalo chase with ceaseless wars, and raided each other for firearms, horses, and scalps until the whole area from the Rockies to the Great Lakes became a perpetual battlefield" (p.256).

241 Fire was a preferred means of corralling game animals, and signalling over long distances

These animals, so frightened of fire, always flee from it, and in the end find themselves so tightly packed together that they can be killed to the very last one. A group of hunters never comes back without having killed three or four hundred. But, for fear of running into, or harming each other, the different groups agree on how to proceed. There are punishments due to those who violate these rules, or who, in leaving their position give the buffalo a means of escape. The guilty ones are stripped of everything; their guns are taken away, their hut overturned — even chiefs are subjected to this as if they were ordinary folk.[242]

Other Animals They Trap

"The other animals whose flesh or pelts are sought after by Savages, are usually caught on snow with traps or nooses. Some of these are: deer, the wildcat, the weasel, squirrels, porcupine, ermine, hare, rabbits, and everything we consider smaller furry animals.

"The deer, a species very common in Canada, does not differ much from the European type, but we have observed that when young, they have striped hair of different colours, and then it falls out and is replaced by hair of the usual colour.[243] This animal is not at all frightened, is easily approached, and seems like a friend to humans. A female that has become friendly does not go off into the bush unless she is in heat, and when she takes leave of the male, she returns to the lodging of her master. When the time comes to give birth, she returns to the forest again, stays there for a few days with her young, then

---

to warn of enemies and the like. It was also used to clear huge expanses of forest undergrowth in Northeastern locales, and in the Midwest, to prepare enormous expanses of grassland for fresh growth, thus to attract herds of buffalo and deer as easy marks. See especially Chapter Four, "Fire," in Krech, *The Ecological Indian*. In this scene, Delaporte relates that they killed three or four hundred buffalo, which have a meat they don't like to eat except for parts of the female, unless pressed by hunger. Another favourite method used for mass killings of buffalo in the Western parts of North America was to drive countless of them over a cliff to their death. Supporters of this method say it made rational sense; critics, that it was needlessly cruel and wasteful of a diminishing resource. "Head-Smashed-In Buffalo Jump" near Fort Macleod, Alberta, is a famous cliff — now a Unesco World Heritage Site — that was used to kill buffalo in very large numbers as early as 8,000 BC, and ceasing only 150 years ago. Fire was also often used to frighten animals into killing areas or to make them run over cliffs. Sometimes such fires got out of control and burned hundreds — even thousands — of square miles of forest and pasture.

242 Here is yet another indication of social ranking.

243 Some studies report a half million deerskins traded in the middle of the eighteenth century. Indians had always traded deerskins for what they valued, and got drawn deeply into the European trade of deerskins (up to a million hides per year) for other goods, but most damaging of all, for rum and brandy. Once on the precipice of extinction, the white-tail deer population is now a great recovery story. There are an estimated 25 million white-tail deer roaming North America. Almost every day of the year I see a handful of them grazing on my own rural property in Ontario.

leaves them, returns to the village, and visits them regularly. If it is considered alright to follow her to gather up her nurslings, she continues to take care of them in the master's cabin. It is astonishing that our French people do not have herds of them in their settlements.

"The wildcats are themselves true hunters who live only on the animals they manage to trap, and which they pursue even to the tops of the loftiest trees. Their meat is white and good to eat, and their hair and pelt are among the most beautiful of this country.

Ingenuity of the Black Fox

"Even more valued are the pelts of certain black foxes of the northern mountains; but they are quite rare due to the difficulty in catching them. They give chase to river birds in an ingenious fashion. They advance on their prey a little in the water. Then they back away and perform lots of somersaults on the bank. The ducks and the bustard-birds, and other aquatic animals, amused and diverted as they are by this frolic, approach them. And then, when the enemy sees them close at hand, he at first freezes quite motionless, so as not to alarm them; he only swings his tail to get them to come even closer; and ... they are stupid enough to fall into his trap! For then, the fox suddenly jumps upon his prey — and he rarely misses. The dogs have been trained in the same routine — and they wage a cruel war against the foxes."

The Work of Those Who Stay Home, and Their Settlements

Field work, building, moving cabins, the preparation of clothing and of food, is the main occupation of the Savages who remain sedentary[244] in the villages. They are the ones who choose a good location for their villages, and usually they set them up in the middle of open high ground that provides a view of the surrounding countryside; nearby are a few brooks that serve them as a natural source of water. They clear a space in the middle of all this for their assemblies. The settlements most vulnerable to enemy attack are fortified with a high stockade made of a triple row of posts, interlaced and sheathed with tough bark. They often have small entrenchments or

---

244 The distinction is between Indians who stay in one area only as long as they have animals to hunt and fertile land, before relocating and resettling in a new area, and hunter-gatherer natives who are more nomadic and get their food from hunting wild animals and picking available wild berries, and the like. Some writers believe the quasi-sedentary Huron, for example, relocated every eight to ten years, depending on the exhaustion-rate of local resources. But these distinctions are crucial in both ancient and modern discussions of land-ownership and "sovereignty," as it is difficult to imagine granting permanent rights of land ownership, or "sovereignty" over an area of land to a people who may once have farmed it or hunted it out, but then vacated it forever, just because they were once there in the past.

secondary defensive structures that they fill with stones they use to defend themselves from the heights of their fort, and storage for water which they use to put out fires. You can only go in or out of the fort by a single opening, and there is always a large space between the stockade and their houses.

The houses rarely exceed a hundred in number. Each house has from three to seven fireplaces, and most of them house several families. They are built close to each other, which always means there is a danger of fire. The pathways between them are not lined up, because each person can build where he wants, as it pleases him. There is no point in looking for either art, nor comfort, nor magnificence in such places: they are made in the perfect image of man in the infancy of the world.[245] Large posts covered with bark are the main building material. This bark takes a long time to prepare, and is taken from the trees when the sap is running. After having stripped off the outside of the tree, and because the bark is at first too uneven, the strips are pressed together so they don't curl in an undesirable way; then they are left to dry. The poles are prepared in the same way, as is the wood necessary for the construction of the building. And when the time comes to begin the work, the young of the village are called upon. A feast is held to entice them; and in less than two days the work is finished, less due to diligence than to the multitude of workers. It is up to individuals to outfit the inside of each cabin according to what they want and the conveniences they consider suitable.

The space in the middle is always the gathering spot, down each side of which a bench is extended for sleeping, and for sitting. It has enough height to protect everyone from dampness, but not enough, for all that, to be unaffected by the smoke, which is always unbearable when you stand up, or are elevated just a little. They spread their rush-mats and furs, and sleep in the same blankets that they wear in the daytime. They have never used pillows. But since being around Europeans, they make a pillow out of a small piece of wood in a rolled-up mat, or of leather padded with deer or moose hair. The bark that is used for the upper surface of the bench and for the canopy, also serves as a closet and a food-locker. All the housekeeping tools are visible, and in the space between one bench and another there are large tubs full of kernels of corn.

The dirtiness of the cabins and the infections which are an unavoidable consequence, would be, for anyone except a Savage, a real torment. Try to imagine where anyone would be able to go to get away among people who only change their rags when they are in tatters. To be truthful, they bathe in

---

245 For European travelers, this sort of description was part of the lure of the exotic, of self-discovery, and the search for an answer to the central question: "Who were we, when we were this undeveloped?" Though they used the word *uncivilized*, rather than the less judgemental term, *undeveloped*.

the river every day in summer, but then they rub themselves all over with oil or animal fat. In the winter, they just live in their own grime, and no matter what the season, you can't go into a home without being driven out by the smell.

There is a door at each end of the cabin, but you never see a lock. At other times, when they go off into the countryside, they are comfortable with just blocking their doors with wood to guard against dogs getting in. They live thus, with no mistrust among them. If any of them are suspicious, they take their belongings to a friend's house, or bury them in a hole covered with their mats. Their proximity to Europeans has taught them that the things they lock up with the greatest care, are not always safe.[246]

Their Land Use, Vegetable Gardens, and More

As these people never fertilize their fields or let them lie fallow, they are soon exhausted, which obliges them to clear other fields in fresh ground, and by necessity to move their habitations elsewhere. Another reason for doing this, is the scarcity of wood, which the women take it upon themselves to collect.[247] The longer a village remains in the same place, the farther away the collectible wood, and after a certain number of years, they can no longer keep up this effort. Then it is necessary to find another spot, and it is the men who are in charge of searching this out. This, they try to do in the neighbouring forests, to save themselves the trouble of hauling everything a long way.

Even though the Europeans have taught them how to use iron[248] to cut, split, and saw wood, most of them stick to their ancient method of strangling the tree with a cord, stripping the bark off, letting it dry out, and eroding the trunk little by little by inserting a small fire into it. They also have stone hatchets made from a piece of very hard rock, that they sharpen by rubbing against a piece of harder rock, which in time and with a lot of work provides them with something in the shape of an ordinary hatchet. The life of a man

---

246 In this passage, Delaporte takes another swipe at the corruption and mistrust that exists among Europeans of his time, and suggests that the natural trust of the Savages is being eroded by this contact.

247 The most reasonable explanation for the fact that Canada's Indians never developed techniques of fallowing, rotation, irrigation, or effective fertilization of crops, is that they never had to: moving the whole village to a new fertile location supplied the resources they needed. Nevertheless, a persistent question must have arisen from the fact that Europeans existed in the same primitive condition as Indians ten thousand years ago. So why did Europeans develop such impressive political and legal systems, tools, and technologies, but Indians did not?

248 A key distinction between the technologically advanced, and the primitive, is the use of metals, and metallurgy. North American Indians, in this respect at least, were a primitive stone-age culture until the arrival of Europeans.

barely suffices to perfect such a tool; and such an item, even one still rough and imperfect, is a precious heritage for an entire family. It is also difficult to fit a handle onto a piece of finished stone. They pick out a young tree, cut off the top, and as if they wanted to graft it, they make a slit, into which they insert a part of the stone. After a while, the drying and shrinking wooden shaft holds the stone so tightly it will never come out. Then they just cut the shaft to the length they prefer.

The Huron women, just like the Iroquois women, do most of the work in the countryside. The grain they plant is corn — otherwise known as Indian corn, or Turkish corn.[249] This constitutes the main food of all settled peoples from one end to the other of North America. Once the snow has melted, they begin their work. The first reshaping of the fields is to gather the stubble and burn it. Then they work the ground to receive the grain. They don't make use of a plough, nor of a lot of other work tools, which don't seem necessary to them and are not even known. A piece of curved wood suffices, with which they turn over the earth and work it lightly. Then they set it up in small round clumps of earth about three feet in diameter and make nine or ten holes in each one into which they throw a few grains of corn which they then cover with the same earth they dug up to make the holes. They do all the heavy work as a group, moving from one field to another, to lend help.

What they own is not separated from other fields either by fences or trenches, and it all looks like the same field. However, there are never fights over boundaries, which they always seem to know how to recognize. The mistress of the field in which a person works distributes to each the amount of grain necessary to seed the part of the field assigned to them. They plant beans beside the corn, which serves as a support for the beanstalks.[250] The Missionary believes that the Savages got the bean plant from us because it doesn't differ much from our green beans. But it is surprising how little use they make of our peas, which have flourished in Canada to a degree not seen in those of Europe. A black, light soil is prepared for pumpkins and watermelons, the seeds for which are started inside the cabin.

These same women take great care to keep their fields neat and to remove weeds entirely until harvest time. This work is also done in common, and

---

249 This is what is otherwise called *maize*, or what English-speaking North Americans call "corn". Most commonly farmed today are crops of so-called "cow-corn" that is used as cattle feed, but is not eaten by humans, and "sweet corn", much loved by humans. This translator's farming friend says racoons will not touch cow-corn. But if there is one ear of sweet corn in a hundred acres of cow corn, they will find it.

250 This custom of planting beanstalks that would climb on corn plants, served also to enrich a soil that the maize plant alone would otherwise more quickly deplete. The customary "three sisters" of Northeastern Indian agriculture usually planted together on small mounds, were squash, corn, and beans.

to make certain that the distribution is equal, they carry a little bundle of coloured sticks with them that mark out the ground they are working. When harvest time comes, they gather the corn, and braid the leaves together, just as we do with onions. Then they spread the corn on large poles above the entry to the cabins. All this is then celebrated with a party and a feast that they mount in the night, and this is the only occasion where the men, who do not take part either in the work or the harvest, are summoned by the women to share their work with them.

To preserve the fruit and vegetables during winter, they rely upon a kind of in-ground granary from which they take daily provisions. These are large holes about four or five feet deep, lined with tree bark, and covered with earth above. The foodstuffs are kept there and are not touched by the frost — the snow covering them from above protects them from it. As for the corn, it is dried on pieces of wood that surround the open space of the cabin. Then the kernels are stripped off, and put in large boxes. Savages prepare it in a variety of ways designed to eliminate defects. While it is still tender, they brown it without separating it from the ear, and it is then when it is the most tasty. They have a special kind that they call *flowered corn*, because it explodes when heated, and opens up like a flower.[251] They use this to honour people they consider distinguished.

Their Porridge, Eating Customs, and Starvation

I have mentioned that their porridge is nothing but a soup made with this commodity. Each morning the women prepare it for the whole family: it is passed around on as many little plates made of bark as there are persons to feed, and each one eats it when he wishes. Hunger is the only clock by which, night or day, these meals are governed. Other than these individual portions, a lot is put aside for any visitors who may show up, whether strangers, or members of the village. Whoever arrives is well-received, and they have barely entered the cabin when they are given a serving of this porridge, which they eat informally, before even saying why they have come.

This porridge is a very light nourishment, and these Indians admit it does not satisfy them unless they add some meat or fish to give it body and taste. With a little foresight and care, they will be able to procure this kind of seasoning throughout the year; however, they don't seem to know anything about managing supplies and of stocking up for the future. The accepted custom is to eat everything at hand when they have it, as if they wanted for nothing, and to suffer from hunger in times of famine. The law of civility and decorum established among them is that whenever someone has good

---

251 This is our "popcorn".

fishing or a good hunt, he shares it with the whole village, and ends up empty-handed due to his generosity. To do otherwise is to dishonour himself.

If this distribution to all has been made and there is still a certain quantity left over, he hosts one of those feasts where everyone comes to eat, and the hunger begins again the next day. It is during hunting season when they are the most vulnerable, and every year there are a few who die. If a hungry family meets up with another family that has not yet finished all its food, the latter do not wait to be asked: they immediately share the little they have left with the newcomers, even at the risk of dying of hunger themselves the next day. Behold the stupidity of these rough people: they dare to charge with inhumanity the very wise, intelligent, and reasonable reply of the ant to the grasshopper, which is the first thing that we — spiritual people, civilized, and humane — learn by heart as children.[252]

The need to which these people find themselves reduced by these kinds of plenty, obliges them to eat everything without distinction, and they find everything they eat to be good. Just as in a time of abundance they do not give the fresh meat time to cure and become tender, and they throw it alive, so to speak, in the pot to boil; they see no problem with serving it smelly and almost rotten. They throw whole frogs into the pot and then swallow them without disgust. They dry out the entrails of a deer without emptying them first, and find them just as tasty as we do the sweetmeats of a goose. They drink the fat of a bear, and seal, and eel oil, and the tallow of our candles is a real treat for them. They have a kind of corn they allow to rot in the swamps, and which they love to eat with a passion. Once they pull it out of the mud, they lick the smelly rotten water that runs out with pleasure. They eat all sorts of bitter and wild fruit, without even giving them the time to ripen, for fear that others may beat them to it and take them first. To harvest all the fruit from a tree, they cut it down at the base first. Some call this the image of despotism.

A Culture Shock for the Missionary

What revolts a European the most who finds himself among these barbarians, is when he finds himself obliged to eat with them. Nothing, in effect,

---

252 The reference is to Aesop's *Fable, The Ant and the Grasshopper* as follows: "The Ants were spending a fine winter's day drying grain collected in the summertime. A Grasshopper, dying from hunger, passed by and earnestly begged for a little food. The Ants asked him, "Why did you not treasure up food during the summer?" He replied, "I didn't have enough time. I passed the days in singing." They then said in derision: "If you were foolish enough to sing all the summer, you must dance supper-less to bed in the winter." In this example we see two incompatible moral foundations in conflict. The first seems to be a native ethic that privileges selflessness — the willingness of one person to share with another in need, even at risk to himself. The second privileges the notion of reason as a means of survival for all, even if it means some may die as a means to this more secure end for all.

is more disgusting. After having filled a pot with meat, they make it boil at most three quarters of an hour, remove it from the fire, serve it on bowls made of bark, and share it with everyone in the cabin. Each person bites into it as if into a piece of bread. About this, the Missionary told me that the Hurons, noticing his repugnance, asked him why he was not eating? "You have to overcome this," they added. "Is this so difficult for a man who prays so perfectly? We overcome a lot to believe in what you tell us, even though we don't see evidence of it." And so, the Missionary, told me, "there was nothing more to debate. You just had to do as they do, to earn their confidence."

Of Plants, Threads, and the Grapevine

Among all that this country produces, you will find neither hemp, nor flax. The ground there naturally produces lots of fibrous plants that the women make use of without a lot of effort. They draw out a kind of thread of white wood bark from which they make lots of little things, especially bags to hold food. They weave the hair of deer or buffalo, or other animals into them, stained with different colours from the juices of certain plants. In place of thread, they use dried gut and filaments taken from the nerves of animals, tiny strings of very thin animal hide, or tiny roots that they use cleanly and with great skill.

The grapevine is not unknown in Canada. It grows in the forest, in certain regions where we see as many as we do trees, to the top of which it climbs. They have a large base and grow many grapes, but the berries are only as large as a pea, because the vines are not trimmed or cultivated. They are barely ripe, when they become food for the bears, who will climb even the largest trees to get them. The birds manage to harvest all the grapes in the entire forest.

Indian Maple Syrup

If these people have never developed the art of making wine, like us, they know how to get a syrup from the maple tree that is delicious, and they make a sugar with it almost as good as our own.[253] As soon as the sap begins to

---

[253] Although it is often believed to be a primordial Indian custom, the Indians of North America almost certainly learned how to make maple syrup sugar from Europeans. The Brazilian sugar trade was ruined by the Dutch in 1635, and in order to satisfy European demand the islands of the West Indies used slave labour. The monopolies formed there drove out the smallholders, who then migrated to New England, where about 1,200 of them were settled between 1643 and 1647, a century before this book was published. Delaporte took much of his information about Indian maple-sugaring from Pierre Francois Xavier de Charlevoix who, in his *Journal of a Voyage to North America* (written in 1720, published in 1744, translated by Louise Kellog, 1923), writes that although Indians made use of the sap of the maple, "It is certain they were ignorant of the art of making sugar from it, which we have since learnt [taught] them" (p.192). See: Carol Mason,

run, they make a notch in the trunk of the tree, and by means of a piece they insert in it, and over which the sap runs as on a gutter, it is received into a pail set below. For it to run in abundance, there has to have been lots of snow on the ground; it must be below freezing the night before; and the weather must be calm, and not too cold. For to the extent that the sap thickens, it runs less freely, and after a while, it stops entirely. Maple sap is very refreshing, and leaves a taste of sugar in the mouth that is quite agreeable. It is also really good for breathing and your lungs, and no matter how much you drink, it never does any harm. If it is boiled a few times, it becomes a syrup that is drunk with pleasure; and to make sugar it suffices to let it boil until it gets to the right consistency. It purifies all by itself without adding anything else to it. You just have to be careful not to cook it too much, and to skim off the foam properly. If it is left to harden too much as a syrup, it becomes oily and takes on the taste of honey. The plane tree, the ash, and the walnut tree also give a kind of sap which the Savages make into a syrup, but it produces less, and is not as good.

Poison Ivy

A plant that is unique in Canada is called Poison Ivy, the name of which is not sufficiently expressive to communicate all the effects it can produce. They are more, or less noticeable according to the temperament of those who go near it. Some, just from looking at it, will come down with a very violent fever, along with scabs that are very bothersome and an incredible itchiness all over their body. For others, it only bothers them if they touch it, and the part touched looks like leprosy. The only remedy is patience, for it eventually dissipates.

Ginseng, that celebrated and marvellous plant, is found in many places in Canada. It has virtues there, and produces prodigies of wellbeing just like in China. The Americans say it can render women fertile, just as the Chinese swear it makes men vigorous: it is as much sought after in Peking as in Quebec.

I remain, etc.

At Quebec, April 8, 1749.

"A Sweet Small Something: Maple Sugaring in the New World" in James A. Clifton, *The Invented Indian: Cultural Fictions and Government Policies* (New Brunswick, USA: Transaction Publishers, 2007), pp. 91-105.

Letter 107

CANADA ~ CONTINUED

I AM far more interested, Madam, in helping you understand the Savages, than the country they inhabit.[254] Nevertheless, I need to say a few words about it, and I will begin talking about the village of Lorette.[255] It is a journey of about three leagues from Quebec City, and the Huron Christians have a chapel there built on the model of the one of which it carries the name. It looks quite the same, and insofar as it was possible, the same dimensions were kept. The support of the faithful there is quite impressive, and almost as many miracles are reported there as at its namesake in Italy.[256] It is situated in a deserted and wild place, where the devotions of the inhabitants is just like that of the ancient recluses of the Egyptian desert.[257] They have the simplicity and frankness of those who first inhabited the world, a lively faith, and a moral innocence that is incredible. They sing the prayers and the canticles of the church in their own language in two choirs, the men on one side, the women on the other, and the fervour and the simplicity that shines through in all their religious exercises is unmatched. It is true that

---

254 Here, Delaporte underlines his critique of all travel writers who preceded him, which he emphasized in his "Notice to Readers": he does not want to dwell on descriptions of the physical land. He committed himself, rather, to sharing insights into the lives and customs of the people of each country.

255 L'Ancienne-Lorette (Old Lorette was first established in 1697), is today a suburb of and an enclave within Quebec City. It was merged with Quebec City on January 1, 2002 as part of the 2000–2006 municipal reorganization in Quebec, but after a 2004 referendum it was reconstituted as a separate city on January 1, 2006. Its history dates back to 1674 when a group of Hurons fleeing war with the Iroquois settled here under the protection of the French. They left after a few decades and French settlers took over the land.

256 The Holy House of Loreto, Italy, is one of the most revered Marian shrines in the world. Since medieval times, the Holy House has been believed to be the very home in which the Virgin Mary lived, conceived and raised the young Jesus, and that it was miraculously transported to Italy.

257 The Thebaid is a region of ancient Egypt comprising the thirteen southernmost nomes (pastoral regions) of Upper Egypt, from Abydos to Aswan.

the care taken to ensure that there is no slackening of the faith could not be greater. Intoxicating beverages are banned by a solemn public vow, and any transgressions are punished with public penitence. Relapses result in banishment of the guilty one to a place that serves as an exile and for piety. Peace and duty reign equally everywhere there, and the entire village seems to live as one family according to the maxims of the Gospel. Christianity destroys the arrogance and the spirit of independence that characterizes their nation, and has turned them into men who submit to all the practices it has pleased missionaries to prescribe for them.

Christians Among the Huron

Accompanied by a man of this faith, you may judge whether or not I was well-received by these good people.[258] After a full military reception by the Warriors, and a welcome by the crowd, we began a general feast, where I paid the bill, and received all the honours. The men ate on one side, and the women on the other. The women gave witness to their gratitude through their silence and modesty; the men, with songs and dances. At first, they sat on the ground like monkeys; then, from time to time, one of them got up, moved slowly to the middle of the crowd, turned his head from one side to another, hummed a tune, and expressed himself in poorly-articulated words. Sometimes he sang a war song, sometimes a song of death, for as they don't drink any wine, they don't sing drinking songs, and are not advised to sing about their love lives. When one finishes, another takes his place, and this goes on until the guests thank them; which would happen earlier without a little indulgence. The speech given on these occasions, is what is most worthwhile: the reason for the feast is explained in a few words, and praises of the one who paid for it all are not forgotten.

The Missionaries had a lot of difficulty at first, persuading this people about the maxims of the Gospel. The difficulty was not in getting them to listen; but one ought not to believe they are convinced of something just because they listen and seem to approve of what has been taught. In general, they all fear quarreling, and whether due to kindness, convenience, or laziness, they always give the impression of being persuaded by things they don't understand, and don't want to understand. We have seen them attend our churches with a diligence, modesty, and show of reverence that indicated the most sincere desire to know and embrace the truth, and then leave, and say

---

258 In this passage, Delaporte goes one step further in personalizing his narrative technique by encouraging the woman to whom his putative letter is sent to judge his reception in the event he is about to relate. This gives his readers almost a sense of eavesdropping on a very private conversation.

to the Missionary: "You had no one to pray with you; I felt for you in your loneliness, and thought I should keep you company. But now that I see others are prepared to render you the same service, it's okay for me to leave you." Many have gone so far as to ask for and to receive baptism, and after having fulfilled all the duties of a good Christian successfully for quite a while, they announced that they only did it to please the Father who was pressing them to change their religion.

However, it is not always a proof that they are not convinced of the truths we teach them just because they refuse to practice them. We have seen those for whom no doubt whatsoever lingered on the articles of our faith, and who even made their vows publicly, but who still did not want to convert. One of them was on his deathbed, when some fire fell onto his blanket. As soon as everyone jumped up to put the fire out, he exclaimed: "It's not worth it," he said. "I know I ought to burn in hell forever, so a little sooner, or a little later: is that worth all the trouble you are making for yourself?"

But it took a long time to extract vows from them in favour of our dogmas. First of all, the Hurons would come up with arguments that would disconcert the Missionaries. "We agree," they would say, "that what you teach us is very beautiful, and very true. But it is only good for you people, who have nothing in common with us. Your way of life, your language, your dress, are different from ours, so why would your prayers not differ just as much? You don't find it so bad that we dress in the manner of our country, that we live on what it produces, and that we speak the language natural to us. In the same way, we approve that you are preserving your own ways; we do not ask you to change your culture for ours. If the Great Spirit had wanted us all — you, and us — to live in the same paradise after death, why would he not have had us all born and living in the same place and the same way, here below? He wants us to be happy in our own way, as he does you in yours, and he would not have put us in places so distant from each other, if his plan had been to unite us. None of us has the ability to cross the seas to attract you to come to our homeland, so why do you go to this trouble to lead us to your heaven? Just ask yourselves: do we exert the same pressure to lead you to ours? The huge expanse of water that naturally separates us seems to say that all men are not made to live in the same home in this world, and nothing proves that they are meant to live together in the next." As firm as they were in this principle, it was difficult to move them from it, and so their conversion was a matter of grace, rather than of reasoning.[259]

---

[259] This is an interesting side-comment. Delaporte, and the Jesuits who came to Canada to convert the Indians were Catholics. Much of the post-Reformation distinction between many Protestant Christians, and Catholic Christians, is the distinction between faith and reason. Many Protestants stake their beliefs upon the motto; *sola fide* (by "faith alone"), whereas in the Catholic

Huron Intelligence and Craftiness

Of all the people of Canada, it is the Hurons who are the most intelligent. They can carry dissimulation to incredible excesses, and this characteristic has long since contributed to make them feared, as has their hard work, their fertile inventiveness, their eloquence, and their acts of bravery. In a word, this is the one nation of the continent in which we notice the greatest faults, and the greatest virtues.[260] Their true name is the *Wendat*; the name *Huron* was given them by the French who, upon seeing these barbarians with their short hair put up in such a bizarre fashion, cried out the first time they saw them: "*quelles hures!*" and got used to calling them Hurons.[261] For a long time they have had the reputation of being bold and crafty thieves; and even today, even among those who show the most disinterest and faithfulness, you have to watch over your food supplies with extreme care, as these are a temptation for Savages who are always hungry and accustomed to thinking of everything necessary for life as their common property.[262]

In addition to the obstacles to their conversion that arise from the character and prejudices of these people, we can add others that come from their Tricksters that are no less difficult to overcome. These charlatans, so fearful of losing the esteem assumed in them due to the practice of their art, would (if Missionaries became assigned to their country) attempt to render them odious. They have figured out that they would have a lot less difficulty in doing this, if many of the Savages already had the notion that the French religion does not agree with Indians. So because the Jesuits were obliged to hide somewhere to say their daily prayers, the Tricksters made the locals believe that the prayers of the Jesuits were evil spells. Soon, everything the Hurons saw in their hands which they did not understand the use of, was, according to them, something destined to attract evil. The Jesuits had to get rid of a pendulum clock and a weather vane, just because the Indians swore that the first would bring death, and the second, bad weather.

---

tradition, especially since the adoption of the work of Saint Thomas Aquinas (1225–1274) as the central theological work of the Catholic religion, the belief that God can be known through reason as well, has been central to Catholic doctrine (see Thomas's "Five Ways" to prove the existence of God). Perhaps Delaporte is saying that the Indians seemed impervious to logical reasoning?

260 That all human beings have great faults and great virtues, and that the one true faith is the only means to steer them away from the former and toward the latter, would have been accepted doctrine in catholic France of the time.

261 The name is derived from the old French word *huron*, meaning "a bristly or unkempt knave," and was apparently applied to the Hurons by the first French in Canada.

262 In this comment Delaporte could be issuing a warning to French readers about the negative social and economic consequences of the egalitarianism that in his time was part of a raging public discussion in France: when people believe that all property should be held in common, expect a reign of thievery.

Add to these difficulties the ones that arise from imposing such strict laws and demanding obligations on men who derive their glory (and for whom happiness consists) in not being bothered about much, and in following all the inclinations of their nature. When we praise the superiority of the Christian God over other gods, they reply: "Each nation has its gods, and even if our misfortune is to have gods weaker than yours, ought we, for that reason, to abandon them?"

The constancy and courage of the Missionaries, the delicate reasoning they placed before their listeners, and the unshakeable patience with which they endured the most undignified treatments, would eventually efface the angry attitudes expressed toward these religious men. Not only would they succeed in calming the initial angriness of this embittered and irritable people, but they would even manage to become popular with them, and make them obey.

Christianity at Quebec

Perhaps nothing contributed more to the progress of the Christian religion in Canada than the creation of a Jesuit College at Quebec. René de Rohault, the eldest son of the Marquis de Gamache,[263] having obtained the consent of his family to enter the Society of Jesus; and his parents who loved him so tenderly — knowing that he so ardently wished to found a College in this part of America, granted him this satisfaction, and for this offered him ten thousand *ecus*,[264] which was accepted. The Savages, on whom a great deal of effort was expended to make them see the use they would get from such a settlement, came to it from all the regions around the capital. As no effort was spared to feed them well whenever they came to the College, they hastened to entrust their children to those who were so willing to feed them and raise them. In this way, little by little, they were made more sociable, and to the extent that they became attached to the French, they were less distant from the Christian verities.

What added to their confidence in the Missionaries, was an epidemic sickness that spread from one village to all the others, and threatened the whole nation with death.[265] It was a kind of dysentery which, in a matter days led

---

263 Though a considerable sum was granted by Rene de Rohault to foster Jesuit establishments in Quebec as early as 1626, it was not until the 18th March, 1637, that the authority to build on, "twelve arpents of land, in the vicinity of Fort St.Louis" was granted to the Jesuit Fathers.

264 Any of various old French coins, especially a silver five-franc piece — from Old French *escu*, which is from the Latin *scūtum*, for *shield* (from the shield stamped on the coin). The *ecu* was also a European Currency Unit based on the composite value of several different currencies in the European Union, and it functioned as both the reserve asset, and the accounting unit of the European Monetary System, to be replaced by the *euro* only in 1999.

265 The devastation of European diseases to which they had no immunity that was suffered by native populations in the New World, which began with contact with the Whiteman, amounted

most of those attacked by it to the tomb. The French were not exempt — but they all got better, which produced two good results. The first was that those who believed these sorts of events to be evils brought by the Missionaries, disabused themselves of this view when they saw them struck by the same sickness. The second, was that these barbarians learned better how to deal with their sickness by following the same treatment as the French.

There was interest in their conversion in other places besides Canada; and in Paris, and throughout the kingdom, there was a saintly eagerness to contribute to this. Many communities engaged in public prayers, and all the grandees of the Court became of the same view. There was a proposal to establish the Ursulines and the Hospitallers[266] at Quebec, and among the girls of these two institutions, it was a question of which was preferred. The Duchess of Aiguillon[267] wanted to be the founder of the Hotel Dieu hospital, and asked for the help of the religious women of Dieppe, who were ready to leave on the first ships. A young widow, Madam de la Peltrie,[268] offered to take charge of the Ursulines, and consecrated all her worldly goods as well as herself to this good cause. From Alençon, where she lived, she got herself to Paris to set up the affairs of the foundation, then went to Tours to look for religious women, and finally she got to Dieppe, where she embarked with the Hospitallers and the several Jesuits who were in charge.

---

to one of the largest unintended near-extinctions in human history. This was devastating, for as Buffon had observed, the native populations of North America were already quite small and Indians did not seem to reproduce as fast as Europeans. Krech, in *The Ecological Indian* writes that "In 1700, 92 million people lived in Europe and only 2 million in North America, and one century later, the figures were 145 million, and 5 million" (p.94). He points out that Europeans who began settling there in serious numbers had come to a "widowed" land. Some scholars believe that the Indian population of North America today is about what it was at the time of Columbus. The contentious claims of more than 600 Canadian Indian nations to "sovereignty", when most of their nations consist of fewer than a thousand Indians each, provokes understandable questions about the meaning of the term *sovereignty*, for they are really what one scholar has described as "bantam" nations. Especially disturbing to many is their apartheid-like insistence on blood rights and blood tribal membership

266 The term Ursulines refers to a number of religious institutes of the Catholic Church. The best known group was founded in 1535 at Brescia, Italy, by St. Angela Merici, for the education of girls and the care of the sick and needy. The Religious Hospitallers of Saint Joseph (also known as Réligieuses hospitalières de Saint-Joseph) was a religious order founded in La Fleche, France by the Venerable Jerome le Royer de la Dauversiere, and Venerable Marie de la Ferre.

267 Marie de Vignerot de Pontcourlay, Marquise of Combalet and Duchesse d'Aiguillon; niece of Cardinal Richelieu. Born 1604, died at Paris, 1675.

268 Mme de La Peltrie was influenced by the *Jesuit Relations* to devote her life and fortune to North American Indian missions. Eager to leave for New France, Mme de La Peltrie went to Paris and consulted M. Vincent de Paul. When she was unable to find space for her baggage on the ships leaving for America, she chartered a vessel at her own expense and loaded it with provisions and furnishings. She arrived in New France with a number of Ursulines, including Marie de l'Incarnation, who was to be the religious founder of the Order of Ursulines.

Everything was done to make the Savages understand how important it was that they only had their interests at heart, for these same women, raised in plenty, and so delicately, had left behind a sweet and quiet life, and exposed themselves to the perils of the sea to come and instruct Indian children and look after the sick.

The day of their arrival was a festival for the town of Quebec. All work ceased. All the shops were closed. The Governor welcomed these Christian heroines on the river bank, at the head of troops in full dress, and to the sound of cannon booming. These young girls, in the first throes of their joy, kissed the ground of which they had so long been dreaming, and that they vowed to soak with the sweat of their work, and even with their blood, if necessary. They were led off the ship among the cheers of the crowd, straight to the cathedral, where the *Te Deum* was sung as a thanksgiving. The French, milling about with the Savages, and even the unbelievers mixed in with Christians, did not hesitate to shout cries of joy and to shower blessings upon them.

A Christian Tribe!

No other person in France could assist more efficaciously with the zeal of these Missionaries than the Commander of Sillery.[269] He came up with the idea of forming a special tribe of Savages made up solely of Christians, who could be protected both from the threats of the Iroquois (by way of the help that we could send them from Quebec); and from hunger, by way of the care we would take to show them how to cultivate the earth.[270] With this in mind, he sent workers to Canada, who picked out a good place to live on the north bank of the St. Lawrence River — a place that has ever since borne the name of Sillery. The Hurons, who were not informed of this project, were keen on its being done, and asked the Missionaries about it. But the Jesuits behaved as if they didn't know the intentions of the Commander, and wanted to wait

---

269 Sillery, now a suburb of Quebec City, was named for Noël Brûlart de Sillery (1577–1640), a Knight of Malta, and a wealthy and successful French diplomat who renounced worldly goods to became a Catholic priest. He provided the funds for the establishment of this settlement for native American converts to Catholicism in 1638. The settlement became the home of up to 40 Algonquin Christian families, who lived there most of the year, excluding the hunting season. Missionaries to New France, such as Jacques Gravier, studied with the natives at Sillery to learn their languages before going to more distant settlements. By the early 18th century he had compiled a nearly 600-page dictionary of Kaskaskia Illinois-French. Many of the community's natives eventually fell victim to epidemics of European infectious diseases, to which they had no natural immunity, and the settlement was largely depopulated by the late 1680s.

270 As mentioned in previous notes, Indians in Canada did not know how to work agricultural land so as not to exhaust it. Instead, they would stay in one location where good soil, hunting, and wood-gathering for fuel were plentiful, until all were exhausted, and then move to a new location and start over.

for his consent. Of course they knew very well this was his plan; but their caution seemed all the more necessary, as the Savages persuade themselves either that we owe them something, or that it is in our best interest to grant them, what we give them too easily.

Consent was finally given, and a dozen Huron families professing the Christian religion, took possession of the location and began living there. They were not alone for long. In a few years this dwelling place became a populated community that gradually accustomed itself to all the duties of civilized life. The proximity of Quebec served to shape these new inhabitants, and inspired in them the kind of polity commensurate with their nature.

On the Way to Trois-Rivieres

In leaving Lorette, we took the road to Trois Rivieres, a small village in a charming spot, about twenty-five leagues from Quebec. It is built on a sandy hillside that is only barren in the spot it occupies. In all other respects, it is surrounded by everything that makes a place to live enjoyable, and a city opulent. The St. Lawrence River is at its feet, and beyond it we see only cultivated countryside, fertile, and crowned with the most beautiful forests. The three rivers that mix their water with the St. Lawrence not far from here, give their name to this village. It owes its existence to the trade it began to do in this spot with the Savages of different nations at the colony's beginning. The French built a fort there, with its own Governor, and ever since it has been one of the most important forts in New France. Today there are no more than eight hundred persons, among which are the Récollets,[271] the Hospitallers, a General Staff, and a court of law of which the President has the title of Lieutenant General. Nearby, the village has a very productive iron mine, and Lake Saint-Pierre, which is seven leagues long and produces excellent fish.

During my stay in Trois-Rivieres, the delegates of a Huron village brought in some very beautiful pelts, which they exchanged for brandy. "Follow them to their village," the Missionary said to me, "and you will see to what excesses these people surrender themselves on account of their liquor. Each day they distribute as much to each person as is necessary to inebriate them, and all of it is drunk in less than two days. They begin at sunset, and the whole night the countryside echoes with horrible shouts. You would think all the devils had escaped from hell, or all the inhabitants were bitterly at each others' throats.

---

271 The Récollets, a reformed branch of the Franciscan family, came to France at the end of the sixteenth century. Their main objective was to observe the Rule of St Francis more strictly, and like other semi-autonomous branches, they came under the minister-general of the Franciscans. They came to New France in 1615 and were present at various times in Acadia, Newfoundland and Quebec.

We set out on Lake Saint Pierre to get to the Richelieu Islands, which are at the other end of the lake. This area has for a long time been the theatre for many bloody scenes during the Iroquois war.[272] They used these islands for ambushes and for retreat. They committed cruelties there, the telling of which would horrify you. I prefer to tell you about the intrepid and valuable actions of two Canadians who deserve to be remembered unto posterity. I will only tell you what the Missionary witnessed, without altering his story.

"To protect themselves from the fury of the Iroquois, forts of a certain kind were built in each Parish where the inhabitants could take refuge at the first alarm. Sentinels kept watch day and night, with a few cannons to warn the enemy to stay back, or else to call for help. These forts were only large enclosures surrounded with stockades that had a few small fortifications within. The church and the Master's house were enclosed, and there was still enough room, in case of need, to shelter the women, children, and animals.

The Assault on Madame de Verchères

"A few Iroquois, knowing that Madame de Verchères,[273] the Lady of the Parish of that name, near the Richelieu Islands, was there almost alone, decided to scale the stockade. A few shots from a rifle that were fired as soon as the first sounds were heard, sent them scattering; but they soon came back, and were once again repulsed; and what caused them the greatest astonishment, was to see only one woman, and to see her everywhere. That woman was Madam de Verchères, who came out with such a determined look on her face that you would have thought she had an entire garrison behind her. She fought in this way for two days, with a courage and a presence of mind that would have made an old soldier proud. And in the end she made the enemy retreat, for fear of having their retreat blocked by a rescue force that was soon to arrive.

Bravery of the Master's Daughter

"A few years later, another war party from the same nation, much larger than the first, appeared in view of the same fort while the inhabitants were busy

---

272 In support of his Huron and Algonquin trading partners, Samuel de Champlain shot and killed two Iroquois chiefs in 1609 at Ticonderoga, near the lake in Upper New York State that now bears his name. Some argue that this incident helped touch off a long, bitter war between the French and the Iroquois, others, that it created a brief period of peaceful relations. Like many of North America's Indians, the Iroquois possessed a strong military organization, and through skilful use of ambush and knowledge of the terrain, they nearly destroyed New France in the first half of the 1600s. After close to a century of warfare between 1609 and 1701, the Treaty of Montreal established peace between the Iroquois and New France.

273 Jarret de Verchères, Marie-Madeleine (b.1678, at Verchères, Quebec, d.1747). Delaporte prints her name without a *grave* accent over the second *e*.

in the countryside. The Iroquois, finding them all dispersed and without any defence, seized them one after the other and marched them toward the fort. The Master's daughter,[274] sixteen years of age, was two hundred paces from it. At the first shout she heard, she ran back to the fort for safety. But the Savages followed her, and one of them caught up to her just as she put her foot in the door. But as he had seized her only by her shawl, she let it go, escaped, and closed the door after her. There was only one soldier in the fort, and a group of women who, at the sight of their husbands who were held prisoner, let out cries of lamentation. But this young woman, having lost neither her heart nor her head, began by tucking up her hair and tying it in a knot, took a hat and a man's clothing, and then locked all the women up, because their groaning and tears would only encourage the enemy. Then, she shot off a cannon, and a few rifles, and showed herself, at one moment with her soldier, at another on one fortification, then on a different one, changing her clothes once again, and always shooting so successfully that the Iroquois believed there were a lot of people in the fort, and by the time a detachment, alerted by the cannon shot, advanced to rescue the fort, the enemy had already disappeared.

Wealth and Poverty in the New World

"In terms of its revenue, the fortress of Verchères is insignificant," continued the Missionary, "and in general, the lords of the Parish are not wealthy anywhere in Canada. As this country was only one big forest when the French began to settle here, those to whom the manors were given were not the sort of people capable of improving their value on their own. These were the officers and the gentlemen of communities that did not have sufficient funds to maintain the number of workers necessary. So it was essential to settle residents here who, before being able to gather up the necessities of life, had to work very hard, and put up all the money themselves. Thus, they could not hire themselves out to the Lords except for a modest fee, such that with the Lord's income,[275] which was not much, the grist-mill rights and the

---

274 Madeleine de Verchères.

275 Habitants (settlers, farmers) in New France were largely defined by their relationship to a seigneur (a Lord). Seigneurs were primarily nobles or clergy members from France who were given large pieces of land that were referred to as fiefs or seigneuries. Such a system created a traditional peasant-lord relationship by establishing a landed elite. The habitant-seigneurial relationship that emerged in New France, however, had a few key differences from those in France. The wealth of the land was primarily built through its development by the habitants. When a habitant was granted the title deed to a lot, he had to agree to accept a variety of annual charges and restrictions. Rent was the most important of these, and could be set in money, produce, or labour. The seigneur was obligated to build a gristmill for his tenants, and they in turn were required to grind their grain there and provide the seigneur with one sack of flour out of every fourteen. The

smallholding farm, a piece of land with two leagues frontage and an unlimited depth, did not produce a lot in a country with such a small population. Without doubt, that is one of the reasons that persuaded the Court in France to permit lords and gentlemen living in Canada to engage in commerce, whether by land or sea, without being investigated or held to account for having avoided taxes. The life led by these Lords on their lands naturally calls to memory those patriarchs who were not in the least adverse to sharing the labours of the country with their domestic workers. None of them has a right of patronage, which is reserved for the bishop; as much for the reason that he is in a better position than others to judge the capacities of the subjects, as because the share that accrues to the priests is paid out of the tithe paid to the bishop.

"There are a few families of Savages settled on the properties of the Lords of this parish; but they are the smallest number of inhabitants, most of whom are French-Canadian. The situation of the latter would be a happy one if they knew how to benefit from it. For they have no taxes or tariffs, and get bread, meat, and fish, at really good prices. The land there is fertile, and I know of no other such healthy climate, nor a more agreeable country. There is no particular sickness that holds sway here; the fields and the forests here are filled with health-giving plants, and the trees produce healing balms of admirable quality. These advantages should at least hold those here, whom Providence caused to be born here; but frivolousness, aversion to hard work, and the spirit of independence cause a lot of them to leave, and thus keep the population of the colony low. It is true that wine, fabrics, and everything that is imported from France is very expensive here. The ones who complain the most are the officers on salary.

"As a dowry, the women on the whole only bring their husbands their high spirits, friendship, their charms, and an impressive fertility. There are more nobles here than in our other colonies; the King keeps a lot of troops here, and many retired military men have settled here. That's what has populated the country with gentlemen, who do nothing without making themselves quite comfortable. There would be even fewer if trade was forbidden to them, and if hunting and fishing were not a common right.

The Creoles

"I know few men less involved than the Creoles. They dissipate with as much ease as they give themselves difficulty in acquiring anything. They love the great outdoors, and when they are young get used to the wandering life.

---

seigneur also had the right to a specific number of days of forced labour (called a *corvée*) by the habitants, and could claim rights over fishing, timber and common pastures.

The example, and their frequenting with the natural inhabitants, for whom liberty is the supreme value, is more than sufficient to form this characteristic. They are very lively, and their women in particular are strong, courageous, resourceful, and capable of handling serious matters.

"I should add to this picture of our Canadians, the high opinion they have of themselves, which inspires in them a confidence that enables them to undertake and execute the most difficult things. They have a wonderful community spirit, the advantage of height, and well-proportioned bodies. The strength of their temperament does not always redound to their advantage: they get old and worn out at a very young age. It is believed to be the fault of the parents, who do not watch over their children sufficiently to prevent them from ruining their health at an age when, once ruined, there is no recourse. Their agility and skill are without equal, and even the most capable Indians do not handle their canoes any better even in the most dangerous waters, nor shoot more accurately in the hunt. No one can match their genius for mechanical things; they almost have no need of a teacher to excel in this, and we see many of them who succeed in all the trades without having served any apprenticeship. But a depth of indolence renders these happy aptitudes useless. Those who live in the countryside spend all winter seriously close to a hot stove, between their pipe and their brandy. When spring calls them to the indispensable work of the land, they work superficially, without any fertilizer, sowing seeds carelessly, and then go back to their profound laziness to wait for the harvest.

"In a country where the inhabitants are either too lazy, or too proud to hire themselves out by the day, each family is reduced to bringing in the harvest by itself, and we don't see the joy that animates the harvesters who have gathered during fine days of summer to cut the vast fields together. The Canadian harvest is only of a few crops of each type: a little hay and tobacco, some apples for cider, some cabbage, and some onions. That's more or less all that makes up their crops.

Creole Laziness and Dissipation

"This excess of negligence or laziness can arise from many causes: first of all, the excessive cold of winter which, in stopping the flow of the rivers blocks the activities of the men. Secondly, there is the habit of resting for eight months, which, as the continuation of a season so rigorous, then makes work unbearable, even on the beautiful days. Finally, there is the passion for military life that has been intentionally excited in these courageous men, that results in disgusting them with farm work.

"The inhabitants of the towns — especially of the capital — spend winter, as they do summer, in a general non-stop dissipation. They don't seem to have any interest in the wonders of nature, nor any taste for the pleasures of the imagination. Amusing themselves is their only passion, and when they are gathered together, dancing is the delight of all ages. This life gives the greatest sway to the women, who have all the charms — with the exception of that sensitivity of soul which alone confers the value and the charm of beauty. Lively, gay, coquettish and courteous, they are more flattered to inspire love, than to feel it. One notices in both the sexes, more devoutness than virtue, more religion than integrity, and less honesty than honour. Idleness, prejudice, and frivolity would not have become so prominent in Canada if, in the first days of colonization the government had known how to occupy the minds of the colonists with useful and solid objectives.

The Abuses of Military Authority

Without exception, all the colonist there owed a blind obedience to a purely military authority. The slow and steady march of law was not known there. The will of the commander or of his lieutenants was an oracle that could not be questioned — a terrible decree to which all had to submit without question. Reprieves, remonstrations, and excuses were all crimes in the eyes of a despot who had usurped the power either to punish, or to absolve, by his word alone; who held reward and punishment, recompense and destitution, and the right to imprison, within his hands, with no need for even the shadow of an offence; and the right — even more terrible, to make all the irregularities of his own caprice respected as if they were acts of justice.

"Authority this dangerous was upheld right up until a tribunal for judging all the suits in the colony was set up in the capital. The custom of Paris, modified to suit local circumstances, supplied the code for these laws.

Finance, and Bankruptcy of the Colony

"With respect to finances, the administration of them is hardly known in Canada except for a tax payable to a seigneur of one twelfth of the value of land sold by a tenant; a minor contribution for the inhabitants of Quebec and Montreal for the upkeep of the fortifications of these places; a few duties, but still too high, on entry, and on the export of goods and merchandise. All these things did not produce a tax, or a revenue of two-hundred and sixty thousand pounds.[276] Land was not taxed by the government, but even so it did not entirely enjoy an exemption. From the first days of the colony it was as if it were strangled in the cradle by granting to officers and gentlemen properties of two to four leagues frontage, with unlimited depth. These great

---

276 The French Pound note was valued at ten French Francs.

landowners, disabled by the mediocrity of their means, and with no experience in farming to make such vast lands profitable, were obliged to distribute their land to working people in return for a perpetual fee. This tax, although mediocre, kept a lot of lazy people going, at the expense of the only class of citizens with which a colony ought to be populated.

"So many immediate obstacles placed on the progress of agriculture, mired the colonists in the impossibility of paying for what they ought to have been taking from the home country. The Ministry was so convinced, that after having always obstinately refused to establish manufactures in America, it now believed it ought even to encourage them there. But its tardy invitations only produced a feeble response, especially due to the losses the colony suffered because of the English, who reduced it more than once to extremities, and still encroach upon it even for a few scraps. May it please God himself that the English do not make themselves masters of the whole country! That time, alas, is perhaps only too close!" cried the Missionary, and I saw his eyes well up with tears. "No, no, it is not far off," he said, "for our unhappy New-France, if we are able to judge the future by the present."

Then, with that assured tone of voice made possible by a knowledge of facts and places, of men and of nations, along with his well-considered experience, he added: "In the beginnings of the possession of Canada, the French hardly sent any money there. The little of it that those who came to settle here subsequently brought with them, did not stay long, because the needs of the colony meant that it promptly left again. That was a problem that slowed commerce, and retarded the progress of agriculture. For all its American settlements, the Court had a kind of money made signified by a certain coin that ideally had a value a quarter stronger than the other species of money that circulated in the home country. But as this expedient did not produce the advantage that was promised, it was judged more convenient to substitute paper money for metal for the payment of the troops and the other expenses of government. This strategy succeeded until we ceased carrying out the engagements contracted by the administrators of the colony. As the bills of exchange which they drew on the treasury of the home country were not paid, they were debased. They were liquidated at a discount, and this crisis restored the use of silver currency to Canada. The merchants, and all those who had remittances to make in France, finding it cumbersome, costly, and dangerous to send coins there, were among the first to demand the restoration of paper money. Bills were printed which carried the Coat of Arms of France and of Navarre.[277] They are signed by the Governor, the

---

277 Henry IV became the first Bourbon king of France in 1589. Bourbon monarchs then unified France with the small Spanish/Basque kingdom of Navarre, which Henry's father had acquired by marriage in 1555, and they ruled until the 1792 overthrow of the monarchy during the French

Intendant, and the Controller. There are bills of twenty-four, twelve, six, and three pounds; and coins of thirty, fifteen, and seven-pence in fixed public monies. Their combined values do not rise above a million pounds, and when this sum is insufficient for public needs, it is supplemented by orders signed only by the Intendant. The least of these is for twenty sous, and the most is for a hundred pounds.

"These different paper notes circulating in the colony were substitutes for silver money until the month of October. This is the slowest season, when the ships leave Canada. Then all this paper money was converted into bills of exchange, which had to be honoured in France by the government, which was supposed to have set their value. But a day will come — and that day is perhaps not so far off — when the amount will have increased so much that the treasury of the prince, being insufficient, will find it necessary to defer payment. An unfortunate war will inflate their number to the point where they will be discounted. Then goods will be priced outrageously, and then, due to the enormous cost of the war, the biggest consumer will be the King, and it will be him alone who will back the defaulted paper money and the damage caused by the high cost of living. The Minister will then be forced to suspend payment of the letters of exchange, until they have cleared up the source of the problem and set the real value: the masses will be frightened.

"The annual expenditures of the government of Canada, which did not exceed 400,000 francs in 1729, and which until the present time[278] have never risen above 1,700,000 pounds, will have no limits. Each year it will rise by many millions, and of that prodigious sum, there will perhaps be owing, when peace comes, more than 80,000,000 pounds. We will get to the bottom of the source of this debt, and the enormous misappropriations that gave rise to it will deepen in significance according as the fading of it from memory of the time and place will permit. The corrupt officials who were the most guilty, will be forced to pay restitution; the pretensions of the creditors will be discussed; and we can only hope that the good will of the nation will insist that the minister in charge of this operation, the men who will not fear the threats of credit, who will scorn the exertions of fortune, and who will not be either surprised by such artifices, nor worn out by their hardships, will preserve the delicate balance between the public interest and the rights of individuals with a just and steady hand.

Revolution. Navarre is today a semi-autonomous province of Spain. Henry IV, who ruled France until his death in 1610, was very supportive of Samuel Champlain's efforts to establish New France in North America.

278 Delaporte must here be referring to the date he gives for the writing of Tome IX of *Le Voyageur François*, or 1749.

The English to Conquer Quebec

While these disorders were getting underway in the finances of Canada, the English were eager to make conquests there; and for us to oppose this, we would have recourse to our typical resource: we would build forts that would make them envious. Thus would hostilities begin between the English and the French, authorized, if not admitted by the two Courts. The flag of Britain would finally receive orders to attack ours, and finally, an open war would be declared between the two countries. The English would begin by seizing Port Royal as a means of gaining entry to Canada. We would see their navy coming up the St. Lawrence River; their flag would appear in front of Quebec; this unhappy village would suffer under the yoke of the conqueror; peace treaties would firm up this conquest, and would add greatly to the total of English possessions in North America."[279]

Given that in general all the colonies of America are made up of rejects and, so to speak, of the dregs of nations, we must render justice to those of Canada, in that the source of almost all the families that still live there today is quite pure, with no dishonourable stains. The first inhabitants there were either labourers always engaged in useful work, or people who came here to find refuge from the wars of religion that were fracturing the kingdom. It's not that we didn't sometimes see people who, because of the terrible state of their affairs were seeking exile, or some others that France and their families were glad to be rid of. But as these were few in number, and care was taken not to let them associate with each other too much, we have to believe that they have reformed themselves according to the good examples right before their eyes. This is more or less all that you might want to know about the inhabitants of Canada — which I will leave in a few days to go to Boston, the capital of New England.

I remain, etc.

From Quebec, April 15, 1749.

---

279 The Battle of the Plains of Abraham (13 September, 1759) was a pivotal moment in the Seven Years' War and in the history of Canada. A British invasion force led by General James Wolfe defeated French troops under the Marquis de Montcalm, leading to the surrender of Quebec to the British. This volume of *Le Voyageur François* was published after this date, but the narrative is situated prior to the conquest, in 1749. Delaporte was writing about a possible future event that in fact had already transpired, and of which he was already aware.

APPENDIX

NOTICE TO READER
~ by ~
L'ABBÉ JOSEPH DELAPORTE
from his "AVERTISSEMENT" PREFACE to Vol. 1

~ of ~

Le Voyageur François
(Paris, France; Chez Vincent, 1765)

THE immense collection of travel documents available would fill a large library, and the reading of them would take a lifetime. Following a plan organized by the English, and corrected by him, L'abbé Prèvost reduced a prodigious number of these stories (tales more likely to frighten by their sheer number, than to excite one's curiosity with respect to what they contain of interest) to a certain number of volumes.[280]

But leaving aside for the moment the general weakness of his plan, and its extreme confusion of details, Prèvost's *History* has been criticized for its tedious repetitions and excessive wordiness. Moreover, his objective was not achieved: the collection suffers for a paucity of overland expeditions, which

---

280 Antoine François Prévost (1697-1763), usually known simply as the Abbé Prévost, was a French author and novelist. Among his many works was the 15 volume *Histoire générale des voyages* (General History of Travel) in 15 vols., Paris, 1746-1759), which was a compilation of different and often conflicting English travel accounts. The Abbé Joseph Delaporte (1714-1779), as explained in this Notice to Readers, wrote the first 28 volumes of the 42 volume series of *Le Voyageur François* (*The French Traveler* — published between *1765 and 1795*) in an effort to improve on Prèvost's work by shifting the emphasis from a style of travel-narrative focused primarily on rendering the traveler's personal experiences, to a style with emphasis on the nature of the country and people experienced.

is to say, of all that part of the ancient world where the most interesting things happened. Some sense of the present condition of these celebrated places, the revolutions they have experienced, and the invaluable remains of monuments that attract the attention of travelers, would have completed this grand *History*.

It is at this point that the stories of our French Traveler begin. And even if the two first volumes had no other use than to serve as a supplement to Prèvost's *General History of Travel*, that is a benefit for which the Public ought to be grateful. But its objective is far broader.

By incorporating the flame of philosophy and scientific observation in his travel accounts, our traveler is able to draw out useful knowledge that he is able to share with fellow citizens. Namely, all the things that are bound to excite the curiosity of a philosophical reader: the laws, customs, traditions, religions, governments, commerce, the sciences, arts, styles, clothing, natural products — in short, the knowledge of all countries and nations of the world, starting with the people of Asia — are the subject of all his letters.

He only devotes his attention to what seems to him to deserve appropriate attention, and as his main aim is to interest and to instruct, anything that does not produce these two results does not seem to him worthy of his remarks. Only rarely will he tell his readers what he feels personally about something. And never do the preparations for a voyage, nor the small incidents that arise on occasion, or that are imagined, or speculated during a long trip, take the place of a more interesting account.

It is not important to know the history of the traveler, but rather, of the countries where he has traveled.

www.ingramcontent.com/pod-product-compliance
Lightning Source LLC
Chambersburg PA
CBHW081355070526
44583CB00020B/2560